ANDREW AND VIOLET

The Story of my Grandparents

Gloria Brown

Gloria (Hellier) Brown

DRC Publishing

3 Parliament Street
St. John's, Newfoundland and Labrador A1A 2Y6
Telephone: (709) 726-0960
E-mail: staceypj@nl.rogers.com
www.drcpublishingnl.com

© Gloria (Hellier) Brown, 2014

Library and Archives Canada Cataloguing in Publication

(Hellier) Brown, Gloria, author
Andrew and Violet : the story of my grandparents / Gloria (Hellier) Brown.

ISBN 978-1-926689-74-6 (pbk.)

1. Smith, Andrew, 1895-1970. 2. Smith, Violet, 1902-2002. 3. World War, 1914-1918--Veterans--Newfoundland and Labrador--Biography. 4. Dildo (Trinity Bay, N.L.)--Biography. I. Title.

FC2199.D54Z48 2014   971.8   C2014-903309-5
Pictures   Cover Layout
                              -Steven-Shane Martin
                              Cover and All Photos
                              -Supplied by author

Layout/Design/Cover By Steven-Shane Martin
e-mail: martinstevenshane@gmail.com

We acknowledge the financial support of the Government of Canada through the Canada Book Fund for our publishing activities.

To Hilda and Jim Barrett

Every question I asked of them was treated as important, no matter how trivial it seemed. Jim passed away unexpectedly on April 20, 2013. I dedicate this book to them, with love and gratitude.

Jim, Hilda and Brian Barrett

INTRODUCTION

I am the oldest grandchild of my maternal grandparents, Andrew and Violet Smith. They were typical of many outport Newfoundlanders in the early 1900s but their lives were marked with great challenges and tragedy. It was important to record their story as a legacy for my own children. It quickly became a Newfoundland history lesson.

This endeavor motivated me to travel to France and Belgium to see the Royal Newfoundland Regiment battle sites where my grandfather fought, and to Ayr, Scotland, to find the original home of his Scottish girlfriend and my mother's namesake. Andrew was fearless as a runner, one of the most dangerous of wartime jobs. I am left incredulous as to what all soldiers, British and German, endured. I have the utmost respect for what the Newfoundland Regiment was able to accomplish.

This is a tribute to my mother, Rea, my primary source of information, and her two sisters, Alma and Hilda. Some of the stories I had heard before. Some I had not. Some I had forgotten. It is my hope our ancestors come alive and assume memorable personalities through these anecdotes.

Thank you to those who helped fill in the smaller pieces of the puzzle. Thank you to my brother Rob, for encouraging me to get personal. Thank you to my daughter, Carla, for her editing advice and her husband, Bob Welland, for his technical and creative support. Thank you immensely to my husband Carl, "Brownie," for his patience. I could not have done it without him.

Gloria (Hellier) Brown

Contents

THE SOLDIER

Andrew Smith

Royal Newfoundland Regiment, Service # 1393

My maternal grandparents were Andrew and Violet Smith of Dildo in Trinity Bay, Newfoundland. My grandfather fought for the Royal Newfoundland Regiment in World War I and returned a war hero with a Military Medal for his courage on the battlefield. He defied the odds and survived four years in the precarious role as a runner, its casualty rate second only to stretcher bearers. He died when I was 20. My grandmother lived to her 100th year and died in 2002.

In everyone's lifetime, there are opportunities lost. Sometimes, we are acutely aware of their happening. More often, time has passed before we recognize we were altogether oblivious to the possibilities. The latter is my experience.

I am a history buff, reveling in the history of others, recent and long ago. I dabbled in my family tree. It was not until my daughter, Carla, made a quick request in 2007 that I realized the lack of depth of my interest. A family tree, while useful, is but a mix of names and dates. Carla asked that I write a few pages about my grandfather, Andrew, after the birth of her son, Russell Andrew Welland. It was a simple request that became a race against time as I scrambled to find people who remembered Andrew and Violet. Carla's request became a revelation, a lighting of a spark within me that I preserve their story. Within a month of the request, I make plans to visit France and Belgium for the first time to visit the battle sites of the Royal Newfoundland Regiment in World War I. It was an opportunity to vacation with our son, Kraig, living in Scotland. His French is good. He earned his keep as navigator and translator.

Andrew Ralph Smith was working at the Anglo-Newfoundland Development Company paper mill in Grand Falls, Newfoundland, when World War I began in 1914. He traveled to St. John's and enlisted in the Newfoundland Regiment on April 9 or 10, 1915, the date differs in his files. His age was 20 years and 8 months. According to his military records, in the Canadian National Archives in Ottawa and The Rooms in St. John's, Andrew's height was listed as 5'5". Upon demobilization in 1919, it was listed as 5' 7", a curious difference which may simply mean the measurement was taken when he was wearing his boots. His friend, Levi Hollett, #1539, was 5'9" upon entry and 5'11" upon demobilization, also a discrepancy of two inches. Compared to today, many of the Regiment were small men. Andrew weighed 133 lbs. His chest measurement at rest was 32", expanding to 35". His father, William, would receive an allotment of 60 cents per day taken from his pay of $1.50 a day plus 10 cents field allowance. This is typical of most soldiers' files. He likely spent the first months of training in Pleasantville, Quidi Vidi Lake, in St John's and received inoculations on May 17, June 2 and June 25 (at sea), according to his medical chart.

Andrew was given the Regimental number 1393. On the same day, George Frederick Newhook, also from Dildo, was given number 1391. Was this more than a coincidence they enlisted at the same time? On June 20, 1915, they were two of 242 Regiment members of F Company and 85 Naval Reservists who boarded the 17,500 ton, 600 foot long Armed Merchant Cruiser, the *Calgarian*, and made a 19 day crossing overseas. They were the 6th Newfoundland contingent. They took their own hammocks, blankets and cooks. The *Calgarian* escorted three submarines. They disembarked at Liverpool and reached Stob's Camp, Scotland, July 10, bringing the Regiment's total to 1500 men. This number was but a small part of the 100,000 newly enlisted civilians which the British Army had to train. It was a daunting task.

Herbert Hellier

The *Calgarian* was launched April, 1913. Its primary role was to be an armed escort for troops and passengers across the Atlantic. It was in Halifax harbour, Nova Scotia, during the Halifax Explosion on December 6, 1917, and provided rescue and medical support as the city was devastated by the collision of the Norwegian ship, *SS Imo*, and the French ship,

SS Mont Blanc, loaded with explosives. Three months later, the *Calgarian* was torpedoed by the German submarine, *U-19*, off Raithlin Island, Northern Ireland, on March 1, 1918, with a loss of 49 men. It was one of 46 ships sunk by the *U-19*.

It is noteworthy that my other grandfather, Herbert Stanley Hellier, Service # X 1381 of the Royal Navy, was on the *Calgarian* when it sank in 1918. He enlisted on November 14, 1914, when he was 18. He was 5 feet 5 ½ inches tall with light hair and gray eyes. He and other survivors spent time in the ocean before being picked up and brought to Londonderry the next day. He had survived a previous sinking of a ship by torpedo. He served on the *Calypso, Vivid I and III, Zaria, Chieftain, Briton* and *Satellite*. He was one of 1,964 Newfoundlanders who did not join the Regiment but the Royal Naval Reserve. After the war in 1919, Herb volunteered for mine sweeping duty in the North Sea.

After three weeks at Stob's Camp, Andrew's Company was moved to a new Regimental Depot at Ayr, where he trained for three months. His speed and agility may have been noted. His second cousin, Lloyd George, observed, "As a boy, he was quick and fast and could often outperform lads much older than himself in races and other physical activities engaged by young people."

Andrew was to be a runner, also known as messenger. There were telephones and telegraphs, but cables between the front lines and Headquarters were often destroyed. Important communications along the lines of rear command then depended on messages carried to the front lines by runners. For longer distances, they were trained to use bicycles. The work required physical stamina, daring and cunning as a runner was a favorite target of enemy snipers and machine gun crews. Running meant making quick dashes between trenches, through barbed wire, water and mud filled holes, across terrain infiltrated by the enemy. Runners did not usually carry a rifle.

They were allowed a pistol and a knife. In the chaos of the battlefield, it was sometimes difficult to find the designated officer. In addition to relaying messages, they were expected to familiarize themselves with the trenches so they could guide newcomer troops in the right direction. The terrain changed as trenches collapsed under shell fire, and the runner should be more familiar with them than anyone.

The first 500 to enlist in the Newfoundland Regiment were known as The Blue Puttees, named for the blue flannel wrapped around their legs from their ankles to their knees. Regular khaki cloth was in short supply at that time. Many of the Blue Puttees were from the City of St. John's. They had their first baptism of fire at Gallipoli in Turkey, September, 1915.

Andrew was not a Blue Puttee and he did not go to Turkey. On October 3, 1915, he left Southampton for Rouen, France. This appears to be his first foray to the front. In Rouen, new troops were given 10 more days of grueling training at the "Bullpen." Typically, the route from the French ports to the front lines was achieved through full day marches and impromptu billeting in the villages enroute. Each soldier was weighted with 60 pounds of equipment and marching was a means of keeping fit and instilling discipline.

In the spring of 1916, the Regiment took part in intensive training for the Battle of the Somme. When they arrived in the village of Beaumont Hamel, the battle site, the Germans put up a sign that said "Hello, Red Man." The native people occupying Newfoundland, until they became extinct in 1829, were the Beothuk. They were known for painting their bodies, homes, weapons and canoes with red ochre, hence the name.

The first day of the Battle of the Somme was July 1, 1916, the worst days fighting in British military history. Half of the 120,000 British who fought that day became casualties, over 19,000 dead. In less than 30 minutes, the Newfoundland Regiment suffered the second highest casualty rate of any other, a shocking price to pay, because in most places the attack failed altogether. It was supposed to last one day. It lasted five months. The sting of Beaumont Hamel left its mark forever on the young men of the Newfoundland Regiment and on the people of Newfoundland. July 1, which is a happy Canada Day long weekend for the rest of the country, is a still a somber day of reflection for Newfoundlanders. After a couple of nights in Paris, it is the first stop on our pilgrimage.

Beaumont Hamel

I am full of nervous energy as I set out for Beaumont Hamel. It is a 30-hectare memorial, the largest of the five caribou sites in France and Belgium commemorating all Newfoundlanders who fought in the Great War. At the entrance, a large bronze caribou statue is perched on a mound of boulders. The statues, by the English sculptor, Basil Gotto, are the same in all five sites and in Bowring Park, St. John's. Mounted on rocky crags, they look in the direction of the enemy. Beaumont Hamel is much larger than the other sites. It has a new Visitor's Center, opened July 1, 2001, with the history of the Royal Newfoundland Regiment. It is one of few battle sites in France with remarkably well preserved trenches and craters.

Beaumont Hamel was in the middle of the 15 mile front. In the first wave of the assault, at 7:30 AM, four battalions from the 86th and 87th Brigades failed to reach the German lines and were trapped in No Man's Land. Two support battalions from the 88th Brigade, the Newfoundlanders and the 1st Essex, were ordered to advance at 8:45 AM. Because of the congestion of dead and wounded soldiers in their trenches, the Essex Regiment was unable to get into position. Lieutenant Colonel A. L. Hadow, the English commanding officer of the Newfoundland Regiment, gave the order from Major General Sir Beauvoir de Lisle at Headquarters to advance. In order to get to the battlefield, the Newfoundlanders had to go an extra 270 yards overland in full view of the Germans.

When they went over the top at 9:15 AM, they were the only troops moving. Despite the odds against their survival, they went "with chins tucked down as if walking into a blizzard" although it was a hot sunny day. They did not waver. They were mowed down in waves. Many did not make it past their own front line. Most were shot in the first 100 to 200 yards. Within 15 to 20 minutes, 85% of the Regiment was dead or wounded. It was virtually wiped out with 710 out of roughly

800 men killed, wounded or missing. Only 68 responded to roll call the next day. All 25 officers were killed or wounded. Most did not see a German or fire their rifles. The carnage was later blamed on inept British leadership and poor intelligence and communications.

During the battle, most of the British and Newfoundland casualties were in their own four belts of barbed wire. They had cut too few gaps to allow the men through. Private Anthony Stacey, #466, watched from a forward trench with Lt. Col. Hadow. He recalled that these gaps were "a proper trap for our boys, as the enemy set the sights of the machine guns on the gaps in the barbed wire and fired."

Lt. Col. Hadow, wrote, "During the night and evening unwounded survivors managed to crawl back to our lines and by next morning 68 had answered their names in addition to the stretcher bearers and the HQ runners." Andrew's name was not on the list of those who answered roll call on July 2 or July 6. Was he running messages in the Communications Trenches to the Brigade Headquarters 100 yards behind the firing line? Hadow's report said the 68 did not include the runners. Was he one of the 100 men in the 10 percent reserve? We know he did not go over the top, as it was called, with the Regiment to slaughter.

Major General de Lisle wrote of the Newfoundland Regiment, "When the order to attack was given, every man moved forward to his appointed objective in his appointed place as if on parade. There were no waverers, no stragglers and not a man looked back. It was a magnificent display of valor and its assault only failed of success because dead men can advance no further." This was cold comfort to families back home.

The plight of the Regiment was described by a German survivor. "We thought the attack was over. Then, an hour later, the unbelievable took place. A second wave of British attackers," (The Newfoundland Regiment) "picking their way through their own dead and wounded, bayonets held high, came down the slope towards us. We had reloaded and simply opened fire once again. In half an hour, they were all dead or dying or pinned down, unable to move. It was curious, but they all seemed to have mirrors fixed to their backpacks. Even the worst shots among us could hit them with ease. The distance, 200 yards at the most. It was slaughter, slaughter, slaughter." The mirrors were tiny tin triangles worn on the backs of the uniforms for easy identification by their own troops. It also provided an easy target for the enemy. German machine guns overheated!

It is impossible to imagine the emotion and shock on this, one of the Regiment's first big battles. The week-long allied artillery barrage that preceded the attack, that was supposed to pulverize the enemy, had done little damage. Most Germans were unhurt, protected in three rows of deep trenches. They had been manning this part of the line for 20 months and their defences were formidable.

The British had a serious problem with their mortar shells. About half were duds! Many of the experienced staff making them went to war and Britain was unable to train new workers fast enough to keep up with the increased demand. Poorly paid munitions workers were given a bonus if they exceeded their quota and that led to hurried work and substandard shells such as those used at Hamel.

Prior to the battle, there was so much activity by the British compared to the German, that the British were lulled into a false sense of security. During two night time raids, June 25 and 27, a Newfoundland scouting team of 57 men, led by Captain Bert Butler, #146, realized the actual German preparedness as six men were killed and Butler was amongst 13 wounded. More casualties were avoided by the quick action of Fredrick

O'Neill, # 402, who retrieved an enemy bomb and threw it back. The bomb burst upon leaving his hand, leaving him severely wounded. On the first raid, they realized the enemy wire had survived the shelling. British cutters were unable to cut through the heavier wire which also had more barbs per yard than the British wire. On the second raid, they came under heavy fire. Butler received the Military Cross for his efforts, the first of four honors he received in the war. He warned against the attack. It was dismissed by Headquarters as nervousness by inexperienced troops.

On our first day at Beaumont Hamel, Jessica Walsh, our tour guide from St. John's, tells us the caribou was chosen by the Regiment as its symbol because it is native to Newfoundland, travels in herds and never leaves its wounded behind. The Regiment's pin has a caribou head within a wreath of laurel leaves. Above the head is a crown and below is a scroll with the words Royal Newfoundland Regiment. I am a proud owner of a pin, a surprise EBay Christmas gift from my son, Kraig.

As I walk St. John's Road, where the Newfoundland Regiment dug its trench, I slip on wet grass and fall flat on my face. As I lay there, the wind knocked out of me, I peer towards No Man's Land, the small area between the German and British trenches. It is apparent from this perspective, that the British were disadvantaged. They were on a rise of land above the Germans. When the British soldiers went over the top, they were in full view of the enemy. They never had a chance.

The skeleton of the single tree to survive the devastation in No Man's Land, which the soldiers called The Danger Tree, has been petrified to preserve it in its place. The Danger Tree is less than half way between the British and German front lines and marks the furthest advance made by Newfoundlanders on that awful day.

The Danger Tree

On the walkway below the caribou are three large plaques with the names of all the Newfoundlanders in the Great War with no known graves. Duplicate plaques are in Bowring Park in St. John's, Newfoundland. Reverently, we scan the names. There are 14 sets of brothers, Evans, Ferguson, Jones, Kelly, Knight, Morris, Penney, Pike, Pinsent, Porter, Ross, Snow, Taylor and White. The Ayer merchant family from St. John's lost 4 grandsons. At the Y Ravine cemetery there are 428 graves and at the Hawthorne Ridge cemeteries there are 367 graves. Soldiers are buried two to a site so they are not alone on foreign land. I find two headstones with the numbers of 1396 and 1399. Andrew's number was 1393.

I am curious as to the fates of the other soldiers who enlisted on or about the same time as my grandfather. I research the 11 soldiers from #1390 to #1400. According to their files, they enlisted in St. John's the same day as Andrew and crossed the Atlantic with him on the *Calgarian*. I am unable to identify #1398. Of the remaining ten soldiers, only Mark Wiseman, #1390, of Trinity, Thomas Joseph Flynn, #1397, of St. John's, and my grandfather survived.

Six were killed at Beaumont Hamel. They include:
#1391- George Newhook from Dildo
#1392- Thomas Seymour from Gooseberry Island
#1395- Augustus Patrick Whalen from St. John's
#1396- William Masters from Harbour Buffett
#1399- Augustus Penney from Holyrood
#1400- Harold Gordon Coish from Ladle Cove
The seventh soldier, Hector Pearce #1394, from Clarenville, was killed on April 14, 1917 at Monchy. William and Maud Pearce lost a younger son, Clyde, the following year, September 28, 1917, in Belgium.

The families of the fallen in the Newfoundland Regiment did not receive word as to the fate of their loved ones right away. George Newhook was listed as missing in a letter to his mother, Lizzie, dated July 31, 1916. It was not until November 23, 1916, that the families were sent a form letter. The first paragraph read, "For some time past the Imperial Government have been making enquiries in relation to those men of the First Newfoundland Regiment who have been reported missing since the action of the 1st July. I very much regret to state, however, that from the correspondence which has taken place, a copy of which I enclose, it is evident that none of them are Prisoners of War in Germany, and the authorities are, therefore, reluctantly forced to the conclusion that all these gallant men, whose names are given in the enclosed list, and one of whom was very dear to you, were killed in that fateful action on the 1st of July." It was bleak Christmas mail for hundreds of Newfoundland households.

There is a large Scottish presence at Beaumont Hamel. On November 13, 1916, the kilted 51st Scottish Highland Division defeated the Germans at Hamel in the Battle of the Ancre. The Highland Division's diary stated, "The ground over which the advance was made was still littered with the skeletons, clad in rags, which represented the men who had fallen in the attack of July 1st." At Hunter's Cemetery there is a statue of a kilted Scottish soldier to commemorate the costly victory, much of it intense hand to hand combat. Next to the statue is a circular memorial in the spot where a German shell killed over 40 Scottish soldiers.

Father Thomas Nangle

Our two hour tour is over as the site is closing. We stay overnight in a French farmhouse. Kraig has to bend his head as the doorways are only six feet. The farmhouse is like thousands of others which dot the countryside. During the war they provided cover for the Allies and the Germans as their owners fled the destruction of their properties. They were a preferred location for sniper fire. We return to Beaumont Hamel the next morning, a sunny day. The grass has been cut and smells like hay. Sheep not there the previous day are grazing. It reminds me of visiting Dildo in summertime when I was a little girl.

Inside the Visitor's Center, one wall contains in large print the names of the communities from which the Newfoundland soldiers came including Dildo and Dildo Harbour. There is a panoramic photo of the Regiment in uniform. If Andrew is in the photo, we are unable to pick him out. Small faces are shaded by caps. Kraig observes that many of the soldiers look like mere boys.

After two visits and four hours on the site, I am reluctant to leave. It is a special place. I am sad because so many lives were lost, so many mistakes were made. Despite its origins, it is a beautiful and peaceful place. It is like the unofficial motto of the Newfoundland Regiment, "Better than the best." Inscribed at the entrance are the words, "Tread softly here – Go reverently and slow," the opening words to the epitaph by John Oxenham.

One man is to be given credit for the idea and implementation of this memorial. He was Father Tom Nangle, a Catholic Chaplin, who served in the Regiment from 1916 to 1918. He was popular with all troops, regardless of denomination. He came up with the idea of "The Trail of the Caribou," memorials in five significant Regiment battlefields in France and Belgium. Tirelessly he looked for donations, visiting many communities in Newfoundland, with funds of $10,000 raised largely by the Women's Patriotic Association. He dealt with French and Belgium landowners to buy their land, negotiating with 250 for the purchase of Beaumont Hamel alone. He commissioned the sculpting of the six caribou by Gotto. He hired Rudolph Cochius who had designed Bowring Park in St. John's, to supervise the construction of the sites. He continued his mission to make Beaumont Hamel "Holy Ground" until the original building was completed in 1925.

Father Nangle had another overwhelming responsibility. When the family of Private Henry Horwood, # 3694, asked for information about their son's death on October 20, 1918, they received this reply. "Major T. Nangle has been for some time engaged in the location and registering of soldier's graves in the different areas of war and having them concentrated into recognized military cemeteries. When each grave has been removed, it will be photographed and a copy sent to the next of kin. It is hoped that Major Nangle will be successful in registering Pte. Horwood's grave in which event you will be notified without delay." The job took its toll. He left the priesthood in 1921 and never returned to Newfoundland. He moved to Rhodesia in Africa, married and had four children. He died in 1972.

Gueudecourt

After Beaumont Hamel we head for Gueudecourt, the first memorial completed by Nangle. Enroute is the British monument at Theipval that bears the names of 73,367 British World War I soldiers whose bodies were never found. Like this and so many memorials and gravesites, Gueudecourt is in the middle of nowhere, on a narrow country road in the midst of rolling countryside and farmland. It is hunting season and the only signs of life are hunters with guns and dogs flushing out small birds and game in the fields. Their gunfire makes us nervous. It disturbs the peace. Towns seem deserted. We see more sheep and cows than people. Fields are mostly plowed with the exception of corn stalks still in the ground. Potatoes just harvested are heaped in high mounds. Buildings are red brick with some stone and stucco construction. Windows are covered with lace. Red geraniums are a favorite flower. Church spires and modern windmills for electricity break the horizon.

The countryside is an appropriate setting for so many graves, all immaculately kept with thousands of identical white headstones. Cemeteries represent many countries including Britain, Canada, Ireland, Scotland, Australia, New Zealand, Egypt, India and Newfoundland. There are 13 German gravesites where soldiers are buried under black crosses but they are not well signed or advertised. We do not see German graves and I am left to ponder, while the Germans were the enemy, were their wartime experiences no different from ours? Along the narrow roads, there are signs reading "Front Line" with a date. Without these reminders, one would never guess it was the site of so much death and destruction 100 years ago.

In the three months after Beaumont Hamel, Regiment numbers were boosted by new recruits. On October 8, they returned to the Somme. At Gueudecort, October 10-12, 1916, in wet muddy conditions, the Newfoundland Regiment captured a German stronghold and held the front line under heavy fire for 40 hours. It was the only British success that day. They paid dearly with a 60% casualty rate, 239 men. For most of the Regiment, it was their first experience fighting with fists, grenades and using a bayonet to kill. Andrew may not have been at Gueudecort as his file states he rejoined his battalion October 14, 1916.

Monchy-le-Preux

The next caribou is in the village of Monchy-le-Preux. It is inaccessible to us, closed off by a fence to ensure the privacy of the residents in nearby homes. Considering that 611 Newfoundlanders fought here with a 75% casualty rate, we are disappointed in the general description on the plaque. Monchy was the second worst day of the war for the Regiment, next to Beaumont Hamel. Upon reflection we rationalize that the Newfoundland Regiment was but a small part of the British force and it is logical the plaques would refer to the British and not a Newfoundland presence. After the war, Andrew's family associated the word "Monchy" with a reverent nod in acknowledgement of that horrific day.

The Canadians captured Vimy Ridge April 9-12, 1917, taking more than 4000 German prisoners. Nearby, about 15 miles south of Vimy, was the destroyed village of Monchy, newly gained by the British and of strategic importance to both British and Germans because it provided a panoramic view of the surrounding countryside. About 1500 men of the Newfoundland Regiment and the 1st Essex Battalion were sent to relieve the troops in Monchy.

Their orders were to capture Shrapnel Trench on the German front line. Their right flank was not protected, a flawed plan, and they were routed, cut off from Monchy. Two companies of the Regiment were surrounded on all four sides and were quickly decimated. Escape was impossible. Bodies of Newfoundlanders and the Essex littered the fields. Of the 166 Newfoundlanders who died at Monchy, 137 have no known graves. The Regiment suffered 460 causalities, the 1st Essex, 602. Despite the German success, they were denied the town of Monchy by the heroics of the Newfoundland Regiment's Commander, Lt. Col. James Forbes-Robertson and a group of 10 men. While most Newfoundlanders have heard of Beaumont Hamel, fewer are aware of Monchy, but the sacrifice and heroics of the Regiment were the same. Despite the losses, some say that Monchy was also the Regiment's greatest victory.

Something remarkable happened at Monchy-le-Preux. After the successful German counter attack on the Newfoundland and Essex Regiments, some 300 Germans left the battlefield and moved in on Monchy in what was perceived as an easy capture. They could not have foreseen the courage of Lt. Colonel Forbes-Robertson and 10 men, nine Newfoundlanders and one from Essex.

Lt. Col. Hadow and Lt. Col. Forbes-Robertson

When Forbes-Robertson realized the situation, he took 16 men from his village Headquarters, gathered up guns and ammunition from the dead and wounded and crawled 100 yards over open ground to a trench behind a hedge to make his stand. Four were killed and two wounded along the way. Forbes-Robertson's plan to "cause a diversion for a quarter of an hour" turned into a nine hour standoff! Initially, the men rapid fired their Lee Enfield rifles, the fire so disproportionate to their numbers that the Germans did not press the attack. They had no idea their enemy numbered only ten. Runner Private Albert Rose, #1826, succeeded in getting back to headquarters but there were no reinforcements. Despite orders to the contrary, he rejoined his comrades on the firing line. As time passed and ammunition ran low, rapid fire was replaced by sniping. Every bullet was made to count by waiting until the enemy was at close range. Monchy was saved. Anthony McAllister, in his book "The Greatest Gallantry," says that Forbes-Robertson's "courageous performance at Monchy earned him the admiration and respect if not the affection of the whole battalion. There is no doubt that Forbes-Robertson was directly responsible for reestablishing the esprit de corps of the Regiment." For his heroics at Monchy, he received the

Distinguished Service Order, second to the Victoria Cross. The RNR did not have a commanding officer from Newfoundland because the British army believed colonial troops should be led by colonels from the British Regular forces.

Masnieres

The fourth caribou is near Arras (Aw-ras), a Flemish town rebuilt after the war. Under Arras is a network of tunnels and caverns called Les Boves that were begun in the 10th century and expanded during the war as a refuge for soldiers and citizens. Father Nangle wanted the caribou erected in La Grande Place, the cobblestoned central square, which we overlook from our hotel. It would have been a more prominent and visible location, but the caribou is tucked away outside the small village of Masnieres, closer to the battle site, near the St. Quentin Canal.

At the Battle of Cambrai, November 20, 1917, the Allied Great Experiment was to use 380 tanks to smash the well fortified German Hindenburg Line, which the Germans thought was impregnable. Next to the Line was the town of Cambrai, a vital supply centre for the Germans, and Masnieres, one of their main strongholds.

The British tank attack was successful in penetrating the Hindenburg Line and they had the initial advantage. When one of their tanks attempted to cross the main iron bridge over the St Quentin Canal, it collapsed. Some of the Newfoundland Regiment and South Wales Borderers held the north side of the canal for two days. On one day alone, the Germans attacked nine times. The Regiment clung on, rebuffing the enemy.

The Germans rallied with new troops. Most of the Allied tanks were broken or destroyed. After the successful German counter offensive, Allied Headquarters, six miles away, realized the position could not be maintained and on December 4, ordered a withdrawal. It was part of a major battle with no victor. Each side lost over 40,000 men. The small Newfoundland Regiment suffered 450 casualties, 248 in the first two days. Lance Corporal John Shiwak, #1735, an Inuit trapper from Labrador, was killed with six others by an exploding German shell. He was the Regiment's leading sniper and scout, one of the best snipers in the British forces. His death was a severe blow.

Caribou at Masnieres

As the war progressed, the Newfoundland Regiment found it increasingly frustrating to be mistaken by the enemy as Canadians as their uniforms came from the same suppliers used by the Canadian army. Newfoundland was still a British Colony. It did not become a province of Canada until 1949. The loss of so many Newfoundland lives resulted in a determination for many in the RNR to be the regiment most fearless and most feared and they left their mark. The Regiment's ferocity was viewed as revenge for Beaumont Hamel. Alf Pretty, Andrew's second cousin and a Korean War veteran, 1950 to 1953, says that the Germans soon came to recognize and fear the Newfoundlanders.

The Regiment acquired a reputation for courage, tenacity and sacrifice. After Masnieres at the Battle of Cambrai in November, 1917, King George V bestowed on them the word "Royal" renaming them the Royal Newfoundland Regiment in recognition of their exceptional valor. Brigadier-General H. Nelson, Commander of the 88th Brigade, said, "I don't care what happens to me now; I have commanded the most wonderful troops in the world, who have fought the best fight any man can see and live. I feel my career has been crowned." I was disappointed this is not noted on the plaque. The prefix Royal had been awarded only twice before to regiments in wartime, in 1665 and 1885. It is a rare distinction.

Vimy

Kraig in trenches of Vimy

On Monday morning we visit Vimy, the most impressive Canadian World War I monument in France. The white stone monument with its soaring pillars and grandiose sculptures is a fitting memorial to the 66,000 Canadians who died. 11,285 names of those whose bodies were never found are engraved in the stone. The Canadians won the battle decisively but as important, it was the first time they attacked and triumphed as a Canadian force, not a British. Unfortunately, the Allies were not able to capitalize on the victory because they did not expect it and did not have a follow up plan. Like Beaumont Hamel, the site is one of few where original trenches and tunnels remain. At Beaumont Hamel the German and British trenches are a football field apart. At Vimy, they are only 25 meters (80 feet) apart. Unbelievable! It is incomprehensible that they could be so close, dug in for so many months in a stalemate, preparing for the inevitable battle. For two years, Vimy had been held by the Germans. In January of 1917, Lieutenant General Julian Byng of the Canadian corps was given orders for a Canadian attack in April.

We take a tour of the Grange, an original Canadian underground tunnel, 8 to 10 feet below ground. It is one of 12 tunnels or subways dug on the Canadian side. They were dug by hand, 24 hours a day, eight hour shifts. Soil in sandbags was passed through the tunnels by men lying on their sides all night long. The bags were disposed of at night, distributed naturally on the landscape in a way that the enemy was not aware of the magnitude of the digging. 50,000 horses and mules were used to facilitate the work. When they finished, they had dug over six miles of tunnels with water lines, electrical wires, medical stations, cooking facilities and ammunition stores. There were 3000 kilometers of wire for telephone and telegram service and glass insulators like Andrew later used working for United Towns Electric Co. in Dildo and kept in his store.

Short and narrow trenches or tunnels, 30 to 50 yards long, called saps, were dug by both sides into No Man's Land, beyond the barbed wire. They were close enough to enemy lines that they were used as listening posts. This was called manning the sap head. Sappers were not allowed to talk as voices could be heard by the enemy. Saps were sometimes filled with explosives. In the weeks prior to the attack at Vimy, 200 mines detonated by sappers took a heavy toll on the Germans.

At Vimy Ridge, Canadian trenches were a match for the Germans. Byng and Major-General Arthur Currie made other significant changes from tactics used by the British Army for many generations. All Canadian soldiers, whatever their rank, were fully briefed about the plan of attack with the exception of the actual date. They were organized into smaller platoons where each was taught not only his own job but also the jobs of the other men in his unit. They perfected a rolling barrage through meticulous practice and repeated dry runs, known as the Vimy Glide. Past battles were preceded by an artillery barrage, followed by waves of soldiers going over the top. At Vimy, the artillery, led by Lt.-Col. Andrew McNaughton, provided a continuous moving cover for the soldiers as they followed directly behind. The pace across No Man's Land was set at 100 yards every three minutes. They had to be in sync or they would be hit by their own shells.

Prior to the attack, machine guns, nicknamed Emma Gees, arched over the enemy lines 24 hours a day, for many days. This was known as indirect fire as the main objective was not necessarily to kill but to deny the enemy opportunity to move men, food and supplies. Aerial balloons tracked the damage. At Beaumont Hamel, without these balloons, the British did not know their weeklong bombardment had been a failure.

In the underground tunnel it is possible to see how primitively they lived. The tour guide helps us imagine crowded, dark, filthy conditions. Soldiers lived with the smells of body odor, wet wool, tobacco, and human waste. Despite the wooden walkway, mud was ever present. After half an hour underground, I am chilled with the dampness despite the fact that it is a beautiful sunny day. Kraig, who is 6 foot 2 inches tall, hits his head and has to watch for beams the rest of the tour. To our absolute surprise and delight, our guide's tour is devoted to the runner. What are the odds that she chooses a role so personal to me? I have goose bumps. Our group consists of British high school students and I am emotional telling them about my grandfather.

Smaller men were chosen to be runners for a taller man was a bigger target. Some runners lived only four or five days. It was a dangerous job. Runners were perceived as trustworthy men as the lives of their regiment could depend on them. It was a position of prestige and respect. They worked in pairs in case one was wounded or killed, and they were not allowed to stop if the other was hit. There could be up to eight runners working various parts of a line. Runners wore special red bands (brassards) on their left arms so their troops would recognize them in the trenches and move to one side to allow them to pass. Unfortunately this made them easier targets for the enemy. Adolf Hitler was a German runner in World War I.

In the Grange we are shown four small rooms dug off the main tunnel, bedroom for the runners, bedroom for the Commanding Officer, the communications room and the officers' mess. They were small cave like spaces with dirt walls, floors and ceilings. The runners' room was off the communication room where officers made decisions. The bedroom measures about 8 x 10 feet. Today it has two makeshift beds. In 1917 it had up to 12 beds, stacked on top of and besides one another. They were called hot beds. As fast as one was vacated, it was filled with another runner. It is impossible to imagine 12 men sleeping in that space. Aside from that of the Commanding Officer, this was the only other bedroom, a sign of the importance of runners and the recognition that they needed their rest to have their wits about them. Runners like Andrew did not have this luxury above ground.

A Runner's bed at Vimy

Belgium

After Vimy we continue to Belgium for the last of our caribou hunt for that is how I perceive it. We hope to find the train station at Ledeghem, now spelled Ledegem and pronounced Leed-em. Ledeghem was the site of the last Newfoundland Regiment battle, the Battle of Courtrai. The final caribou is in the town of Harlebeke, outside Kortrijk, pronounced Kor-trick, on the side of a busy road. I first looked on the map for Courtrai and it did not exist. After this war, many places began using their earlier Flemish names. Nothing is simple.

The summer and autumn of 1917 in northern France and Flanders saw record breaking rainfalls, resulting in incredibly muddy battlefields. In the Battle of Langemarck at the Steenbeck River, on August 15, 1917, the Regiment crossed the Floating Swamp, 400 yards of deep oozing bog which gave no foothold. Holding their rifles over their heads while struggling in the mire, they hoped not to be hit or lose their boots in the mud. The torrential rain, combined with fog, continued for the Battle of Poelcappelle on October 9, 1917. Broembeek

Creek had swollen to a river. Soldiers were rain sodden and covered from head to toe in mud. The Regimental Diary states that all wires were cut by enemy shelling. Communication was by runners only. The swamp swallowed up the wounded and claimed many lives.

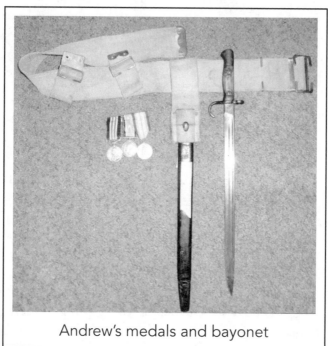

Andrew's medals and bayonet

Stretcher bearer, Patrick O'Neill, #2263, braved the swamp repeatedly "to bring back the wounded to the Dressing Station at Ruisseux Farm. He personally took charge of the Company stretcher bearers and had all cases cleared very promptly." Awarded a Military Medal, O'Neill was killed 23 days later on October 9, 1917.

Andrew, called Andy and Smitty by his comrades, was a scrapper, one of 54 men enlisted from the outports of Dildo and New Harbour. Fifteen were killed. Of the 54, Cpl. Levi Hollett and Andrew were decorated. Andrew's Military Medal was awarded to non commissioned ranks for acts of bravery on the recommendation of a Commander in Chief in the field, the enlisted soldier's equivalent of the Military Cross. It was created by King George V, in March, 1916, half way through the war. One quarter (27) of the 108 Newfoundlanders awarded the Military Medal were killed in action.

Levi Hollett

Levi Hollett was awarded a DCM, Distinguished Conduct Medal, and the French and Belgium Croix de Guerre. The DCM is the second highest award for gallantry in action, after the Victoria Cross, for non commissioned ranks. The Regiment received 31 DCMs. The Croix de Guerre recognized acts of heroism with enemy forces. Levi was one of eight Newfoundland recipients. He acted alone and single handedly destroyed a sniper's post to capture a dugout firing on his platoon in the Battle of Broembeek, (Poelcappelle), in Belgium, October, 1917.

The popular Battalion Transport Officer, Lt. Stanley Goodyear, #334, from Grand Falls, a tall man with an air of invincibility, was killed at Broembeek. He was awarded the Military Cross posthumously "for most conspicuous consistent and continuous good work as transport officer of the Battalion during the past eighteen months in France. His resourcefulness invariably overcomes all difficulties." At one time, he disobeyed a British Officer's stop order. Goodyear, on horseback, charged with his team and wagons past the check point into the battlefield with his Regiment's supplies. He was one of five brothers serving in the war. Two survived.

In April, 1918, as a result of low numbers, the Regiment was withdrawn from active service and assigned guard duty at Sir Douglas Haig's General Headquarters at Montreuil. For two and a half years, the Regiment was proud to fight as part of the 88th Brigade of the 29th, and their removal from it was viewed as a blow by the remaining Newfoundland troops. On April 26, 1918, they were inspected by Brigadier General Bernard Freyberg, the youngest general in the British Army at 27.

They were to meet again. In October, 1918, in Steenbeck, Belgium, while the Regiment was under fire, an officer on horseback shouted to them, "Who are you?" "Newfoundlanders," they replied. Freyberg exclaimed, "Thank God. My left flank is safe. Now for my right." It was the ultimate compliment from a man they admired.

In August, the tide turned in the Allied favor. The Regiment was sent back to the trenches in Belgium, a bleak battleground many had fought before. The Battle of Ypres began September 28, 1918, at Polygon Wood and Keiberg Ridge. The final Newfoundland Regiment battle began around a tiny hamlet called Drie Masten.

Ledgehem is enroute, a very small town. Finding the train station is no easy task. It has been a private residence for over

60 years. A small plaque on the building verifies it as the former station built in 1889. The railway tracks have been removed and we are seeing the back of the station from the road. I feel almost giddy and can't wipe the grin off my face but we must leave as it is getting dark. I wish we had more time.

9. HET OUD STATIONSGEBOUW

Railway Station at Ledgehem 1918

On October 2, the Newfoundland Regiment took over the train station and 500 yards of railway track for four days, resisting heavy German machine gun fire, leaving the night of October 6-7. Their Headquarters was moved to the Telford farm October 4. I think it is noteworthy that we are at the train station October 8. The British forces cleaned up, rested and waited until October 14. The Royal Newfoundland Regiment waited in the shelter of the railway embankment that night until zero hour, 5:35 AM. They ended at the de Beurt farm, about 100 to 200 yards from Drie Masten. The Beurt ridge was in the village of Winckle St. Eloi.

On the morning of October 14, 1918, smoke from weapons and explosives combined with a heavy mist to make fog thick as pea soup. This gave the Regiment an early advantage as they could not be seen by the Germans. When the fog lifted, however, they were pinned down in sunshine in full view of the enemy as they tried to cross a stream, the Wulfdambeek, too wide to jump and six feet deep. Gunfire prevented further advance. Attempts were made to storm the German battery with more casualties and without success.

Private Tommy Ricketts, #3102, a member of the Lewis Gun detachment, volunteered to go forward with section commander, Lance Corporal Matthew Brazil, #1368, to try to eliminate the troublesome battery. Ricketts engaged them at close range, his Lewis gun a new lightweight machine gun, which could shoot 500 to 600 rounds per minute and was effective up to 650 yards. It was nicknamed the Belgian rattlesnake. He ran out of ammunition 300 yards from the Germans. Without hesitation, he doubled back, crawling 100 yards of bullet swept ground, returning with more ammunition before the enemy was able to regroup. Brazil provided covering fire with his rifle. Second Lieutenant Stanley Newman, #36, led the platoon into the battery and a nearby farm, capturing machine guns and German prisoners.

On that day, near the little hamlet of Drie Masten, Tommy Ricketts won the highest of British military honors, the Victoria Cross. A 15-year old boy soldier, he joined the Regiment in 1917, marking an X on his enlistment paper, saying he was 18 years, 3 months old. When King George V pinned the Cross on Ricketts's chest, he said, "This is the youngest VC in my army." His older brother, George Ricketts, # 1703, went missing in action, presumed dead, December 3, 1917.

For his role, Newman received the Military Cross. Brazil received a Distinguished Conduct Medal. Ricketts and Brazil both received France's highest honor, the Croix de Guerre. Brazil's family did not receive his Croix de Guerre until 1983, after Brazil had died, because the Military had responded to an inquiry by Brazil in 1939 saying there was no record of his having been given the honor.

It was on this same day, October 14, during the Battle of Ledgehem in The Last Hundred Days, that Andrew was awarded the Military Medal for bravery in the field. Andrew, as well as Doyle Curtis, #1552, and William P. King, #2577, won Military Medals for their service as company runners. The fog and when it lifted, the exposure to enemy guns made it difficult to coordinate an attack. The course of action had to be communicated to and from Headquarters with each success and failure. This was the job of the runners. On October 18, Private Andrew Smith was appointed Acting Corporal.

Twenty-six Regiment members were killed and less than half the men were able to continue the two day, seven mile trek to the River Lys to attack Vichte. The retreating Germans had blown up the bridges and fired on the Regiment as they paddled and rafted across the river on October 20 to spend the night huddled in the pouring rain. On the 24th, one of Andrew's D Company billets was blown up, wiping out most of his platoon. People of Belgium came into the streets to welcome their liberators, only to fall victim to German shells. On October 27, the Regiment withdrew for a much deserved rest, their numbers depleted to 256, one quarter of their strength. Two days later, Andrew was granted a leave. Two weeks later the war came to an end.

Unfortunately, on October 20, in the battle of Lys, William P. King was killed in action. He was a small man, 5' 3" and 126 pounds., which made him an excellent candidate for a runner. He had returned to the battlefield only two months earlier after a lengthy recovery from severe gunshot wounds to his buttock, left forearm, lower chin and jaw, suffered in April, 1917.

Fourteen Regiment members received Military Medals for their courage at Ledgehem. In 2007 we discovered this letter addressed to Andrew's mother, Julia, in his military file. The surviving family was unaware of its existence. While the files of all fourteen soldiers acknowledge their receipt of the medal, only eight include a personal letter recording the actual deed for which it was given. We are fortunate that Andrew's was one of those. It was a wonderful find!

April 15, 1919
Mrs. Julia Smith

I beg to quote hereunder the details of the deed for which the Military Medal was awarded your son #1393, Pte. Andrew Smith, Royal Newfoundland Regiment, taken from supplement to The London Gazette.

Ledgehem. Authority, Daily Orders, 1st Battalion, 9/11/18. For conspicuous gallantry and devotion to duty, on the 14th October 1918, during the advance from LEDGEHEM towards the LYS River, this man was acting as Company runner. During the whole of the day, he repeatedly carried messages from the front line to Battalion Headquarters and back over ground swept by machine gun fire and by snipers. On one occasion when two runners had been sniped before they had gone 100 yards, Pte. Smith at once volunteered to take the message and get it back to Battalion Headquarters. Throughout the day he showed a complete disregard of danger.

Please accept my congratulations and assurance of the appreciation of the conduct of your son.

Yours faithfully, MINISTER OF MILITA.

William's parents, William and Mary King, Southside Battery, St. John's, received a similar letter stating the heroic actions of their late son.

"For conspicuous gallantry and devotion to duty. On the 14th October 1918, during the advance from LEDGEHEM towards LYS, this man was acting as Company runner. During the whole of the day he carried messages back to Battn. HQ

often under heavy fire. Especially when his Company was held up at NEERHOF during the advance, he carried messages continuously back to Battn. HQ. On each occasion he had to cross about 200 to 300 yards of open ground swept by enemy MG fire."

The Curtis family was informed:

"This man has always shown gallantry and coolness in the face of the enemy. During the October operations, he was most valuable as a runner, always willing, and showed an utter disregard of all dangers when a message had to be delivered."

Hamor Gardner, # 645, of British Harbour, in charge of the transport of ammunition to the battle site, "showed great presence of mind when he hitched up his horses and wagons and galloped through a heavy enemy barrage, bringing his convoy with him, saving it and rejoining the Regiment." He was also awarded a Military Medal.

Andrew's Military Medal

After war was declared in August 1914, Governor Davidson cabled to London of his Newfoundland recruits, "The men have been enrolled from all ranks of society; they are of fine physique, rather short in stature but thick set and enduring. They are also handymen and very hardy and accustomed to hard work and little food. With almost no exceptions, the men are abstemious – they will render a good account of themselves." (Abstemious means sparing in eating and drinking). These attributes were to hold them in good stead. By the end of the war, 6241 Newfoundlanders had served in the Regiment, 35.6% of the island's men between the ages of 19 and 35. Fatalities claimed one quarter of the Regiment. Casualties (dead plus wounded) stood at an astounding 72%. By 1917 this little army that didn't have enough funds to send its troops oversees with weapons, had evolved into one of the most respected and decorated units in the British army.

We realize, given the staggering losses of the Regiment, that Andrew was very fortunate to have survived where so many died. In the beautiful countryside that is Northern France we also realize the consequences for the French people and their culture if they had not been able to survive the invasion of their country. In a moving ceremony at Ypres, the street is closed every night at 8 PM beneath the Menin Gate Memorial and the local Fire Brigade sounds the Last Post. In this act of daily remembrance the local residents open their windows and doors and stand quietly with visitors to the site to show respect. The Royal Newfoundland Regiment marched under this impressive gate three times, in 1916, 1917 and 1918. The gate was destroyed and has been rebuilt as a memorial.

Trench Warfare

It is impressive that Andrew spent almost four years in the trenches, when the average survival rate for a front line soldier was a mere few months. The survival rate for runners was less. It is more impressive, after all the death and destruction he witnessed, that he remained a happy and caring person. Today, in Newfoundland and Labrador, to be a descendent of a member of the Royal Newfoundland Regiment is an honor.

Andrew's military file has never been seen by his family. While the letter to his mother describing the deed for which he won the Military Medal is my biggest thrill, the file provides other glimpses into my grandfather's life at this time. I am excited to learn the surname and address of his Scottish girlfriend for we have known her only as Rea.

WWI Soldier Receiving Mail. Print from Andrew's sister, Blanche

Money, or rather a shortage of it, was a problem for many soldiers on the Front. On November 5, 1917, Andrew sent a telegram to his parents, "On leave from France. Cable five pounds through Minister Militia." On November 10, he cabled the Victoria Street office, "Wire on money at once to Post

Office Ayr if arrived." It did not. His file records a Cancellation of Allotment was signed by Andrew in the field in France on January 7, 1918, witnessed by Captain H. Rendell. Effective January 31, 1918, it cancelled his parents' allotment of 60 cents a day. Subsequent correspondence indicates his mother sent the money and followed up with a letter as to its whereabouts but the money was never received. One month later, in a letter from France on February 12, 1918, he wrote to the Pay and Records office, "I have an idea that my pay was made up wrong." On March 11, 1918, it was acknowledged he had not been paid for 28 days and was credited with £6:6:7.

Perusing Andrew's file, I find reference to only three leaves to the UK. The first is August, 1916. The second is November 4 to 18, 1917. The third leave was two days after his company withdrew from Ledgehem, from October 29 to November 12, 1918. His leave ended one day after the armistice. A soldier was lucky to get two weeks leave a year.

Mail is an important part of a soldier's life. Under trench conditions, it is remarkable delivery was even possible. Regiment files do not generally record parcels. The file of Private Reginald Cheater, # 3670, is unique. Cheater enlisted April 23, 1917. After training, he joined his battalion in the field, November 14, 1917. Nineteen days later, he went missing at Cambrai. Sadly, he died of pneumonia as a German Prisoner of War on April 25, 1918. His parents, John and Annie, from Greenspond, sent him three parcels. The list gives invaluable insight into the contents and the cost of same in 1917.

September 24, 1917:
2 pairs stockings ($2.00), 1 lb. raisins (.17), 1 plug tobacco (.15), 1 pack cigarettes (.15), postage (.24), for a total of $2.71
November 15, 1917:
1 lb. tobacco (.85), 1 towel (.25), 1 cake of Pears soap (.17), 1 handkerchief (.15), postage (.24), for a total of $1.66

December 16, 1917:

1 cake ($1.00), 1/2 cheese (.20), 1 lb. cube sugar (.15), candy (.10), 1 black chocolate (.10), postage (.74), for a total of $2.29

It is noteworthy that the third parcel was sent after Cheater was captured but his parents were not notified of his POW status until January 14, 1918.

With so much of Andrew's life fading into the past, snippets have reappeared in unexpected ways. In 2006 his daughter, Rea, viewed a play called "The Known Soldier" in Gander by Newfoundland playwright, Jeff Pitcher. The play was based on the Battle of Ledgehem and the winning of the Victoria Cross by Tommy Ricketts. While Rea knew her father had fought at Ledgehem, she was not prepared to hear her father's name, Andrew. It gave her goose bumps. At the end of the play, medal winners were announced. She was deeply moved, the emotion noted by my brother, Robert, who emailed Jeff Pitcher. In turn, Jeff phoned Rea, a gesture much appreciated.

Like many veterans Andrew did not talk much about his wartime experiences. He lived it and knew there was no glorification in it. When he did talk, it was generally about the intolerable life in the trenches; the rats, frogs, slugs, horned beetles, flies, lice, shelling, cave-ins, hunger, and the lack of any kind of comfort or personal hygiene. They wore the same clothing for weeks, even months. They suffered from parasites and infections. 146 Regiment members died because of disease such as dysentery, caused by the filthy conditions. Andrew's legs were sometimes black as coal due to poor circulation in the muddy, damp and cold conditions.

They lived for weeks on bully beef (canned corn beef), and tea with stale bread or biscuits, and pozzy, a plum and apple jam. Sometimes, when supply lines were cut, they'd have nothing to eat for days. Andrew recalled being so hungry he threw up blood. The hard French bread was a far cry from the soft white bread which was a staple of their Newfoundland diet. They fantasized about eating real food and sleeping in a real bed. The constant smoking and difficulty in cleaning one's teeth contributed to an infectious disease known as Trench Mouth, resulting in foul breath and bleeding gums. At home, most families were unaware of the barbarous conditions. They were told only the glory of war.

Trenches accumulated water during rainfall, creating mud which was often knee deep. Wooden slats called duckboards were laid together like track to make walkways in the mud, although these were often lacking. Heavy rains and enemy shelling caused trench walls to collapse. Soldiers dug sleeping holes like small caves in the sides of trenches known as funk holes. After frequent cave ins when men were buried alive, these were forbidden. Andrew told his grandson, Robert, of one such time when he was sleeping with buddies and received a direct hit. They were being smothered with dirt and logs. They managed to frantically claw themselves out to safety.

Rea recalls her father saying that when he was exhausted and could not take another step, he wished for a piece of paper to put over his face before he slept. Was this to block out the light or a desire for privacy? Or was it to discourage the rats from walking on his face, a problem well documented in the trench warfare of World War I? Black and brown rats numbered in the tens of millions. Brown Somme rats grew big as cats as they fed on corpses. They roamed the trenches, eating unprotected food and bloated bodies, spreading infection, disturbing sleep and being a constant nuisance. They crawled in the bedrolls of soldiers while they slept. A single rat could produce up to 900 babies a year! Soldiers made games of killing them.

To a newcomer, the smells emanating from the trenches were nauseating. Soldiers learned to live with the stagnant mud, rotting sandbags, poison gas, and everyday smells of overflowing cess pits, body and feet odor, wet wool, cigarette smoke, cooked and rotten food. Lime was spread to reduce the incidence of infection. The most disturbing was the smell of decaying bodies, the smell of death.

Andrew and Hardy Rideout 1966

When Andrew first met his sister Violet's second husband, Hardy Rideout, #3144, they were astonished to realize they had met in the trenches. Andrew was lousy, stripped of his clothing and covered in red bite marks. He was using a cigarette to burn out lice. They used candles to burn the fluff in the seams in which the lice laid their eggs. This was known as reading their shirts. They turned their clothes inside out and flattened the seams. If they were lucky enough to have a cake of soap to rub, it was easier to burn the lice without burning their uniforms. Lice (cooties) congregated in the seams and even when the clothes were washed, their eggs (nits) remained. The itch was relentless. The most difficult spot was under the belt at the back. Soldiers scratched themselves raw and wore their underwear inside out to get relief.

There were three kinds of lice, head (nits), pubic (crabs) and body (chats). Body lice were the most problematic. They caused Trench Fever, sometimes called Five Day Fever, although this was not identified until 1918, at the end of the war. Recovery could take several weeks., Many shaved their heads to discourage nits. They had chatting parties when they sat around picking lice out of each other's hair and clothing. Lice made a popping sound when burned and had a sour stale smell. Men killed them between their fingernails. The spurt of blood from each dead louse provided some satisfaction, but this "war" could not be won. The lice were inescapable.

Trenches were dug by soldiers, back breaking work, often in the dark. Most trenches were five feet deep. The soil dug was put in sandbags stacked two to three feet deep to make a parapet in front of the trenches. Many front lines were on sites of previous battlegrounds. The digging uncovered rusty cans and wire, broken rifles and bodies of friend and foe. Trenches were not dug in straight lines. They were usually zigzagged, in staggered lines. The opposing sides dug their trenches facing one another, often only 100 to 300 yards apart, separated by No Man's Land. They required constant maintenance.

There was a Trench Cycle. Soldiers rotated, serving time in the front (fire) line trench, followed by time in support, then in reserve, ending with a period of rest, before starting all over again. Time in support, reserve and rest could still be under fire, depending on the situation. The Newfoundland Regiment was not in the front line but in support at Beaumont Hamel. The three lines were joined by communication trenches. A lot of rest time was spent filling sandbags and carrying duckboards and other supplies to the front line. The word "rest" is deceiving.

The reserve trench was the destination of stretcher bearers with their wounded, before they were sent to the Casualty Clearing Station for medical attention. A scene of desperation, the stench of soiled clothing combined with the retching and moans of wounded and dying men. Whether they were in front, support, reserve or rest, they lived in narrow trenches, open to weather and enemy fire, in crowded unsanitary conditions.

Movement in the trenches was restricted during the day. Soldiers had to be forever mindful of keeping their heads low and walking in a crouch as enemy snipers were a constant threat. Newcomers were especially vulnerable. There were inspections, mealtimes, cleaning of guns and equipment, upkeep of trenches, duckboards, latrines and sandbags, and pumping out of water. The thunderous roar of artillery fire was constant. They spent much of their trench time smoking, digging, patrolling, raiding and waiting for the inevitable.

At night, trenches came to life as more could be risked under cover of darkness. Fresh troops relieved the old. Vital food, water and maintenance supplies arrived. Wiring inspection parties from both sides went out most nights into No Man's Land. The irony is that sometimes they stumbled upon one other. They had a dilemma. If they chose to shoot, the noise would bring machine gunfire from both sides. They would surely all die. Sometimes they chose to fight with fists and sometimes they went their separate ways.

Soldiers etched out what little comfort they could with only two issue blankets. In the bitter cold of winter, in icy muck and snow filled trenches, they were not allowed a fire as smoke would give away their position. The winter of 1916 in France was one of the coldest on record. Many suffered from frostbite. Chilled to the bone, they huddled together for warmth, an ideal environment for the spreading of lice. Conditions were gruesome. Senses were numbed by fear and fatigue.

Aside from chatting parties, men rubbed their feet with grease before changing into dry socks. At the beginning of the war, Trench Foot was a serious problem for both sides, as feet were constantly cold and wet. If untreated, gangrene set in and toes, feet and legs had to be amputated. All British troops were ordered to carry three pairs of dry socks and to change them twice a day. Officers carried out regular foot inspections.

The women of Newfoundland were encouraged to knit socks for the British army and include their names in the toes. In the January 16, 1915 edition of the *Twillingate Sun* newspaper, they were instructed "to knit near to 3 rows of white for 10 inch socks, blue for 10 ½ inch socks and red for 11 inch socks. Rib the leg and top of the foot. Length of leg is 14 inches." Two weeks later was the remarkable story of Maggie Osmond of Morton's Harbour. Her knit socks were one of 1143 pairs sent by the Women's Patriotic Society to the St. John's Ambulance Association in England. While in England on medical leave, her son, Douglas Osmond, #306, swapped socks with another soldier who had been given the socks with Maggie's name. The newspaper article was dated January 30, 1915, and Douglas was to die July 8, 1916, of wounds to the face and thighs suffered at Beaumont Hamel.

Andrew told his family that early in the war, there was an unofficial truce at Christmas with Germans in the opposing trenches, that the war took a holiday! The Christmas Truce of 1914 was extraordinary. It was not an organized event which involved all soldiers but rather small clusters of men, usually privates and non commissioned officers. Against the backdrop of thousands of candle-lit pine trees distributed to the German troops, they tentatively reached out to one another. They held joint burial services, sang Christmas carols, exchanged food and cigarettes and took photographs. In subsequent years, the commanders of both sides were determined the events of 1914 would not be repeated. This understanding, not to use weapons at Christmas or when the soldiers were at rest, was given the name, "Live and Let Live." It was fragile at best.

The Regiment spent a pleasant Christmas in 1914 in Fort George, Scotland. Their second Christmas was fierce fighting in the trenches in Turkey. Christmas 1916 was celebrated in Camps-en-Amienois, a village 35 miles from Beaumont Hamel, and in 1917, the village of Fressin, 40 miles from Arras. . To get to Fressin, they trudged for three days and 33 miles through deep snow but they did not complain. They had endured enough mud and rain.

We learn so much and are reminded again of the tragedy of war. With the use of modern weapons such as the machine gun, the old ways of battle resulted in a waste of life on a scale the world had never seen. World War I became a war of attrition. The grim sacrifice of lives was viewed as a means to an end, with the victor being the one who could outlast the other.

The trench system was flawed. After Headquarters made its plan, the commanders in the field were unable to exercise their own judgment or make decisions based on the new reality of the battle site. While discipline is critical to the success of a military operation, Headquarters was far away and communications poor. I can only guess the stress on the runners. The officers in the changing field were committed to continue with the original plan whether or not it was still the best course. The element of surprise was lost and once in a lifetime opportunities missed.

My brother, Robert, had a fascination with all things military. He badgered our grandfather with wartime questions but was usually ignored. There was an exception. Andrew told of the ugly side of war. One of the Regiment members was shot and fell into a muddy shell hole. They listened to him calling for help. He could not crawl out and was sinking to a muddy death, which unfortunately, happened often. They could not save him for enemy fire was too intense. He called that he was going to kill himself and with his grenade, that is what he did.

Andrew was born with a caul, a portion of amniotic sac over his face. This was considered good luck. Folklore had it that such a person would not drown or die in a foreign place. His mother took comfort in that. There is no record of hospitalization in his file. The closest he came to injury was when the heel of his boot was shot right off his foot. Alma recalls him saying, "If ya thought I ran fast before, ya can imagine how fast I ran after!"

Levi Hollett was wounded, in his right thigh at Beaumont Hamel and in his left hand at Masineres. Andrew's friend, Jonathon Taylor Gosse, #2629, was also wounded twice.

Jonathon Gosse

On one occasion Andrew and Jonathon Gosse were on leave in Scotland with little money. At a boxing match free for the military, volunteers were encouraged to fight the winner. In a few minutes Andrew knocked him down and left with a fist full of cash! It was a popular story they liked to tell when the two got together years later with their buddies. The family rarely heard stories first hand. There were more snippets. By using thread he tied to trees as his guide, Andrew led a group of troops trapped by Germans to safety. In another incident Violet said Andrew captured a German pilot when he "pitched" after his plane crashed.

A favorite memory was when Andrew and a couple of buddies smelled fresh coffee brewing in a farm house. Upon entry, they saw hot cups sitting on the table. They realized the enemy was hiding in the cellar, their weapons against the wall, out of reach. They stripped the Germans of their valuables. Andrew took a gold pocket watch. He also took a pair of German boots for they were better than his own. The hob nails in the soles of his boots may have helped extend the life of the soles but they sent vibrations through the feet and legs with every step. The story always ended with how much they enjoyed the coffee!

Andrew brought the gold watch home to Newfoundland. It sat on the mantle of the Front Room for 30 years. It was exquisite, its face surrounded by a circle of rubies. By depressing a button on the back, the inner workings of the watch were revealed as well as the engraved name of its German owner. Andrew's daughter, Alma, naively brought the non working watch to a "jeweler" in Argentia to be fixed as a surprise for her father. Far too innocent, it did not occur to her that he might steal the valuable piece, which he claimed he lost. Ashamed at not ever retrieving it, Alma did not own up to her deed for many years.

It was said by his family that Andrew twice lost his rank but only one time is recorded in his file. "Insolence to an officer" occurred August 22, 1918 and the decision to demote him to Lance Corporal from Acting Corporal was noted on August 24th. On that day, the Regiment was not in the battlefield but guarding General Headquarters in Montreuil. The Regiment diary from that day read, "Battalion went short route march. Very hot." What Andrew did to be demoted is not in his file. His daughters remember it was said he once challenged an officer who insisted on lighting matches for cigarettes in the trench which could give away their location to the Germans. Another time he questioned a liquor ration (toddy) to an officer who had already received his share.

Rum was given after, rather than before an offensive, and during cold weather, to add to their tea. Soldiers were rationed to two ounces a day. The rum came in one gallon earthenware jugs from Ypres marked S.R.D. These initials may stand for Supply Reserve Depot or Service Ration Depot or Special Red Demerara, 186 proof Jamaican rum, but to the men, it was "Seldom Reaches Destination," "Sergeants Rarely Deliver" or "Soon Runs Dry!"

Levi Hollett's records show he was forfeited seniority six months for drunk and disorderly conduct on High Street after 21:30. Levi's offences happened on November 23, 1918, after the end of the war! When Levi came home from Buchans and Corner Brook, he and Andrew laughed and talked about old times over a few beer. Loss of rank and docked pay were the usual punishments for undesirable behavior which ranged from drunkenness to being absent or late for parade.

Captain Herbert Rendell

Andrew did reflect on the fate of Captain Herbert Rendell, # 93, from St. John's, commander of his Company. Andrew had just run a message at Keiberg Ridge near Passchendaele in Belgium. They were under heavy machine gun fire from Germans, many holed up in local farmhouses. It had been raining heavily. The troop's clothes were soaked through. Rendell asked what the conditions were like in the muddy battle zone. Andrew replied it was bad, there were snipers everywhere. Instinctively the Captain rose to the top of the trench to view the situation. Andrew protested, "I wouldn't do that, sir, if I was you," but it was too late. The Captain was shot in the throat. It was reported on Sunday, September 29, 1918, at 1:25 PM, that Captain Rendell, M.C. M.I.D., was killed in action near Zonnebeke at 11 AM. He was 29 years old.

Herbert Rendell

An eye witness report from Second Lieutenant McHenry stated he died instantly. The officer commanding 1st Battalion reported that he lived two minutes. Andrew was with him when he died. Traditionally only officers' names were recorded so Andrew's name or his accounting of the incident would not be used in the report. It was the runner's duty to report the death of an officer to Headquarters. The captain's death struck a chord with Andrew. He was encouraged to share his memories with Captain Rendell's family but he was reluctant to do so.

Page 2 of Andrew's pay book, dated December, 1917, reads:
   Regiment – Newfoundland
   Company – E
   No. – 1393 Rank – Private
   Name in full – Andrew Smith
   Date of Attestation – 10 – 4 – 15
   Age on Enlistment – 20 years

On the bottom of page 3, is Andrew's signature, A. Smith, above that of H. Rendell, Capt. It is poignant to see that Rendell's signature is the most frequent in Andrew's book, 17 times in nine months, and to note that he last signed his name on September 17, 1918, 12 days before he was killed.

Captain Rendell's parents were Dr. Herbert Sr. and Eliza (Clift) Rendell, a prominent St. John's family who lived on Duckworth Street. Dr. Rendell was the first superintendent of the Sanatorium. He died in 1952 at the age of 94. After Herbert was killed, his father wrote the London office to learn details of his son's death and burial. He inquired about the whereabouts of his son's Military Cross, awarded after the Battle of Masineres. A younger son, Second Lieutenant Clifford Rendell, #621, died as a result of a wound at Beaumont Hamel. His right leg required amputation and there were hopes for a recovery. Cablegrams reveal that a Herbert and Miss Mary Rendell were at his side in the hospital in France. Unfortunately, Clifford died of septicemia, blood poisoning, on July 22, 1916. He was 21 years old.

In France, on January 3, 1919, Acting Corporal Smith was appointed to Acting Sergeant. On January 30th he embarked for home on the *Corisican*. His time in service had been three years, eleven months and two weeks, a total of 1453 days, two weeks shy of four years. On discharge, he received a war gratuity of six months, net amount due $420.00, and a clothing allowance of $60.00.

On September 12, 1919, Andrew sent a telegraph from Grand Falls. "Will be at St. John's sixteenth to receive my decoration. Andrew Smith." Military Medals to be awarded to:

2577 Pte. William King *Killed in action October 20, 1918*
3603 Pte. Edward O'Brien *Killed in action October 21, 1918*
2318 Pte. Maurice Power

2603 Cpl. Richard Power
1393 Sgt. Andrew Smith
3156 Cpl. Heber Trask   *Killed in action October 25, 1918*

The letter listed the six names and regimental numbers. It did not record that three of the soldiers had been killed. Research revealed the untimely deaths of King, Trask and O'Brien three weeks before the war ended, medals awarded posthumously.

BUCKINGHAM PALACE.

The Queen and I wish you God-speed, and a safe return to your homes and dear ones.

A grateful Mother Country is proud of your splendid services characterized by unsurpassed devotion and courage.

George R.I.

Andrew's letter from King George V

Trask, O'Brien and Richard Power won their Military Medals the same day as Andrew, for their efforts in capturing enemy pillboxes. Richard Power had already received a Distinguished Service Medal and the French Croix de Guerre and Bronze Star. Maurice Power captured four enemy snipers holed up in a farmhouse and returned unscathed with bullet holes in his jacket. The next day, O'Brien died of a wound to the throat.

I am left wondering about the medal presentation ceremony. Who was in attendance with my grandfather? Thomas Trask, father of Heber, replied that he would not attend "owing to my circumstances at this particular season and being rather unwell." Richard Power from Cupids was away at the Labrador Fishery. In a letter dated, September 6, 1919, Dr. Herbert Rendell Sr., father of Captain Rendell, replied that he was attending the ceremony on the 16th. He wrote "that it would be my son's wish that his (Military) Cross should be presented to his mother." Were Andrew and Dr. Rendell at the Investiture the same time? My grandfather would have made the connection. How did he feel?

The Dornier Do-X

The DO-X in Dildo, 1932

Andrew saw German uniforms again after the war. On May 19, 1932, the German flying boat, the Do-X, was forced to land and stay overnight in Trinity Bay on a transatlantic flight from New York to Germany. Thick fog made it impossible to land in St. John's as scheduled. It found shelter in Dildo Harbour. Many people who had hoped to see the DO-X in St. John's converged on Dildo for this once in a lifetime opportunity. Some petrol was brought in and the DO-X completed its refueling in Holyrood when the fog lifted. Captain Friedrich Christiansen, sighting the only telephone in the community running to the Smith home, sent a party of officers to use their phone for assistance.

How did Andrew feel at seeing the approach of and hearing the German accents of the crew in his home 14 years after the war? It must have brought back memories but he was not a man to hold grudges. He understood the futility of that. He put it in the past where it belonged and treated them with courtesy and respect.

One of his daughter Rea's first memories for she was only three and a half years old, was of seeing the uniformed airmen, sitting in the eating room awaiting phone calls about their fuel. Her mother gave them a lunch. In thanks, Andrew and Violet and their five children were invited to tour the gigantic aircraft. Florence was 10, Gerald was 7, Lendo was 5 and Alma was an infant. Rea remembers being taken to the DO-X in a little boat and looking up at the huge plane but she has no memory of entering the plane or being on it! She does remember their being dressed in their Sunday best for the occasion.

Built in Germany in 1929, the DO-X was the largest and most powerful flying boat in the world. Weighing 55 tons, it was 33 feet high and 134 feet long with a wing span of 157 feet. Mounted on top of its wings were six pairs of engines. It had three decks. On Saturday, May 21, it left St. John's with over 6000 gallons of fuel, so heavy it completed the first five hours skimming the waves of the Atlantic Ocean. It guzzled up fuel, 400 gallons of gas per hour. Plagued with difficulties, the decision was made to stop flying the DO-X in 1934. Despite its limitations, it was an extraordinary feat in its time. It was destroyed in The Museum of Aviation in Berlin during RAF air raids in World War II.

Lance Corporal A. Smith

My original war photo of my grandfather was given to my mother by his Aunt Millie Pinsent. For years it was on mom's closet shelf, missing its frame and I fretted over its care. I was fortunate to find a duplicate of the military issue 14 x 20 inch oval frame in an antique shop. The photographer's name is signed, J.C. Evely, Freshwater, Bay de Verde. Three war photos were taken at the beginning of the war. They bear the names of the recipients, his father, mother and his Aunt Millie. Andrew wears a Lance Corporal stripe on his sleeve.

In a fourth war photo, Andrew is wearing three chevrons, the rank of Sergeant, taken at the end of the war. This was the portrait hanging in the Front Room of his home in his lifetime. Something is odd. At first glance, Andrew's hand appears to be resting on the chair but the chair is behind him and his arm is forward of his body. The chair may be part of a backdrop rather than a prop? The lower portion of the portrait has been touched up by the photographer.

Sergeant Andrew Smith

I have always been intrigued by this portrait. One cannot help but compare the photos, taken four years apart. There are those who might warn that we see only what we want to see. There is a danger in assuming the portrait should reflect the toll war has taken on the soldier and it may not be so. I try to keep an open mind but a thinner weary face looks back at me. I see a difference.

THE GIRLFRIEND

The June 26, 2009, wedding of our son, Kraig, to Kirstie McLeod, in Edinburgh, Scotland, provides the perfect opportunity to visit Ayr (pronounced Air), on Scotland's southwest coast. Ayr was the site of the Regimental Depot where Andrew trained before going to France. His military file preserves a pledge he signed there, October 2, 1916.

Andrew met a local girl in Ayr. Her name was Rea C. Scott. She lived with her family at Amelia Field Cottage in Prestwick, Ayr, on Waterloo Road. The relationship was serious enough he arranged an allotment of money for her while fighting in France. The story goes that upon arrival at her door during his leave in 1916, her mother told him they thought he was dead and Rea was seeing another man. She pleaded that he not pursue Rea. He heeded her request. One can only imagine the emotions which led to his request forwarded to Rea on August 25, 1916. Private A. Smith, 1393, "Wishes to stop allotment please. Sent forms - - -" This is recorded in his military file.

Andrew must have corresponded with his sister, Violet Sanger, and spoke his girlfriend's name. How else can one explain that a year later, on August 29, 1917, his sister gave her first child the unusual name, Rea? It is commonly spelled Rhea. Eleven years later, when his second daughter was born, Andrew gave her the same name. Two other descendents bear her name, granddaughter Rea (Smith) Hendry and great granddaughter Rea Wallace. My grandmother was often asked if it bothered her that his niece and daughter were named after his Scottish girlfriend. Violet's answer was that you had to live during the war to understand and since he had no contact with Rea after he returned, it was a wartime thing and she understood that. When Rea and Alma were girls, a small framed photo of Rea Scott hung in their bedroom. Sadly, the photo is missing.

Our first stop is Ayr Cemetery. The Newfoundland Regiment plot is well cared for, with manicured grass, perennials and shrubs. Other wartime headstones in the cemetery do not have the same care. A groundskeeper confirms that someone comes weekly to care for the Newfoundland graves but his Scottish brogue makes it difficult to grasp all he says. I wish I had Kirstie's help with the translation but I had run back to speak to him and she was nowhere in sight.

Regiment headstones in Ayr Cemetery

There are 14 headstones, a Celtic cross embossed with a caribou and a stone bearing the Regiment names buried elsewhere in Scotland. We leave with an appreciation for the Ayrshire people whose respect for the Regiment is evident in their care for our dead.

The Tourist Information Center has no knowledge of the Newfoundland Regiment. They send us to the local history section of the library where precious little information is available. On August 17, 1916, the Royal Burgh of Ayr was gifted an "exceptionally fine specimen of a mounted caribou head" as a souvenir of the gratitude of Newfoundlanders for the kindness rendered to their fighting men! A more useful piece of information is the location of the Regimental training field. It is Newton Park, a 20 minute walk.

During World War I, Newton Park was requisitioned as a training field for the Regiment. Today it is a park with lawn bowling greens, tennis courts, a playground area and a pond. Ayr is home to Scottish lawn bowls. Unfortunately there are no signs designating its use during World War I. Kirstie finds a brief note on a website which says the local people called the members of the Newfoundland Regiment "the Foondies," whom they held in great affection and high regard. It is a shame so little public information pertinent to the Regiment has survived.

After our trip, I find more Regimental history in Scotland in, "The Fighting Newfoundlander," by Colonel G.W.L. Nicholson. The first troops were trained at Pond Camp on the Salisbury Plain for seven weeks and then Fort George, Inverness, for ten weeks. From February until May, 1915, they were the only non-Scottish troops ever to garrison Edinburgh Castle. At first resistant to the idea, the locals eventually concluded, "The young colonials were no sae bad." From Edinburgh they moved to Stob's Camp, Harwick, for 12 weeks. As the number of Newfoundland troops grew, their Headquarters and four senior companies moved to Aldershot. The remainder went to Ayr. After a complaint from the Chief Constable of Ayr of the rowdiness of the Regiment, they were moved temporarily to a tented camp at Barry Links for the summer of 1917. This was significant for the honor of the Regiment was at stake. When they returned to Ayr, they were given a warm and noisy welcome by the townspeople. Many had Ayr brides. "The Auld Toon of Ayr" was their home away from home. Each time they left for the Front, they were given a royal sendoff by the people. The feeling was mutual.

Ayr had a racecourse where the Regiment drilled and exercised on the track daily. They were billeted in Newton Park School and the Grandstand buildings. Officers stayed in Wellington Square near the sea front. Their commander was a retired Liverpool officer, Major C. W. Whitaker. During the Regiment's two and one half years in Ayr, he developed an admiration for his Newfoundland troops. They learned how to build trenches and string barbed wire. Local experts and veteran Newfoundland officers taught them about weapons. The Regiment was treated well.

After Newton Park, we hurry towards our next destination, Waterloo Road. We know from Andrew's records that Rea Scott lived there. It is a 10 minute walk beyond Newton Park. Waterloo Road is in an adjoining community called Prestwick.

You can imagine our amazement when we turn the corner of Waterloo Road. On the first house on our left, 3 Waterloo Road, I spy a little sign "Amelia Field Cottage" in the top left hand corner, the address and cottage name found in Andrew's war records. We stand there laughing in disbelief! It is a small gray stone structure on the corner of Waterloo and Arran Park, the only surviving structure on the block between Prestwick Road, Waterloo Road and Arran Park, because a modern Aldi supermarket occupies the remaining property. A teenage girl in the garden believes the original cottage housed two families because it has two front doors and two chimneys. Across the street are a number of modern duplex homes. It is a miracle the cottage survived.

We have found the home of my Mom's namesake. If the folklore of Rea Scott's mother discouraging Andrew in the pursuit of her daughter is true, it makes sense that a mom may not want her child to be in a serious relationship with a wartime soldier from a country overseas. One can only speculate.

Exhilarated, Brownie and I, Kraig and Kirstie, our daughter, Tracy, her husband, John MacPherson, and our grandson, Owen, head for the beach. Ayr boasts a large beach and esplanade. It exceeds our expectations. In 1208, King William the Lion designated an area by the beach for such things as sheep grazing, denying any development. In 1894, the Burgh of Ayr had the foresight to again confirm the 44.5 acres, known as the Low Green, be for public recreation only. It has an outdoor adventure playground and public washrooms. A road separates the Low Green from a wide sandy beach. It would have been a logical place for a visiting soldier to enjoy. I imagine it would have been a popular gathering place.

After a quick fish and chips and soft ice cream on a park bench, I phone my mom in Newfoundland to tell her of our success. We relax on the beach a couple of hours. Tracy, Owen and I go into the shallow water, surprisingly warm for the ocean. Owen finds two pieces of seaweed and makes them his pet eels. He is happy, a perfect ending to a long day.

Today Ayr is a pretty town. Its population is 46,000. Its streets date back to the 1200s. It is one of the most important harbours on the west coast of Scotland. It is built on the River Ayr, which was first bridged in 1250. This "Auld Brig" is still used by pedestrians. Andrew and his fellow Newfoundlanders would have had to walk the bridge in order to get from their quarters in Newton Park to the town center.

It is 7:30 PM, time to go back to Edinburgh. I wonder if my grandfather went to Edinburgh by train. Looking out the windows, the countryside is very rural, with rolling green hills and golf courses and the ocean is visible much of the way to Glasgow. In Scotland, in June and July, it is daylight at 3:30 AM and it does not get dark until 10:30 PM. I reflect on the day. I wish I had the knowledge and the sense as a teenager to have asked my grandfather about Scotland. He may not have talked to me about the fighting but I believe he would have been open to telling me about Ayr. Aunt Hilda reminds me that Nan believed in youth we are denied the wisdom age affords us. It is true. I remember the story when Andrew won a fistful of money after winning a boxing match while on leave in Scotland with his friend Jonathon Gosse. Was it in Ayr?

I am content. There are many pieces of my puzzle still missing but I am pleased to have added a few more, Ayr, Newton Park and Amelia Field Cottage.

Amelia Field Cottage

VIOLET HIGDON

Four generations: Gloria, Rea, Violet and Carla 1991

My grandmother, Violet Ruth Higdon, was the last of seven children born to Robert Charles Higdon and Annie (Williams). Violet was born on February 11, 1903. Her mother was 40 years old. Her grandfather, Charles Higdon Sr. married Mary "Polly" (George). He came from England as a cooper making barrels for the fish trade. Charles Jr. was one of their eight children, William, Tom, Martin, Sarah, Elizabeth, Mary and Kathleen.

In May, 1996, our daughter, Carla, age 23, visited Violet, her great grandmother, who was 93. Carla had the foresight to record their conversations. The quotes in this book are taken from these tapes. When Rea, Alma and Hilda heard them, they were surprised at their mother's accent. They did not remember it as being so strong.

Her mother, Annie, was a nice woman. "She ne'er said a bad word in her life. I used ta. I haven't fer a long time. I'm ashamed o' me own self." Annie was born to Thomas and Mary Williams in 1862. She had two brothers who drowned while crossing an icy pond carrying flour and molasses. Annie also had a brother named Sam and two sisters, Martha and Hilda. Violet regrets not having a picture of her mother. Violet was 26 years old, married with four children when her mother died. On October 10, 1929, Annie dropped dead in her bedroom. She was 67 years old. Violet says, "Mother was backwards in regards goin' ta church. She hardly e'er went. I was one o' them too. I did fer awhile but I ne'er in years gone by. After I had my children die, I ne'er went after. I give it all up."

Violet's father, Charles Jr., died three years later. He was born in 1854 and died September 1, 1932. He was 78 years old, eight years older than Annie. After Annie died, Charles lived with his son, Tom. Violet said her father "got a good livin', always had full and plenty ta eat, and always had a bit o' mutton or fresh beef ta cook. We ne'er had ta go on the gov'ment." They grew potatoes, carrot and turnip in the garden. They had sheep and a horse. Violet helped her father get firewood. She tackled (harnessed) the horse a good many times, went in the woods, sawed and loaded the wood on the sled, and unloaded when they got home. She was the youngest and her siblings were grown and did not live at home. One morning when her father was tackling the horse, he dropped something and the frightened horse ran away. "I had ta go right across the bridge in New Harbour, chase the horse, get her and bring her back home - a long distance. Poor old Father said if ya hadn't told me, I wouldn't believe it." His severe arthritis made it necessary for him to lean on her every day for support on his walk home from work at Woodman's General Store.

Charles Higdon Jr.

Violet grew up in an old fashioned house, something like her home in Dildo. "We had ta come in o'er a big hill and our house was up in big old trees. I used ta be 'fraid comin' in the night times, 'fraid somethin' come outta the woods. I was real nervous comin' in o'er that hill. I used ta have ta get Father sometimes ta come out. I'd say, come out at 10 o'clock, fer company. He wouldn't sometimes, but if I was late, he'd come out lookin' fer me. Father used ta be always strict on me." She recalled two of her brothers died young. "No doctors then but one o' ours (brothers) had T.B." She hung around with 10 or 12 girls, "always mixin' up with one another. We was happy go lucky."

Violet tells Carla that the old Church of England school in New Harbour was torn down and she walked farther than around the harbour to go to the United Church School. The school was divided into two parts, one for Primmer and one for those above Grade 5. She says, "I didn't want ta be nothin' 'cause I ne'er had sense ta realize. Sure, my gracious, I left school when I was only in Grade 4. When I was 13 or 14 or somethin,' I went ta Grand Falls and I went ta work."

One of her friends was Andrew's sister, Violet, who married Tim Sanger, a foreman in the Grand Falls paper mill. "Me and her was friends. She was always askin' me ta come down. I looked after Violet's children. That's how I come ta go ta Grand Falls in the first beginnin'. Every year she had a baby. She had a big crowd, 14 or more children." Our Violet went to Grand Falls in 1917 to help Violet Sanger with her first child. Andrew was overseas and he and our Violet had not met. After the war, "Violet Sanger didn't like Andrew goin' out with me 'cause she had somebody in view fer him ta marry and she thought Andrew was goin' out with her but Andrew preferred me before he would her. Violet didn't like it. Too bad." (Chuckle) I mean ta say, "I ne'er disliked her or anythin' like that but I ne'er called her Mrs. Sanger or nuttin' like that. It was all Violet and me 'cause Violet was only a poor girl like meself. Imagine, she was a servant girl fer my father's brother's son, a Salvation Army officer, Major Higdon."

Andrew left the UK for Newfoundland January 30, 1919 and arrived home Friday, February 7. He returned to his home town, Dildo, to a hero's welcome. A coach on the train was decorated in honor of the local boys coming home from the war. His brother, Eldred, was at the station with a horse and slide to bring Andrew home. Violet, along with much of the community, was there to see the big event. Violet says, "Me and Mary Higdon was best friends. Mary's mother was dead. She was livin' with her father. She used ta go with Ches Garland. (They later married) They (soldiers) all come from overseas and the train used ta come then and we was in the station and I saw him (Andrew) all dressed up. Sure, I says ta meself, by'e geez, he's some nice lookin' fella. Three nights after he come, I was down ta Mary Higdon's, like I told ya, and Mary, with no mother, used ta have her boyfriend come in her house and so their boyfriends used ta come with her boyfriend. I used ta go there too and two or three girls used ta go there and we used ta have open house like, have say two, three, five or six games o' cards and that's how I met Andrew. He come in that night. When he was comin' out through the gate, one o' the girls, ya know, carryin' on like girls are like, give me a shove (push) and landed me up be alongside Andrew, ya know, fer badness, and he grabbed me. So from that then, we went home ... quick as that! So that's how I come ta meet Andrew." That week, Violet celebrated either her 16th or 17th birthday. Andrew was 24 years old.

Violet's official birth certificate gives her birth date as 1903. When she was 65 and applied for her old age pension, she was denied because officially she was 64. She maintained it was wrong, that she was born in 1902. Mistakes were made in those days and she had no recourse. Hilda has since confirmed that Violet's birth date on the 1921 Newfoundland census as Andrew's wife is listed as 1902.

When Andrew wanted to meet her parents, she was unsure because her father had a habit of stripping down to his one-piece long john underwear in the evenings. Violet recalled that in their courting time after the war, if there was a loud noise, even if the ice cracked, Andrew jumped and dropped to the ground. That winter, as he made the long walks to her home in New Harbour, he said it was too cold to be doing this and they would not be doing it another winter.

Andrew and Violet
Wedding Photo

Andrew went back to Grand Falls to work in the paper mill. Violet followed. This time, she worked part time cleaning offices and Staff rooms at the mill for $5 a month. They returned to Dildo and married December 29, 1920, when she was 18. She had an engagement ring and "a beautiful wedding band, wide as e'er ya believe." They returned to Grand Falls and rented a house before Andrew had to leave his job. He was not well. Violet said he suffered from indigestion. She attributed it to the war when he would go four to five days in the trenches with nothing to eat. He was also exposed to poison gas. They returned to Dildo. Their first child, Florence, was born nine and one half months later. All their lives their affectionate names for each other were An and Vi.

Violet remembers her three children who died of Typhoid Fever, Florence, Gerald and Larry. "Poor Gerald, there was ne'er man in the world like he and not because he died." When Verd was sick, Violet said to Larry, who was almost four, "You stay here, don't go upstairs or you'll get that Typhoid." Larry would say, "Lord dyin' on that Audie," his nickname for Verd.

She talks of Jim Newhook and Pete Pretty, boyfriends of Florence. She tells Carla she has regrets. "Jim just visited me the other day, in his 80's now. Smart fellow, nicest young man you'll see. But at that time, I was death about her goin' with Jim. If I let she, she and Jim would be married and that (Florence's death) would ne'er have happened. He always liked her. He ne'er stopped comin' ta see her, even when she was goin' with Pete Pretty who was overseas." Jim continued to visit Violet regularly, even in the nursing home, until her death.

Violet's mind at 93 is still sharp although she doesn't think so. She says, "I hates ta be shoutin'," as she is hard of hearing. This deafness makes it difficult for Carla's questions to be clearly understood. As a result Violet's answers do not always address the question or she goes off on a tangent as the question triggers another memory. Still, she can name her ten children and most of her grandchildren when they look through the photo albums. She stumbles with the great grandchildren. She says of them, "Sometimes I forgets their names. They're some pretty lil' things. My crowd was pretty good, ya know."

Carla did not think her attempt to record her great grandmother was a success. Young and idealistic, she had not previously spent adult time alone with Violet. Her intent was to record Violet's memories and probably not her opinions. Some of Violet's pronouncements made her squirm. Violet seems to recognize Carla's confusion and is unsure how to address it. She says to Carla, "It's hard ta go back in the background fer ya ta understand. You are third generation. I haven't got the memory I even had last year. I say, Violet, ya must be gettin' off yer head if ya can't remember that. Sometimes I think my brain's not workin'."

Violet was quite blunt in her opinions of the people and events in her life. She praised some and was critical of others. She was realistic about her own family, their strengths and their follies. Like most parents, she had aspirations for her children and grandchildren to amount to something. When they fell short, she was not shy about expressing her frustration, especially if she had harped (preached) to them beforehand of the possible consequences of their actions. They should have known better. That was her nature. She called a spade a spade. She did not mince words. She did not try to color the facts as she saw them. She seemed to view the world in black and white. There was no back door to her. She would not think of herself as being critical but honest with her feelings. She could be outspoken. She could raise her voice. She did not suffer fools gladly. Violet believed, if you make a bad bed, you lie in it. Hilda can still hear her saying, "Keep yer hands busy and the devil outta yer mind." Sometimes people took offense. She was no shrinking violet, pardon the pun!

Even Andrew is not spared. She says, "Guarantee no one in the world like he" and "I wouldn't part with him whatever he done. I forgive him like but not everyone be's like that. I think when ya really likes a man, it's hard ta break it, provided he stays steadfast ta ya." But she is critical of his lifestyle and the lifestyle of some of his friends. Andrew was with them most nights. "Don't take me wrong 'cause Andrew was just as bad. I ne'er kept Andrew home from the time he was off work. On the nights he be away, I ne'er seen him from after supper. He come home 12 o'clock, 1 o'clock. He wouldn't be home with me and the family. On the nights he be home, his friends be with him.

I put up with all that – drinkin' beer and playin' cards. I heard lotsa things said. It's past and gone now. He's gone a good many years now and I'm still here. If it was anyone else but me, would have left Andrew fer long ago, but I ne'er. Probably that's why we kept together 'cause I said, wherever ya goes, ya go. Ya come and go as ya like." Carla asks, "Were you in love with Andrew?" Violet responds quickly, "By sure ya knows I had ta be. I never had a feller. Andrew was my first. Guarantee."

Violet sees alcohol as a root of unhappiness. "No drink is no problems." She viewed it as a problem in her own family. Andrew and his sons liked their beer. Violet says, "It's alright ta settle down providin' you get a husband who's not wasteful but if he's wasteful or drinks and things, it's better not ta have him. It's a tough fight goin' through this world."

Violet may have shown tolerance because she knew they could count on each other. She says, "We worked hard together." Andrew had a steady job and was a good provider. A full time job which did not require the husband leave his home to work was a rare thing. Andrew loved his family. He was a happy man. He was well liked and respected and had a lot of friends. It was she who always said, "He won the MM, ya know." She never said Military Medal but MM. Violet dismisses the age difference between them. "No matter, Andrew didn't die o' age but I'll be dyin' o' my age." (Chuckle). When asked if she was interested in another relationship after Andrew died, she replies, "He's not born yet." She remembers leading the horse while Andrew set potatoes and going into the woods on Saturdays for wood. She recalls a time of no phones or lights, kerosene oil lamps, washing in a pork barrel tub and getting water from a well. "I was buried up from me toes ta me head with work. I ne'er had a minute's peace."

Unlike Andrew, Violet kept pretty much at home. They were opposites in many ways. While her children and household kept her busy, she was also not comfortable in other people's homes, "even with someone belong ta me." They visited Walt and Clara Reid and Mark and Leni Newhook but she worried about making work for people or eating too much food. She could not relax but she was happy to have company, especially people she knew, and served a good meal.

Violet was the disciplinarian. She was strict. For the most part, the children tried not to cross their mother. In her defense Rea says their father was away most days and many evenings. He was the breadwinner. It was considered Violet's job to raise the family. She did not complement her children for a job well done. She worked like a dog and her expectation of them was that they do the same. She did not know how to relax, always had to be doing something. It didn't come easy to her to be light hearted. Her love was not expressed in words but in the effort required to give them food, clothing and a warm and comfortable home, to see that they did not do without. She was not a coddler or a cuddler. Her idea of rearing youngsters was that they pull their weight. She had little tolerance of those who did not. To show her displeasure, she would flick her hand and hit the back of their heads to knock some sense into them. When pitching into (checking) the kids, Violet could be loud and vocal. You were really chastised. If he recognized that Violet was vexed or in a temper, Andrew would say to their daughter, Hilda, "When ya gets yer chores done, I would leave if I was you." In later years, Andrew's advice to Hilda's husband, Jim, was, "If she (your wife) has a racket in the day, take yer hat and go out the door. If she has a racket in the night, turn over and go ta sleep." After a hallabaloo (uproar), it was always best to lay low.

Daughter, Alma, was glad it was her father and not her mother who caught her kissing Earl Cooper one Sunday afternoon. They were sitting on a log in a field. She knew she would never hear the end of it from her mom who was forever preaching to the girls about the dangers of being too friendly with the boys.

Andrew simply said, "What are you two devils up ta? Alma, ya best be gettin' home. It's supper time." She was forever grateful that he did not embarrass her in front of Earl or tell Violet. He never brought it up again.

Violet did not abide or understand people who were mean and people who wasted money. "I think everybody should speak ta ya when ya passes whether you're friends or not. If you're not, have nothin' against one another. Friends should look out fer one another. It's a wonderful way ta be but everybody's not like that. Everybody doesn't got the same feelings." She loaned a lot of money. "I'm not sayin' I was rich but I'm not poor either. I don't want no money from nobody, thank God." She kept her money in her bra or tied it in a sock for there were no local banks. Daughter, Dulcie, liked to tell the story of a customer at a butcher shop where she worked who pulled her money from her bosom. The older lady said, "I reckon they're the only two suckers I can trust!"

Violet and Albert

Violet outlived Andrew by 32 years. She was 67 when he died. After his father's death, Albert thought he was man of the house. Nobody got away with hen-pecking Violet except Albert. Some of the friction was his misguided attempt to protect her such as the time he hid her winter boots because he believed it was too slippery for her to go outside. They were two of a kind, each loudly voicing their opinions, adamant in their beliefs. Both were hard of hearing and not "hearing" the other's point of view.

Violet's daughters and granddaughters were well aware of her view of the woman's role in a marriage. If the relationship was in difficulty, the man was given the benefit of a doubt. He was the breadwinner. "I got the impression ta think that it got ta take somethin' ta break ya up like he's goin' off with another woman or he's really got ta be cruel ta ya. Ya got ta give him reason, then it's yer fault, but if ya don't, it's his fault. It's two o' yas ta make it a go."

Violet had impressive long thick brown hair with auburn highlights. She could sit on it. As a child, it was reddish brown; the color inherited from her father whose hair and moustache were a blasty bough color, like dead branches of a fir or spruce tree. Her daughters were mesmerized when their mother unbraided her hair and it hung in massive waves down her back. Violet bent her head, let the hair fall forward and brushed out the clits (tangles). They watched, fascinated, as she gathered her hair and made small pleats. Pleating was not the same as braiding or plaiting and is not to be confused with the modern French pleat. The hair around the face was divided into five or six sections. Each section was held upright, ends loosely folded and twisted once or twice, allowing the hair near the scalp to pook out, like a fold or a pleat. The twisting of the ends was repeated and the hair was secured to the top of the head with hair pins, not clips. Each pleat overlapped the other. Violet wore her part on the left side.

After pleating around her face, Violet gathered the remainder of her hair to make two plaits or braids. She began each one at the back of her neck and then flicked it over her shoulder to finish. She crossed them at the back of her head, pinning them in place. One long plait overlapped the other to make a bun behind the pleats. Her hair was her crowning glory.

Washing her hair was a chore. Hilda helped rinse it in the kitchen sink. It took hours to dry. She never wore it loose during the day as it was not practical when cooking and looking after children. Most days she wore the braided bun without the pleats. When making bread she wore a bandana or a pair of underwear on her head, as was the custom of the day. She wore the two braids down her shoulders when going to bed.

In the early 1960s, Violet cut and colored her hair for the first time. She and Andrew visited his sisters in Grand Falls and she returned with short hair. She was 60 years old and it was going gray at the roots but her braids were still brown in color. Hilda has her mother's long braids, saved from that day. The hair is shiny with an auburn tint and not a single strand of gray.

The short style may have been easier but did not instill the same pride. She struggled with psoriasis of the scalp, a condition she attributed to Loving Care hair color. She fretted about what people might think was dandruff on her shoulders. She absentmindedly scratched her scalp with her knitting needle. The thick white hair stubbornly refused to keep shape. Her granddaughters were enlisted to help. She lost interest and never learned to do it herself.

Sadly, at 93, she stays upstairs in her bedroom most of the time, "barred in," and rarely goes outside. Visits by family and friends are important but gradually, Violet becomes housebound. She does not want to be a burden to her immediate family. "If I was prefer, I rather go ta a Home, clear o' me own people and then nobody would have no trouble with me." Hilda says, "God forbid she was beholdin' ta ya." It will be another year and a half before she makes the decision to move into a Seniors Home. Granddaughter Lorraine remembers visiting her in the Home on the Barrens and Violet said, "I'm just bidin' my time.

Ya think that livin' ta be so old is a wonerful thing. Do ya realize I don't got nobody belong ta me 'cept the ones I made?"

Randy, Roger, Violet, Rick

When grandson Randy drops by with a trout, Violet says, "I wish I was as good as when I was 40." She shouts, "I'm no good fer nothin' or nobody." Randy teases "I wouldn't want ta be 93." Violet laughingly replies, "Why ya can't go crawl under the ground when ya like afore yer time comes." She says to him, "Ya gettin' some size. You're some beautiful. Ya growed up big." Carla objects and Violet says, "I mean big bone-ded." Inevitably the discussion is who does he or she look like and who is big and not big? Violet clearly prefers big. To her, big is healthy.

Violet missed Andrew terribly but Hilda recalls she had her queer little ways of dealing with it. She would say that it is better for the man to go first as a man has a tendency to make a fool of himself when his wife dies. She had a good man, bar none, and she would not want that to happen to him!

Shortly after his death, she had a series of health issues. She required surgeries to remove her gallbladder and an encapsulated cancerous breast tumor. She survived being hit by a car while visiting her daughter, Dulcie, in Carbonear. She had a hysterectomy. She did manage to avoid the crippling arthritis that affected her father and brother.

After her car accident, granddaughters Tina and Lorraine did housework for her Saturday mornings and washed and set her hair, returning after supper to style it. Joy was given a grocery list to run up to Rex Moore's general store. In the last two to three years before Nan went into a nursing home, she needed help getting in and out of the tub to bathe. Brenda volunteered for the job.

Many of Violet's children and grandchildren have been tested and some have a condition called hypertrophic cardiomyopathy. HCM is genetic and an uncommon disease, affecting 1% of the world population. It contributed to the death of her son, Verd, at age 46. Rea and Alma do not have HCM. There is speculation it was passed down through Andrew. His maternal grandmother, Catherine, remarried after his grandfather died. Some descendents of her second marriage to Joseph Hefford have been diagnosed with the disease.

Tina and Violet

Violet was puzzled why she lived to such an old age. "I look at meself in the mirror and I can't believe how old I got." At age 89 she broke a hip that required surgery. She was not expected to recover or walk again. After two months of hospitalization, the doctor told Hilda to carry her home and keep her away from doctors for he was amazed at her recovery. At age 94 she moved into a senior's home. Just before her 97th birthday Violet broke her other hip. She never walked again without a walker.

She was mentally alert. Just before she died she asked Hilda how much longer before she would be 100. When Hilda replied six months, she said, "I'm not gonna make it." If she was right in her earlier belief that she was born in 1902, she may have lived to be 100! Hilda recalls that on a previous day, her mother said to her, "If you and Tina didn't wake me up and talk ta me so much about this, that and somethin' else, I'd probably be gone by now." Tina and Brenda relieved Hilda on Violet's last day. It was almost as if she waited until they were briefly out of the room. "Not gone a minute," but when Brenda decided against having a cup of tea and turned back, Nan was gone. She died peacefully with her arms crossed and a fist to each cheek. She died of extreme old age according to her death certificate on September 11, 2002 in her 100th year. She was predeceased by five children. She was survived by 5 children, 32 grandchildren, 51 great grandchildren and 5 great great grandchildren.

Before Violet died, she asked to be respectable at her funeral. The previous Christmas Hilda bought her mother a navy suit and blue blouse, burying clothes from money gifted by the children and grandchildren. Adding a soft blue sweater on Violet's arm was Tina's idea as her grandmother was always cold. Violet paid for her funeral and Albert's before she died. The pall bearers were her grandsons Randy, Roger, Ricky, Andy, Claude, and great nephew and neighbor, Carson Smith, Uncle Eldred's grandson. Brenda gave a eulogy from the grandchildren. Family members chose the hymns, "How Great Thou Art, Amazing Grace, Farther Along (Hilda's favorite) and at the cemetery, I Come to the Garden Alone."

Brenda and Violet

My father, Bob, was terminally ill with kidney cancer but insisted on going to the funeral on September 14, 2002. He had given a eulogy for Andrew and his intent had been to do the same for Violet but he was too frail. My sister, Debbie, spoke a tribute on his behalf. Violet had said, "I was the same ta Bob as I was ta me own son." He wrote to her Christmas, 1993, "Since my first visit to Dildo, you have been to me everything a mother could be." He said to Beatrice, Verd's wife, "When we walked through their door, we don't know if we adopted them or if they adopted us." Despite the steep hill, he insisted on going to the cemetery. On the drive back to Gander, they saw a double rainbow. Debbie said in awe, "Nan is on her way." Dad was hospitalized the next day.

ANDREW SMITH

Andrew was larger than life. When I say tell me about my grandfather, the response is always the same. It is an ah hah moment, a brief pause and big smile, followed by, "He was somethin' else," or "He was quite the character," but it is inevitably followed by, "Ya couldn't ask fer better" or "No one like him" or "He was the best kind." The accolades are often funny, like he was, the praise is genuine, the words sincere. He was a passionate man who lived a full life.

Long after his death, daughter Hilda tried on her father's Legion blazer. She is a small woman and I remember the look of absolute shock on her face when she realized it fit her well. This man, who loomed so big in her eyes, was no bigger than she. In his time, when men were smaller, he would have been of average size, but Violet would have been considered tall for she was the taller of the two.

Andrew's eyes were an unusual color, pale blue like Hilda's. He had dark wavy hair and a double crown (two circular swirls at the crown of his head). He loved his suspenders and salt and pepper caps. He had two such caps, flat tweed cloth caps with a peak or brim in the front, a style he wore all his life.

Andrew in a jovial mood

He was an exceptional singer, with a loud booming voice and a big smile. His whole face lit up when he laughed. He bounced his children and grandchildren on his knees as he sang songs like "Squid Jigging Ground," "Pack up your Troubles"and "It's a Long way to Tipperary." My favorite was "Keep on the Sunny side of Life." He lifted his heel and slapped his thigh to the beat. Neighbor, Gertie Smith, loved summer evenings when the windows were open and she could listen to Andrew sing his babies to sleep. Granddaughter, Joy, says when he wasn't singing, he was humming. He affectionately called his daughters and granddaughters "lil' maid." An older girl was called "big maid."

He was an excellent dancer. The popular local square dance was called Lancers. He was light on his feet, took short steps and bounced on his toes. Violet grumbled, "You're worst than the youngsters," as he danced with his daughters on Saturday mornings to the music of the radio.

Andrew enjoyed jokes and was a practical joker. Violet could match his wit. When he returned home late one night, she called from upstairs, "Is that you, Jake?" for Jake was a local man known for fooling around. Andrew roared in laughter, "Deed it is, Vi, I'll be up in a minute." Alma remembers his coming home after having a few too many. Violet was mad as the devil as she helped him upstairs. He mistakenly peed in her shoe, thinking it was the chamber pot. She got a second pair!

Andrew was a happy go lucky person and seldom showed other feelings. In 1950, Alma married an American serviceman, Al Orsak, and moved to Rhode Island. Al was posted to Korea and Alma came home that Christmas, alone. Andrew sensed her sadness and he sang and teased to make her feel better. When it was time for her to go, he disappeared up over the hill, rather than personally say good bye. In a subsequent visit, he went into the garden when she walked down the lane.

Andrew was an avid boxing fan, especially fond of Joe Louis. His friends gathered round his kitchen to thumb through the well worn boxing magazines or listen to the commentary of the latest fight on his radio. Later, a favorite pastime was watching wrestling on Verd's white TV. Violet was right into it with the men as she cheered, booed and pummeled the air, imitating all the moves she had seen.

Andrew took pride in keeping trim. His size belied his strength and agility. Short and wiry, he excelled in all things athletic. As a young man, he was challenged to a fight by a New Harbour lad. Furious that he had been unsuccessful in walking home a girl who chose Andrew instead, he insisted Andrew meet him at a field, a meeting area of young people. Fist fights were an acceptable way of settling disputes so a time was set and a large crowd gathered. They sparred and Andrew knocked him to the ground. When the other youth was taken away, it was realized he had rind from a birch tree wound around his upper torso to better absorb the blows.

Despite his antics, Andrew was viewed as a peacemaker. He had the benefit of a readymade war hero status but he didn't perceive it as such and never talked about it. At community and church Times, his presence was encouraged as alcohol often resulted in a scrap or a racket. Andrew was respected and able to discourage or break up trouble. He wasn't one to start something but he would end it. Alma remembers a fist fight making one devil of a racket. Andrew was alerted. "Jesus Christ, what the hell is goin' on here?" He took the biggest man, Max Cranford, from behind by the collar, put his knee against his butt and pushed him outside. He warned the others, "Now b'ys, enough's enough. Get out or I'll take ya out." The rest of the night was without incident.

Andrew possessed a soldering iron, a company tool and was often asked to fix engines, teakettles, chains, and eye glasses. One Saturday afternoon, when everything was cleaned, Violet exclaimed, "Oh Lord, look what's comin' in the door," as she scrambled to find an old blanket to put under a boat engine. The engine parts were spread out over the kitchen floor. A scattered time he was given food in payment, a fresh fish or duck. Alma says if her father was paid for everything he did, he'd be a millionaire in his day.

It must have been a challenge for Violet, married to Andrew. He was popular for he treated everyone as equal. What you saw was what you got. There were no airs about him. His job of 40 years with the United Towns Electric Company had him in contact with everyone in the community. He was friendly and outgoing, always open for a chat. The house was very busy.

Andrew and Violet 1966

Violet was left to manage the children and the home. She did not have his exuberance or confidence. Did she put few constraints on him because she realized the futility of it? Did she question whether he came up short as a husband? She was proud of him. Did she accept she could do little but grumble? She could certainly speak her mind. Did she feel trapped or is that a modern ponderance? Either way, it must have been difficult for her, not to get swallowed up by his personality.

Friends

One of Andrew's best friends was Chester Reid, son of Ebenezer. Chester was a comedian, a singer and storyteller. Andrew loved him and spent a great deal of time with him, playing cards and having a beer. They regaled everyone with their stories and, like most Newfoundlanders, they talked a mile a minute. Andrew thought his friend was born 100 years too soon, meaning in another time and place, Chester could have been famous for he could make a laugh out of anything. On Carla's tapes, my father, Bob Hellier, says, "Chester would sing a song called "The Cock-a-doodle-doo." It must have had 15 verses to it. I've kicked myself with both feet the same time, a dozen times since that. I never had the sense to copy it all down. I've never heard it since. He could sing away at that. He had a beautiful voice. But when you're young, you don't think about stuff like that. It wasn't so important back those days. It wasn't until Gloria was in university and started working on the family tree that I realized the importance of it."

Gertie and daughters, Evelyn and Gloria

One of Chester's daughters, Gertie, married Levi Thorne, Aunt Evelyn's youngest son. Evelyn was Violet's older sister. Gertie knew Aunt Violet and Uncle Andrew long before she married Levi. "I loved them like me own." When Gertie was 12 and 13 years old, she helped Violet with her small children, braiding Dulcie's hair and washing Albert in the sink. She was happy to do so because Violet gave her 25 cents. When she did housework, neighbor, Eli Rowe, would say, "Oh my, those lil' arms don't look big enough ta wash that floor."

Chester and Maud Reid

Gertie's mother, Maud, had 12 pregnancies but six of the children did not survive infancy, including two sets of twins. Surviving were Lloyd, Gertie, Melva, Ina, Calvin and Glen. Maud went through a lot. She was patient and kind, "ne'er a bad word 'bout anybody came outta her mouth. There was no one in the world that cleaned birds like Maud." Chester was "a wonderful one fer out in the boat." When he made salt fish, he always tucked one under his wool sweater for Andrew. Before Andrew died, he told Gertie he was looking forward to having a game of cards "up there" with her father.

Gertie remembers when her parents' house was hauled on a bed of wooden logs to its present location. A rope was tied around the house. As the large group of men heaved (pulled), Andrew and Chester led them in song. "Now we got a bargain, and it's in Tom Pretty's garden. Haul, b'ys, haul!" When the house was settled in place, Andrew picked up her little sister, Ina, and put her through an open window into their new home.

Gertie says her father and Andrew could be as foolish as odd socks and have everyone in stitches. They were colorful characters, the ringleaders in the group. Gertie fondly calls Andrew "a queer hand."Chester's grand daughter, Gloria, says, "Pappy Reid was a ticket (practical joker). He'd give me a few cents fer ta go ta Walt Reid's fer a bottle o' beer. In actual fact, it was a bottle o' pop but Pappy told me it was beer and I believed him. I'd argue with the crowd o' men gathered in the shop who laughed, G'wan (go on) wit ya, maid. They enjoyed his lil' game, pullin' my leg. They were all in on it."

Florence Smith remembers Chester visiting Andrew at mealtime, his grub bag hung on Andrew's fence. Chester asked for a lookin' glass (mirror). Andrew queried, "What in the name o' blazes do ya want a lookin' glass fer?" Chester, not a blade of hair on his head, replied "I wants ta see if I got e'er mouth." To understand their dry sense of humour, Chester was saying the reason he was not offered a meal could only be because he had no mouth to eat it! Violet laughed, "You bloody fools!"

Owen Reid was a friend of Chester and Andrew. Owen and Chester were not related. Owen married Susanna (Mayne) from Hopeall, a midwife, the second marriage for both. Owen's first wife, Mabel, died of tuberculosis. They had no children. Susanna's first husband, Andrew Higdon, died of a heart attack. They had five children, Ted (Julie Reid), Steve (Margaret Jamison), Andrew (Jenny Cranford), Sadie (Clarence George) and Hilda who died of tuberculosis at age 17. Owen and Susanna had two children, Lewis (Dorothy "Dot" Cooper) and Stella (Thomas Hearn).

Owen Reid

Owen was a tall slim man with a big laugh. Stella loved being with her father, "always in Dad's pockets." He'd say, "My lil' maid, come here, I wants ya." Off they'd go to his fishing stage and share a favorite treat, Old Boy bread and a can of tomatoes. Owen fished in the summer. In winter, he had a contract for A.N.D, Anglo Newfoundland Development Company, cutting logs for the railway. He was funny, happy all day long. Stella cannot remember him unhappy, even when he was dying of Typhoid Fever when she was 13. He was more concerned with his family's welfare, telling Stella to be good and go to school. It was his habit every Christmas to put a load of wood on his mare and give the wood to the Salvation Army and he despaired that it would not happen that year.

Owen nailed a pig's bladder to his kitchen ceiling and issued a challenge to anyone to try and remove it with a kick. The prize was a bottle of black rum. Pigs were raised during the year to be killed in the fall as winter meat. It was common to save the pig's bladder to make a kickball (soccer). Many gave it a try but Andrew was the only one to succeed. "All the b'ys came ta urge him on." Stella watched as he heaved (lifted) himself up off the floor with a big kick and the bladder exploded into bits and pieces. He was some spry. He did not leave with his bottle as the occasion called for a celebration by all.

Owen, Chester, Andrew and friends rolled baccy (tobacco) to make cigarettes for their card games. The winner might take home a brace of rabbits. If they ran out of papers, they cut up brown paper. Popular tobaccos were Bugle, Target and Big Ben. Health risks of tobacco were unknown, smoking commonplace. They smoked like tilts (smoky huts). There were big hee haws all night long.

Their love of life and their antics made them well known. Their shenanigans were their way of making their own fun at a time when life was difficult. Vera Mercer, his sister Blanche's daughter in law, says, "Everybody loved Uncle Andrew. He was somethin', always jokin', carryin' on and playin' tricks." He was the life of the party. He and his friends climbed on Emma Higdon's roof on Boxing Day, put a brin (burlap) bag in the chimney to smoke her out and stole her turkey from the pantry in the back porch. Carla cannot believe that her great grandfather could do such a thing in his 50s! While such activities would not be tolerated today, it was viewed then as entertainment, a story which brought much laughter in its retelling.

Mark and Lenie (Aileen) Newhook

Hilda recalls the Christmas their turkey went missing. Andrew's family enjoyed their Christmas dinner but on Boxing Day, Violet could not find the remainder of the turkey stored in the pantry off the back porch. They visited Mark and Lenie Newhook (pronounced locally as Nook) that night and upon leaving, Mark gave the astonished Violet her empty roaster. The next Christmas, Violet was determined to get even. She looked everywhere in Mark's house but to no avail. She finally asked Mark where he hid his turkey and he pointed with glee to a box wrapped as a present under the Christmas tree. Granddaughter, Chryl, can't believe the kind of stuff they used to do, but these stories became local legends!

Every night at quarter to 6, Andrew's friends congregated in his house to listen to "The Barrelman", a series of Newfoundland stories by Joey Smallwood, and at 8 PM, to the Gerald S. Doyle News Bulletin. Andrew had one of few radios in the area. In winter, Violet never appreciated this activity as their clothing and boots dripped on her floor from the melting snow. Aside from the obvious clean up, she fretted one of her children might slip and hurt themselves. In summer, Andrew left the window in the eating room open and people gathered in the lane by the window to hear the news. It was a highlight for the children too. Rea believes she learned as much from The Barrelman as she did the few times she was able to attend school. Many stayed on to play 120s, a card game. Violet and the children worked their supper and homework and her making bread around the men's schedule.

Violet and their daughter, Florence, followed faithfully the daily radio series, "The Woman in White." Florence was a sentimental type and the program often brought her to tears. Neighbor, Ed George, enjoyed the comedies, "Amos and Andy" (1928-1956) and "Lum and Abner," (1931-1955). Amos and Andy was an African American drama, although its 2 creators were white actors who played black actors. It would not be politically correct today but it was one of the most popular and beloved radio programs for nearly 30 years.

Joey Smallwood became the first premier of Newfoundland in 1949, the driving force behind Newfoundland becoming the tenth province of Canada. He later attributed his success to The Barrelman, which made him a well known radio personality. A Barrelman was a person high in the crow's nest of a ship, on the lookout for danger and land. Smallwood regaled his listeners to "send me stories, true stories, showing how brave are the Newfoundlanders; how hardy they are; how strong they are; what hardships they endure." He said, in his second year, he received 1500 letters from 200 communities in four months. He instilled pride in his listeners and, in the process, he collected invaluable Newfoundland folklore. He was The Barrelman from 1937 to 1943. His starting pay was $30 a week.

The Gerald S. Doyle Radio News Bulletin was as popular as the Barrelman. During World War II, Andrew was intent on listening to the news and following the progress of the war. It was serious business. The children knew to be quiet as their father leaned forward so he could hear every word. In addition to the news, it gave public service announcements, weather reports, shipping schedules, fish prices and personal messages. Most Newfoundlanders travelled to the hospitals in St. John's for treatment of more serious illnesses and recuperated there. The personal messages informed folk back home of births, deaths, funerals, hospitalizations, operations and travel plans. They were vital links to the family and community, especially those who did not have a telephone.

Gerald S. Doyle was a successful businessman with a wide range of drugs, household products and cod liver oil. Oil from cod livers fermenting in a barrel of seawater left a very bad taste and body odor. With the production of odorless cod liver oil, it was easier for Gerald S. Doyle to promote daily doses as a food-tonic. He astutely marketed his goods by travelling the coastal communities, sponsoring the Gerald S. Doyle News Bulletin for 34 years, from 1932 to 1966, and collecting traditional local folk songs. He published five free "Old-Time Songs and Poetry of Newfoundland." The result was the preservation of the songs and Gerald S. Doyle became a household name.

Animals

Andrew and Violet were wonderful with animals. Cats and later crackies (small mutt dogs) were ever present. Violet took delight in the newborn yellow chickens and Andrew looked forward to letting the lambs frolic in the grass in spring. They had a white rat and it was treated like a pet. The children played with it. No one was allowed to hurt it. Neighbor, Florence Smith was petrified. It was free to roam the house during the day and put in a barrel in the store at night. In 1943 or 1944, a plane was forced to land on the road and two airmen came to use the phone. As they sat waiting for instructions, they were fascinated as the rat ran up the sleeves and down the legs of their jumpsuits.

Violet and Dulcie and Albert, holding a
white rat

Andrew loved his horses. Not everyone had a horse but they were invaluable for hauling firewood, plowing gardens and pulling the sleigh in winter. They were not used for recreation. Andrew never owned a saddle. In Rea and Alma's childhood, the horse was Nance. In Hilda's time, the horse was Skip. Andrew bought Skip from Dimmy George, who owned a livery stable, for $100.

Skip loved Verd and followed him everywhere, even to school, then waited for him to come home. Verd always had an apple in his pocket for the horse. If the back door was open, Skip stuck his head in the doorway looking for treats. One such time when Verd was feeding Skip at the door, Hilda asked him to move the horse and Verd said, "No, I'll hold his head and talk ta him and you go under." Fool like, she says, she crawled under Skip's belly. She was half afraid of Skip for he was a tall imposing horse with a long neck. He was reddish brown with two white front hooves.

Alma and Skip, the Horse

Andrew treated his horses well and worried that Lendo drove Skip too hard. One winter, when Lendo was returning with a load of wood, the sled tipped while rounding a curve. The wood fell on Lendo. With only his legs sticking out, he was unable to move. As God would have it, others using the same path found him and brought him home. Andrew was shook up over what might have been but, by the same token, he was livid with Lendo for going too fast. He was proud of Skip because the horse had enough sense not to move after the accident. Those who found Lendo said if the horse had moved, Lendo would have been seriously injured or killed but Lendo was tough as gads (tough as nails). He was a survivor. Nothing seemed to faze him.

When Andrew got older and felt he no longer needed a horse, he sold Skip. Skip would break loose from the new owner, jump fences and travel a long distance repeatedly showing up at Andrew's gate. He felt badly for the horse and was sorry that he sold him.

Final Days

When attending Memorial University, an hour's drive from Dildo, Brownie and I visited my grandparents. When I introduced them, Andrew thought I said Barney and Barney he remained despite Andrew knowing the difference. They liked each other. Both had sunny dispositions. Brownie says, "Andrew had a mischievous twinkle in his eye. It made no difference whether it was his child, neighbor, relative or stranger, he treated them all with kindness and respect."

In March, 1970, Andrew was diagnosed with liver and pancreatic cancer. Andrew and Violet never talked about his condition as each tried to shield the other, even as he became jaundiced. In April, Alma came from Virginia to visit her father and there was snow up to her knees. Rea had phoned her on the quiet. Even Violet did not know she was coming. Alma was nervous for she had not seen her father sick a day in her life except with the Typhoid. When she went to the hospital, he was sitting on the side of the bed and said simply, "I knew ya'd come." It was only the third time he had seen her in 20 years. He added, "Ya come when I'm livin', maid. Ya'll do me no good when I'm gone." The second day, he was asleep. She touched his hand. He woke and said, "O my dear, I was in another land, havin' a beautiful dream 'bout Chester."

When his wartime buddy, Jonathon Gosse, passed away July 1, 1970, Andrew's reply was that of a soldier, "Jonathon has gone o'er the top fer the last time." To Hilda, he said, "Hello, maid. I know ya, maid." In his later years, Andrew often complained of a cold back and feet. Violet sewed flannelette linings in the backs of his shirts. He insisted on warm socks. He said, "Vi, if I gets sick and can't do fer meself, make sure me feet are warm." Now his feet were cold and she fretted. When she left to get a cuppa tea, he said to his daughter in law, Beatrice, "I've seen enough people die. Don't cry fer me. I'm willin' ta go." He asked for Albert Jim Rowe, his neighbor and cousin. "I may need ya today, Albert. I thought I'd linger 'til the fallin' o' the leaves but it don't look like that now." About 5 AM on his last morning, he said, "Vi, go get Florence. I gotta tell her somethin'." Violet did not because of the early hour, afraid she'd fall in the ditch in the dark. Today, their good friend, Florence Smith, still wonders what he wanted to say.

Andrew died at home on July 8, 1970, age 75. His sister, Nellie, sang beautifully at his funeral at the Salvation Army Citadel in Dildo. Hilda sewed her father's war medals onto a black velvet cushion. My father, Bob Hellier, recited the Legion ritual with Jim Reid. Rea sat between her mother and Verd, who was shaking in great distress. Beatrice could not bring herself to go to the funeral, but it was that day she realized she was pregnant with Holly.

The Salvation Army church was full as people came to pay their last respects, one of the largest funerals in Dildo for some time. Andrew was not a church going man but, when he was ill, he developed a strong bond with Captain Bert Goulding of the Salvation Army. United Towns Electric employees were in attendance for the man whose headstone reads, "For all of us he did his best. May God grant him eternal rest." Captain Max Feener played the Last Post.

For years, our annual visit to Dildo was not complete without a visit to Andrew's grave, perched on a hill with a wonderful view. It was not a somber occasion but a celebration of his life, of keeping his memory alive. Nan was pleased to be part of the tradition, accompanying us up the steep hill, and sitting to rest on the concrete wall around the plot where she is now buried.

Violet at Andrew's gravesite 1986

John Reid was a teenager who loved to sing and play guitar. He was encouraged, with a promise of a beer, to accompany Andrew and Chester Reid on their rounds. When they died, John, in his twenties and working in a factory in Toronto, wrote a tribute to his older friends. It reads like a eulogy.

Ode to Chester Reid

He lives down the lane just a short ways from my home.
There with his wife they raised a family of their own.
There they dwelt together until that very day
That the angels in God's garden, they took my friend away.

He lived through the years and at the age of sixty two,
The Lord kind of figured that his work on earth was through.
And now He would answer his final request
To take him to Heaven for his eternal rest.

I'm sure the Lord he planned for him not a night of loneliness
For just a short while after, He took poor Andrew Smith.
Now they'll always be together and they'll never be alone
And we'll see them there someday when Jesus takes us Home.

Poor Andrew was the greatest man. He meant the world to me.
He was a very special friend of poor Chester Reid.
For they enjoyed together all that life was worth.
Happiness they spent with us while they lived here on earth.

So Lord, this is a message to give to them tonight
To send them love from all their friends and their darling wives.
The love comes from the daughters and the sons they will agree
That this is my small tribute to Andrew and Chester Reid.

In later years, John added a final verse:

Many things have changed since then. The wives have now gone Home.
I know they're with the angels now up there on God's great throne.
So memories, that's all I have of my two special friends
So won't you help me sing today my good friends' favorite hymn?

Chorus of the hymn "Will your Anchor Hold?" by P. J. Owens
We have an anchor that keeps the soul
Steadfast and sure while the billows roll;
Fastened to the Rock which cannot move,
Grounded firm and deep in the Saviour's love.

THE BABIES

Andrew and Violet Smith had 10 children.

Annie Florence	Oct. 12, 1921
Andrew Verdun	Nov. 23, 1934
Gerald Silas	July 26, 1924
Lawrence George	April 15, 1937
Orlando Maxwell	Nov. 19, 1926
Edward Albert	Jan. 27, 1941
Rea Edna	Dec 11, 1928
Dulcie Violet	Feb. 7, 1943
Alma Mary	June 26, 1931
Hilda Joy	Sept. 26, 1945

(Bertram and Violet, stillborn twins)

In 1940, the infant and maternal mortality rate in Newfoundland was double that in Canada. In the 1920s and 30s, thousands of Newfoundlanders lived in poverty and suffered from hunger and malnutrition. The scattered and often isolated coastal communities made it difficult to provide doctors and nurses, of which there was a severe shortage. In 1930, there were 83 doctors, 31 in the larger centers. Medical attention was not free and many could not afford to pay a doctor or travel to see one. In an emergency, if a family on government relief managed to pay for a doctor, they risked disqualification from the dole.

When Rea and Alma were small children, there was no local doctor. The only nurse was Nurse Woodman, retired and living in New Harbour. Doctor Bertram Gill, from Bay Roberts, visited the small communities several times a month on scheduled days. If a family needed his services, they put a piece of white cloth on the gate near the road. In Rea's time, the midwives were Susanna Reid and Aunt Bets Pretty. Hilda is 17 years younger than Rea. In her time, the midwife was Clara Pinsent.

Clara Pinsent, daughter, Shirley
and Andrew

Clara's daughter, Shirley, says her mom got $10 to $15 a birth. Health care did not cover childbirth or dental work. Some families could not afford to pay and gave gifts of vegetables or fish. New mothers stayed in bed for nine days and during that time, midwives continued with the care of the baby, mother and family. They were expected to do the cooking, cleaning and mending. When midwives had families of their own, arrangements had to be made. Clara had three children, Helen (Munn George), Shirley (Brian Brown) and Ron (Myrtle Thorne). Their dad, Ken, worked in Buchans. Clara baptized those babies she feared might not survive and her baptisms were recognized by the church.

Families had the option of paying a fee to call a doctor. Rea remembers a fee of $6 a family per year. The fee increased to $7.50 and then $15 with the opening of Markland Hospital. Ken Mercer collected the fees, not an easy job in a time of recession. Violet had frequent requests to phone the hospital, hers being the only pay phone in Dildo for many years. She did not like being asked if the people needing a doctor had paid their fees. She thought it was none of her business. She was only the messenger.

Dulcie

The first hospital outside St. John's was built in 1910 by the A.N.D. Company in Grand Falls, followed by a second in Millertown in 1911. When the Commission of Government took office in 1934, one of its mandates was to provide hospital care to the outports, the rural communities. It established 13 small cottage hospitals, with one to two doctors, some nurses and a bed capacity of two to 30. Maternity care was their main focus.

Markland Cottage Hospital in Whitbourne was one of those, the nearest to Dildo. It opened March, 1935, with 12 beds. It closed in 1985. Dr. Newhook and Nurse Cherry, who was as good as a doctor, were the first medical staff. The bungalow style hospital had a dormitory for nurses and nurse's aides and a beautiful rock garden tended by Nurse Cherry. Newhook was the doctor at Markland for 29 years.

Violet's Pregnancies and Births

Violet said in those days mothers did not tell you about the ways of a man and woman. "Years gone by, people don't got the understandin' they got today. Everythin' was kept close. If ya speak 'bout it, Mother would say that's nothin' for ya ta be talkin' 'bout. If I spoke 'bout someone havin' a baby or somethin', she'd say that's not a nice way ta talk. One o' these days will be time 'nough, when you're o' age." Many first time expectant mothers did not know how their babies were to come out, did not know what to expect when they "took" (labour pains). There were strict codes of modesty and proper behavior for women. Violet puzzled, "If you and yer man got no problems, why should ya want ta mix up (have sex) with somebody else? There is people, I s'pose, who's gonna do that whether they got problems or they hadn't. I means, if I saw a man married and he left his wife, why, I wouldn't have him. If he's no good fer her, he's no good fer me. Why would ya want ta be stuck with he?"

Dulcie, Rea and Albert

Violet was no more forthcoming with her daughters. The words pregnant and menstruation were never used. Her girls learned from older friends or relatives. Violet preached, "Ya be careful 'round the boys now," but there was no further explanation. Female undergarments were clipped together tightly on the clothesline as to be unrecognizable, similarly for the white monthly flannelette squares which were the devil to bleach. They used Gillett's Lye. They were astonished at a neighbor who hung hers out to dry for all to see, white as the living snow. Andrew had no qualms joking about the subject. When Elva (Pollett) Higdon bemoaned she had five sons and no daughters, he mischievously advised that she jump when her husband, Ray, shivered. She chuckled it did not work.

When Violet was 73 years old and visiting Hilda, she listened as Hilda explained ovulation to her daughter, Denise, and niece, Lorraine. Violet took it all in and exclaimed, "In all me born days, I ne'er hear tell o' it. Ya learn somethin' new every day. If I knew that, half the ones I had wouldn't be here now!"

Violet had difficult pregnancies and long labours. She was sick as a dog most of the time. The doctor warned her of the danger of hanging clothes in the tall sharp grass, fearful it might puncture her varicose veins. All her children were born at home, except Hilda, born at Markland Hospital. She almost bled to death with the birth of her first child in 1921. Violet had a midwife but they got a doctor from down the shore who came by horse. Otherwise, "I'd be down in the graveyard, dead. I thought I was gone and I only just come outta it. She (Florence) lived and I got through." Florence was born feet first. "Midwives can born a baby only if everythin's alright." One of her sons, possibly Gerald, was a large baby at birth. There were no scales but Violet said the midwife thought he could have weighed as much as 12 pounds!

Andrew, Violet and granddaughter Tina

While pregnant with Rea, Violet developed pyorrhea, infection of the sockets of the teeth. The doctor pulled all her teeth while she sat in the chair in her kitchen. She was 26 years old and nearly hemorrhaged to death. Old women brought cold stones from the beach to stop the bleeding. For over 20 years, Violet had no teeth, little wonder she was a slow eater. She sliced her meat into tiny pieces. She cut apples in half and scraped them with a spoon. She hated the false teeth she got when Hilda was a little girl and wore them only when she went out or if someone was visiting. Nephew, Bill Sanger, fondly recalls, "Aunt Violet usually wore her false teeth when we arrived, but after a half an hour she was comfortable enough that she took them out and put them in a cup of water on the counter. We took that as a compliment, we must have felt like family to her." She looked normal without them.

Rea and Hilda

Rea remembers when Verd was born. Susanna Reid, the midwife, was upstairs with her mother. The five children were eating while their anxious father paced the floor, casting frequent glances upstairs as men were not allowed to be present at labour and delivery. After the birth, a beaming Andrew, with Verd in arms, proudly showed each of his five children their new brother. A few months later when Verd was crawling, Rea saw Mrs. Reid walking up the lane and said to her mother, "Mrs. Reid is comin'. You'd better change Verd 'cause he has a wet diaper and she could take him back."

Alma with Hilda and Dulcie

Susanna Reid born a good many babies. She delivered Florence Smith's son, Mervin, in her Salvation Army uniform, scurrying from church when she got the call. Susanna was a strong and pleasant woman. She was generous, making baby stuff for newborns and giving her own towels and bedclothes to mothers with none of their own. Her daughter, Stella, remembers her father, Owen, puzzling as to the whereabouts of their quilt as he lay shivering in bed. Susanna discouraged Stella from being a midwife, saying there was no money in it at $5.00 a birth and sometimes she never got a cent. She died at the age of 84.

Violet had her first seven children in 16 years. She was pasty looking. The quick succession of babies depleted her body's resources. Doctor Gill said she was anemic, had a leaky valve, and was not to do heavy work, not even lift a kettle off the stove. She smiled and said she had seven children. On his advice, for years, she drank bottles of clear syrup called hypophosphite. Used in many tonics, phosphorous was believed to be good for the nerves and brain and a deterrent to tuberculosis. Mostly it was prescribed for iron deficiency. Violet drank gallons of Brick's Tasteless and Beef, Iron and Wine and marveled how she never got the Typhoid Fever, that only she and Alma never got sick.

Violet and Hilda 1946

Before the birth of her last two children, Dulcie and Hilda, Andrew and Violet suffered the devastating loss of three children to Typhoid Fever. Albert was born prematurely after the baby, Larry, died. Violet mourned them for years. She had the devil of a time. The word "depression" was unheard of then. Rea now realizes her mother's condition for many years after the deaths of her children in 1941.

Hilda was born at Markland Hospital when her mother was 42 and her father was 51. There was concern as Violet was old to be having a child, born during an early menopause. Rea remembers her father's excitement as he was driven to Markland Hospital to pick up Violet and the baby. It was a Saturday and he was so proud you would swear it was his first child. You wouldn't know but he was 20 years old. The old hospital record of Hilda's birth gives Andrew as her father but fails to mention the name of her mother.

Twins and Triplets

Violet lost twin babies in the late 1930s when she was four or five months pregnant. She was sitting on the kitchen floor straightening a quilt, getting ready to pin. She got an awful start (fright) when Jonathon Gosse came rushing in, upset because his wife, Marion, was having trouble with her pregnancy. He wanted to use their phone to call Dr. Newhook. Jonathon was a quiet and mild man and to see him so agitated, Violet got up quickly. She felt something drop. When the doctor came, he told Violet to go to bed and rest. She did as told but the leaking continued.

On a later date, Dr. Gill from Bay Roberts examined her. He said, "Mrs. Smith, you can stay in bed forever but this baby's not gonna make it." Violet remembered him taking a sharp stick from his bag. He broke her water. The water gushed and to their surprise, there were two babies, a boy and a girl. Quickly, he baptized them, naming the girl, Violet, and the boy, Bertram, after himself. They shivered briefly before they died. Rea remembers her father solemnly going upstairs. There was silence and sadness. Years later when Violet saw her first Barbie doll, she said the twin babies were about that size. She mourned and talked about them for years, marveling that they were perfectly developed, with distinct facial features and fingers and toes. They even had fingernails. She would say, "Nobody'd believe it."

Beatrice, Verd and triplets

Multiple births continued in the family. On December 1, 1956, Verd's wife, Beatrice, gave birth to triplet boys, Randy, Roger and Ricky, at Markland. Beatrice had not seen a doctor prior to the births. It was not until Roger was born at 5:35 AM that Dr. Newhook realized there was another baby. Beatrice was put out for the remainder of the delivery. The other boys were born five hours later. When she awoke, he said, "Well, Beatrice, ya gave us an exciting time. What would ya like ta have?" She replied, "A boy and a girl." He said, "Is that all?" and hugged and kissed her. It was the first time he delivered triplets. A fifth pregnancy resulted in twin girls, Velvet and Veona. They were her seventh and eighth children in five years.

Ricky and Randy were over 5 pounds at birth but Roger was 3 pounds 4 ounces. Dr. Newhook wanted him to stay at Markland after the nine days. Beatrice said, "We go home together. If he stays, we all stay." He reconsidered. "You're stayin' with Violet and Andrew. You'll have lots o' help." When he visited a week or so later, he could not tell which boy was Roger. True to form, Andrew quipped, "Since we brought him home, we've been feedin' him rabbits!"

The parents and grandparents quickly established a feeding, changing and bathing schedule for the triplets. Beatrice alternated breastfeeding the boys while Andrew and Violet bottle-fed the others. The alarm clock was set for 2 AM and 6AM. Beatrice can still see Andrew in his one piece long johns and Violet in her long flannelette nightie and braids coming down the stairs each feeding to help. They were very protective and careful over the boys and visitors had to stand by the stove and get the cold air off them before they could see or hold the babies.

Every week for about a year, Dr. Newhook and Dr. Brett stopped by to check up on the boys. Dr. Fred Brett was the chief medical officer in Green's Harbour, giving Dr. Newhook some much needed help. Roger had a hernia as an infant. On one visit, the two doctors boiled a 50 cent piece on Violet's stove to sterilize and when cooled, they taped it to his belly button and left it in place for a month. It worked. Beatrice says Dr. Brett was a lovely man. She remembers going to his Green's Harbour clinic to get the children vaccinated. She refused a needle for herself. He said, "You come in here. That's what gives the kids confidence in their mother." Dr. Brett died July 27, 2002 at age 81.

Infant Care

Alma and Hilda, 1946

Violet bathed her babies in front of the stove with the oven door down. They wore "wrappers," tight white flannelette bands about two inches wide for the first two to three weeks over their belly buttons. For the first six weeks, they were dressed snugly in "barry coats" or barrows (long nighties) which came up over their feet and fastened at the waist. Inside the nighties were layers of quilted flannelette as there were no plastic pants. When mothers stopped using the long nighties, it was called shortening. It was a special day, the nighties usually replaced with an eyelet dress. There were always safety pins pinned to the bodice of Violet's dress for diapers. They were not easily found otherwise. Before changing diapers, she did what was called holding the baby out. She held the infant between her legs with their back to her belly and put a hand under each thigh until the child peed into a pail on the floor. This saved diapers as they were particularly hard to dry in winter and it helped with toilet training. Baby clothing was on a line over the stove. Babies slept in a rocking crib in the kitchen where it was warm and Violet could keep an eye on them. They slept in the bed with her while they were nursing.

Andrew and Dulcie, one of my favorite pictures!

In the past we believed the children were named by Andrew. This was not so. Violet says, "My sister Evelyn had a daughter Annie, the nicest lil' girl that was e'er on earth. She died o' measles or somethin', no doctors in those days. I said first one I gets, I'm gonna call her after her." Annie was also their mother's name. In Grand Falls, Violet's friend, Maggie, had a nephew, Orlando. They simply liked the name Verdun, as it is spelled in the 1935 and 1945 census, but the family spelled it Verdon and they called him Verd or Audie. Andrew called him Verdie. To his wife, Beatrice, and family, he was known as Vern. Vernon is the spelling on his marriage certificate.

Violet breast fed her babies and made her own baby food. To make "pap," she grated fresh nutmeg and sprinkled it on bread and biscuits mixed with warm water or milk. For good measure, she topped it with a little bit of sugar. For gas or colic, she added a peck (speck) of peppermint to warm water in a bottle. She browned flour in a fry pan for diaper rash. When the children were younger, they also called their father Pap. Violet said, "He always liked the youngsters. He had ta be with them." He often coopied or quot (squat) down, crouched on his heels, to their level. After each of his 10 children was born, they sat between Andrew and Violet where he made it his job to feed them. When Violet was run ragged, having worked herself into a frazzle (frenzy) or in a tear (hurry) trying to keep body and soul together, he took a child or two on his lap and sang. He took great joy in children especially when they were babies and delighted in their laughter when he tickled their bellies.

Nurse Dorothy Cherry

Dorothy Cherry was in her 30s, widowed and had lost a young daughter when she answered an ad by NONIA, the Newfoundland Outport Nursing and Industrial Association. She arrived from Lancashire, England to Lamaline, on the south coast of Newfoundland in January of 1929. On November 18, 1929, a 7.2 magnitude earthquake in the Atlantic Ocean off the Grand Banks caused a tsunami which devastated a 20 mile stretch affecting 40 communities from Lamaline to Lawn, killing 28 people and injuring many others. The news did not reach St. John's for three days and during that time of no assistance, through intense cold, wind and snow, Nurse Cherry trudged on foot and by horseback to provide medical aid. Nearly 500 homes, two dozen schooners and 100 fishing boats were destroyed. She was called the Florence Nightingale of the disaster. Subsequently, she nursed in Heart's Delight and Markland. In 1947, she was honored as a Member of the British Empire for her long years of nursing service in Newfoundland.

Markland cottage hospital

Cherry was a good nurse, albeit brisk and strict. Florence Smith says she was clean as ever clean could be. She kept to herself. Even her closest associates knew nothing about her private life, her tragic past. She was all business but Chester Reid's daughter, Gertie, remembers a special act of kindness. She was hospitalized for two weeks at Markland with blood poisoning after she cut her foot sawing wood with her brother, Lloyd. Cherry brought her a small Christmas tree before she was released on Christmas Eve. In the summer, Cherry took refuge in the flower gardens of Markland. In the winter, she enjoyed knitting socks for soldiers overseas and for the men who worked at the Repeater station in Whitbourne. She ended her career at Markland.

Dr. William Henry Newhook

William Henry Newhook was born in Harbour Breton in 1892. He completed his medical degree at McGill after serving as a sergeant in World War I in France with the Canadian Army Medical Corps. At Markland, his patients came from the communities of Blaketown, South Dildo, Old Shop, Broad Cove, Dildo, New Harbour, Hopeall to Green's Harbour on one side of Trinity Bay. On the other side of the bay he travelled from Whitbourne to Chapel Arm, Norman's Cove, Long Cove, Thornlea, Bellevue, Bellevue Beach to Chance Cove. Roads were poor. He travelled by hand trolley on the railway, horse and sleigh, taxi, and his own car. Bert was responsible many nights, at 2, 3 or 4 AM, to shovel the snow when his dad made emergency calls. The doctor got into the habit of eating at 10:30 PM, usually fruit and oatmeal, to sustain him during these frequent early morning calls. Dr. Newhook's days were long, his caseload heavy.

William Henry Newhook

On a typical day, Dr. Newhook did family chores between 6 and 8 AM, such as tending the vegetable garden, a job he enjoyed for he was an avid gardener. At 9 AM he went to Markland and did rounds until noon. After his meal, he often laid his head on the table and had a power nap. At 1 PM, he went to the addition on the east side of the house called the Surgery. It had his desk, a couple of chairs, an examination table and a dental chair. There would be a lineup of people and cars, in the lane to their house and down the street. There were no appointments. It was first come, first served, which sometimes meant working into the evening.

In the spring, they visited schools and scheduled those who needed tonsils removed in summer. Beatrice was one of five girls from Norman's Cove chosen by Nurse Cherry. The youngest was crying. Dr. Newhook exclaimed, "Do ya think she's ever gonna quiet down?" Beatrice suggested the little girl come to her bed for comfort. He said, "Thanks be ta God, you're a blessing. We were sick and tired of hearin' her bawl."

Rea had a jaw tooth removed by Dr. Newhook. He used cocaine as the local anesthetic, a common dental practice in the early 1900s. Bert remembers the bottles lined up, clearly labeled Cocaine, and the oversize needles with a big syringe. Rea had a bad reaction to the cocaine. Bert says the practice of medicine then could be considered crude by today's standards. You worked with what was available. His friend broke his leg while tobogganing. He watched his father use a piece of wainscoting being installed in the house as a splint.

Dr. Newhook made his own drugs with ingredients shipped by train in crates packed with straw, from McMurdo's, a pharmacy in St. John's. This was a way he could make money for doctors were not well paid. His pockets were filled with quarters, the common charge for most prescriptions. Medicine was dispensed in recycled bottles provided by patients, including rum bottles! Rea remembers a time she made beets. Unbeknownst to her, Albert's medicine was in the vinegar bottle. The beets were spoiled and the medicine wasted.

Dr. Newhook volunteered for the Whitbourne United Church as an organist, the Kiwanis Club, Royal Canadian Legion, the school board. Although it was not on the curriculum, he taught French to the senior grades. He was a ham radio operator and enjoyed sports, especially hockey. Doctor Newhook married twice and both wives had the same first and last names, Elizabeth Roberts! The first was from Gaultois, Newfoundland. She died at age 45 of heart failure. The second was from Nova

Scotia. Bert was the Best Man at the wedding on Christmas Eve, 1951. Dr. Newhook had 11 children, including twins.

On March 29, 1963, he died unexpectedly in the delivery room at Markland of a heart attack. Nurses Audrey (Mercer) Adams and Rosy Torraville finished "borning" the child. Dr. Newhook was 71 years old.

Back: Andrew holding Albert, Alma, Verd
Front: Nephew Bill, niece Nellie, nephew Erwin

THE MEDIC

Andrew had a gift to treat the sick and the dying. Rea and Alma were amazed at their dad and the things he did for he was not an educated man. Before the existence of Markland Hospital, someone was always at their door for medical aid. Andrew was clean, particular and had a great deal of common sense. He dealt with a wide range of issues from infections, bad teeth, broken bones, cuts, fevers, and allergic reactions to bee stings. Violet went with him when he gave enemas. While Andrew was certainly exposed to injury and death during wartime, did the experience give him a knowledge and confidence to tend to people's needs? He used common aids such as bread, baking powder, molasses, myrrh and juniper. Peroxide, iodine, calamine lotion, Vick's Vapor Rub, Mecca Ointment and Minnard's and Sloan's Liniment could be bought at the general store and they were stored in the small mirrored medicine cabinet in the kitchen along with Andrew's shaving supplies.

Andrew treated boils, infected splinters and blackheads. Boils were common, especially on men's necks. He applied pressure to squeeze with two small flat pieces of wood. Violet made a poultice by soaking bread and a raisin in boiling water. It was held in place with a clean cloth, often a strip from an old pillowcase. Violet grumbled "An, we won't have a pillow case ta our name," as he used them for poultices, bandages and slings. He removed fishing hooks from boys' and men's fingers, lips and ears. He filed off the barbs at the end of the hooks, and sanded the ragged edges so he could pull them out. Snow was used as a clotting agent and put on the necks of those suffering from nose bleeds. In summer Andrew used ice from Pretty's General store. It was cut from ponds in winter and buried in sawdust in the icehouse for summer use.

Andrew with horse harness

Sometimes Andrew's knowledge tipped the balance between life and death. In his garden one day he heard neighbor,

Florence Smith, screaming and holding her infant son, Mervin, who had stopped breathing. Today, Florence believes he was overheated, covered with too many blankets. Andrew blew repeatedly into Mervin's mouth until he began to breathe. He had her drop a needle's worth of brandy into a teaspoon of warm water and feed it to the child.

Mrs. Thomas Moore came in great pain with her finger swollen around her wedding band. It was a summer day. Andrew had her go outside in the fresh air because he worried she might faint. For a long time he patiently used a file on her gold band. A shim (sliver) of matchstick behind the ring protected her finger. It seemed to take forever.

It sometimes fell to Andrew to be a mortician. After he tended the dying, he made their caskets. Florence Smith knew someone was dead or dying when she heard Andrew sawing and hammering at odd hours.

Grandson, Claude, watched his grandfather build coffins. They were not rectangular but narrow at the feet and wide at the shoulders. At the point of the shoulders there was not a join but an actual bend in the wood. This process is called kerf bending. Parallel cuts are sawed into the inside surface, half way through the wood. A kerf is the gap left from a saw cut. The wood can be bent without splintering because the kerfs compress together. This method of construction required less lumber.

Andrew believed everyone deserved a brass plate and handles on their casket. The exterior of the casket was covered with a purple fabric tacked neatly in place. For infants or small children, he used pink or blue fabric. He made the casket for his brother Eldred's grandchild, (Phyllis's first child), who died days old, "failure to thrive." Violet made each person a pillow and lined the casket with white satin or flannelette. She was particular and obsessed about germs. After Andrew prepared a body for burial, she made him remove his clothes to be washed immediately and he lathered his hands and arms with Jeye's Fluid, a powerful disinfectant. This was not a paid position.

In Albert and Hilda's time, there was less need for Andrew's services. Markland Hospital was open and more people had cars. Still she remembers him staying up all night with the sick and dying, often accompanied by Violet. He treated over a period of time, Uncle Eldred's son, Bill, who cut his leg badly with a chain saw.

Family

Walter and Lena Pinsent

Andrew had a first cousin, Walter Pinsent, who was ill. He and his wife, Lena (pronounced Lenie), had a toddler, Audrey. Walter was confined to bed in his mother's, Aunt Millie's, house. Lena hung a white towel in the bedroom window when Andrew's help was needed. Andrew's children were instructed to check the window. On one occasion when Walter was expecting Andrew, he threw a pillow at Ralph Pinsent and told him to go away. Walter died in January, 1940. He was 27. Dr. Newhook diagnosed tuberculosis. A letter from a Dr. Fraser, 282 Duckworth Street, St. John's, on November 3, 1939, diagnosed pericarditis, inflammation in the covering of the heart, but the doctor was optimistic for a full recovery. Andrew believed Walter may have been leaded from working underground in the Buchans mines.

Audrey, who had her second birthday in April after her father's death, remembers her mother forever grateful to Andrew for nursing Walter through his final days. The name "Andy Smith" was heard by the small girl as "Annie Mitt," a name she called him for many years before she realized the difference. Walter and Lena married in June of 1937, two and a half years before Walter's death. Lena married Ernest Thorne in September, 1951, but that marriage was also short lived as Ernest died of a heart attack. Audrey's grandfather, Moses Thorne, made caskets in New Harbour. Her grandmother made the lining and Audrey helped her make it fancy by cutting out small diamond shapes. Moses' sister was midwife, Aunt Bets Pretty.

Walter's younger brother, Adolfus "Dolf" Pinsent, came to Andrew for help, bleeding profusely, with three of his fingers nearly severed by his axe while he was cutting splits. Andrew applied a tourniquet and carefully cleaned the fingers. He put splints on both sides of the hand and sent Dolf to Nurse Woodman in New Harbour who said the care he received from Andrew was better than what she could provide. Her response pleased Andrew and he was delighted that Dolf kept the use of his fingers.

Dolph in background, with his sister, Mildred and her husband, Walter Mercer, and their parents, Millie and Bill Pinsent

When grandson Ricky was five, he nearly severed his big toe with an axe despite warnings that he not go near the chopping block in his grandfather's yard. There was blood everywhere. He did not go into their house for help because he knew he had done wrong so he hopped down the road to his mother. The doctor was unavailable so Beatrice and Verd took him back to Pop. "Pop got turpentine, (myrrh from a tree), cleaned the toe and done it up with gauze." The scared little boy was in good hands.

Despite all his expertise, Andrew was unable to help Rea with her asthma. She had her first attack about four months old. They thought it was pneumonia. He sat on her bed night after night, fanning her and saying "Poor lil' devil, poor lil' devil." Violet said Rea was skin and bone, no bigger than a bed fly. Rea lived daily with the smell of Vicks Vapor rub. She inhaled steam from a bowl of hot water and Vicks with a towel over her head. She took Friar's Balsam and sugar to soothe her throat. For years she wore two squares of red flannel (thin wool), one on her chest and one on her back, attached over her shoulders by two straps. Her white undershirt helped keep it in place. She drank so much Gerald S. Doyle cod liver oil that the oil penetrated her shirt and left it yellow except for the two squares next to the flannel which stayed white. Wearing red flannel was a popular treatment for chest ailments. It was supposed to promote perspiration and draw out inflammation. Andrew's mother, Julia, saved goose grease to warm up and use as a chest rub.

When Rea was 14, Dr. Gill prescribed a new medication that made a huge difference. "Heaven," she says. It changed her life completely, enabling her to do things she was not able to do before, including work in St. John's. She renewed the prescription each month by phoning a number to McMurdo's Pharmacy in St. John's and it was mailed to her. She does not know its name. She talked to a McMurdo apprentice named Albert Jenkins, who later established his own store in Gander and became her pharmacist.

It is one thing for a parent to treat the physical ailments of their child, but it is another to recognize and admit that their child has physical and mental impairment, such as Albert. His premature birth was the cause of much concern. He had great difficulty swallowing. Rea ran from the house as her parents struggled to keep Albert alive when he glutched and gagged, for she feared the possibilities. His baby teeth did not last so he could digest only soft food. He had one health crisis after another and they rushed him to Markland Hospital. Andrew and Violet were petrified because he was so small for his age.

They lived with the belief that he would not survive early childhood. He was a happy and handsome little boy. He was able to walk, talk, feed and dress himself. He loved to play and be around people, many of whom looked out for him. Outwardly he looked like a normal child. Soon there was the creeping realization of the reality caused by the circumstances of his birth and they understood the full extent of Albert's difficulties. This was easier when Albert was a child. It became more difficult as they aged and Albert became a man. It was not until he was 34 that Albert was officially deemed unemployable. With very limited resources, Andrew and Violet simply did the best they could.

Albert and Dulcie

Andrew made the casket for his father, William. Rea remembers her grandfather's last days. She was five years old. Grandfather was crazy in stomach pain and it was thought to be cancer although nobody could be sure. Her grandparents lived in the house next door, with son, Eldred, and his family. Andrew tended to his father, keeping watch from a chair outside the bedroom door. When William died on June 5, 1934, at age 67, Andrew dressed him. Rea remembers seeing her grandfather during the wake in his casket, lying on a white pillow. He had a piece of fabric with an open cutwork pattern spread over his face. As a precaution against the spreading of possible germs, William's cup and eating utensils were dumped overboard in deep water. Sometime later the cup washed ashore.

Animals

Roy George, Gerald and Ken
Smith with Amos, the lamb

One of neighbor Ken George's sheep broke her leg while Lendo was firing (throwing) rocks for badness (up to no good). Andrew assumed responsibility for the injured lamb, fitting it with leg splints and keeping it in his front garden until the leg healed. There was no animosity between Ken and Andrew over the incident because they were related, good friends and neighbors.

Andrew spent many days unsuccessfully nursing his first horse. It died of an undiagnosed horse sickness, which affected and resulted in the deaths of horses in the Dildo area. Despite his best efforts, Andrew was unable to save her. He was very upset, saying, "What have I done? I killed the horse," for he had acted out of desperation on another's advice and administered kerosene to the horse's nostrils. She didn't fight him for she knew he was trying to help her. The next day, she died. He blamed himself. Alma watched as Albert Jim Rowe helped him load the horse on a sled to be hauled away by another horse for burial. This same horse had previously lost her foal which was unable to stand on her feet to nurse, did not thrive and died. In its grief, the horse followed Andrew everywhere he went for days because she knew he was the one who had taken away her foal.

Nance, a second horse, had an abscess in her mouth. Andrew fed her small boiled potatoes and the chewing of the soft food resulted in the breaking of the abscess. Skip, the third horse, developed the same condition. Skip trusted Andrew so implicitly that he allowed Andrew to lance the abscess with a sterile knife. Andrew held the harness and talked quietly to the horse during the procedure. Hilda says, "The horse cried 'cause it was a real bad sound," and she had to leave. Skip was devoted to Andrew and listened to him, remaining still until the job was done.

Tuberculosis

The leading cause of death in Newfoundland at this time was tuberculosis, also known as TB or consumption. It was rampant, with a much higher rate than Canada, the United States and Britain. From 1901 to 1975, it is believed that 31,824 Newfoundlanders died of the disease. Violet's brother and Andrew's sister were two of these. The high rate was partially attributed to the habit of families and friends gathering in the kitchen for warmth and to the common habit of spitting tobacco. Tuberculosis is hard to detect until it is active and then it is more difficult to treat. Thousands of survivors suffered from its effects for the rest of their lives.

One of the earliest pioneers in the treatment of tuberculosis was Dr. Herbert Rendell. His son, Herbert Rendell Jr., was killed in 1918 while he was Andrew's Captain in World War I. From 1911 to 1917, Dr. Rendell and Ella Campbell, RN, travelled on his yacht, the *White Knight*, around the island in the summertime. They worked tirelessly to educate people of the causes, prevention and treatment of TB. Dr. Rendell was the first superintendent of the new 52 bed Sanatorium in St. John's in 1917. Ella Campbell was its first nursing superintendent. Sadly, she may have been tubercular when she died of heart failure after having the grippe (influenza), the next year. She was 34 years old.

In 1946, proceeds from the sale of Christmas seals bought an American Naval patrol boat for $14,500, and it was renamed the *Christmas Seal*. It was a floating TB clinic, used until 1970. People from coastal communities stood in line for the boat's visit to get their X-rays and to view the film, "The Silent Menace." The BCG vaccine was used in the 1940s and 1950s, and streptomycin, the first antibiotic remedy for TB, became available in the 1960s.

Andrew and Violet's son, Albert, was said to have had a TB hip. While TB was more common in the lungs, it could also attack bones and joints, the brain and kidneys. Albert broke the hip when he was four or five by falling on a rock while playing ball. For several years, he wore a two inch strap over his shoulder like a sling which was attached by a swivel to another strap on the opposite foot. His leg was bent backwards towards his back. He needed crutches to walk. Violet took it off only before he went to bed when he hopped on one foot. It didn't slow him down. Today, he has one leg slightly shorter than the other.

In 1961 Lendo got tuberculosis, probably in the lumber woods, followed by his wife Emily. Lendo coughed up mucus a long time before going to a doctor. Both were hospitalized in the sanatorium in St. John's, Lendo for 14 months, Emily for 12. Patients usually stayed at the "san" for one to two years but it could be much longer. Initially, it meant absolute rest, no sitting or walking. Andrew and Violet made the trip by bus to St. John's most Sundays. Lendo was furious he was not allowed to see Emily as men and women were put in separate wards, huge rooms, with many beds. He was roary eyed (infuriated) and often threatened to leave. He was not a happy man.

Emily (Cooper) Smith

At first, Emily's brother, Tom, and his wife, Joanne, looked after their children. Then, Andrew and Violet took the three older children, Rea, Joy and Claude. Mr. and Mrs. Charlie and Lizzie Smith (unrelated) looked after Brenda who was three months old. Andrew was 68 years old and because he and Lendo had jobs, they were denied government assistance even though Lendo was ill and could not work. Andrew was upset but he knew many Newfoundland families had it worse. More men died than women and families were left without an income. Children died and some were orphaned. It was a dreaded disease.

THE HOUSE

Dildo wharves and stages

Dildo is a small coastal community in Trinity Bay on the Avalon Peninsula on the east coast of Newfoundland. It was settled in the early 1800s by the Smith, Reid and Pretty families. It had a deep sheltered harbour and an abundance of fish. The catching of squid for bait was big business until the 1930s. It was an important whaling centre until 1972. Today, most people commute to work to larger nearby centers. Like many outport communities, it hopes to become a tourist destination, its name one of its attractions. The origin of the name "Dildo" is unclear. There have been several failed attempts to change it. Newfoundland is known for unusual place names. In 1935, the population was 525. Today, it hovers around 1000. In 2001, it was given the Harrowsmith magazine award as one of the 10 prettiest small towns in Canada.

When Newfoundlanders pronounce the word Newfoundland, it rhymes with understand. They emphasize the last syllable, land, and not the middle syllable, found, which they pronounce fin (as in a fish), and it sounds like NewfinLAND!

I grew up in Gander, an airport town, and Dildo was a world apart. In Dildo, cars and people competed with roaming sheep, dogs and goats on the single dirt road. There were droppings everywhere! The first thing I did was explore my grandfather's store and barn. I dared not cross the road immediately for Mom, fretting about safety, kept a tight rein on us. When the opportunity arose, I scrambled over the bank to the rocky beach, listening to the waves, watching seagulls and enjoying the smells of wood smoke and salt water. I spent hours searching for treasures in the flotsam, small bits of kelp, driftwood, colored twine and sea glass. The wharf was not a safe place, uneven because it was made of skinny limbed out spruce and fir trees. It was littered with rotting cod's heads, thrown away by fishermen gutting their catch on bloodied tables by small sheds known as stages. The stages beckoned to be explored if nobody was around, with their barrels, nets, rusty anchors and fishing gear. Salt cod was spread on adjoining flakes, raised wooden platforms covered with boughs. If I was lucky, I clammered aboard a dory tied up to the wharf, better to see jellyfish floating in the water. Wooden barrels at the stages were filled with fresh cod livers fermenting in seawater in the sun. Despite the putrid smell, older people skimmed off the oil and drank it. It was considered good for your health.

Andrew and Violet's house 1977

Today, some would like to see Dildo Island made into a Heritage site. It was the site of the largest fish hatchery in the world from 1889 to 1896. Dildo Island is a destination of tour boats with hiking, fishing, bird and whale watching options, and a Newfie boil up lunch. Andrew's first cousin Eli Rowe's house and his second cousin Lloyd George's house have been preserved as the Inn By The Bay and The George House Heritage Bed and Breakfast. The neighboring community, New Harbour, is known for its ship building. Four generations of Charles Newhooks made it the greatest family of shipbuilders in Newfoundland history. Dildo and New Harbour shared many services, churches and schools.

Andrew bought his house in Dildo with money his mother saved from his overseas pay and the $420.00 he received as his War Service Gratuity. He gave his Uncle Tom Smith $100 for the land. The house was a shell but out of the weather, important because it could take several winters to get enough wood from Newfoundland's thin trees to start a home. It was built by Llewellyn George before he left to work as postmaster in Grand Falls. Andrew pulled it down to its present location. It was a two storey home, measuring 20' x 25' and has always been a dory buff color (creamy yellow) with green trim. It looked out over the Atlantic Ocean to Dildo Island and over around the cove to Dildo Head.

The house boasted a stained glass door before a 5' x 20' sun porch was added in 1955 and 1956. The glass was textured, allowing for privacy, in shades of purple and green. The four corners were red. Above the door was a wide ornamental crown and rope molding. Under the window was a plaque bearing Andrew's name but everyone used the back door, which was never locked.

Rea in her blue wedding suit in front of the stained glass door

Initially, the house had four bedrooms upstairs and one on the main level. There were no closets. Florence, Rea and Alma shared one bedroom and two beds. Florence had a white single bed with brass knobs. Rea and Alma had a double. The boys shared a front bedroom. Before the smallest of the bed rooms became Albert's room, it housed clotheslines for drying in times of inclement weather. Andrew's Uncle Tom was first given the downstairs bedroom, and when he died, it went to Verd. Only the master had a feather bed. Rea rubbed a cake of Sunlight soap over the inside of the ticking in the feather mattress, to prevent the feathers from coming through. Andrew liked a high bolster pillow.

Before the 1950s, there was no bathroom. They used a chamber pot at night and an outhouse in the barn during the day. One of my first memories visiting my grandparents was seeing a full chamber pot in the morning! Water was brought from a shared well between the house and the root cellar. It was very deep and never dried up. Hilda was five years old when Andrew and neighbor, Len Smith, dug a ditch from the well to each of their adjacent homes. That provided the first running water, in a small sink in their back porch. The following year, Andrew installed a white porcelain sink, draining board and back stop in the kitchen and he converted the boys' bedroom into a bathroom, installing a toilet and sink. There was enough incline in the hill that gravity water was sufficient. They did not need a pump. When a tub was installed, it had only cold water. In 1975, Hilda and Jim bought Violet a hot water tank. She finally had hot running water, no more heating water on the stove. Violet was 72 years old.

In the seldom used Front Room, Violet kept her good dishes in a lovely cabinet next to a black round table and chairs. The room boasted a fancy parlor stove under a white mantle. It was the home of Andrew's official oval war portrait and a large 16" x 20" framed wartime print called "A Woman's Sacrifice." The origins of the print are unknown. It is a poignant picture of a young daughter standing on a windowsill, framed with lace curtains, waving to her father in his soldier's uniform. He waves back at her as he goes through the gate. She is supported by her mother who chooses not to look out the window but bends her head into her daughter's back. An infant lies in a cradle at her feet. The dominant colours are green, blue and gold. Violet bequeathed this print to Rea who imagined, as a child, it was her dad going off to war.

"A Woman's Sacrifice"

The house had a large back porch. On the left was a pantry or back room for storage of pots and pans and food items and preserves. A small room on the right stored the wood for the stove. A wringer washing machine stood in the porch for many years.

The kitchen was the center of activity. The largest room in the house, it was the heart of the home. Everyday dishes were stored in a built in cupboard with glass doors under the stairs. Under the window was a wooden daybed with loose cushions.

It had a reclining back, like a chaise lounge, painted dark green like the Grand Falls Mill canvas on the floor. A baby's rocking crib, a rocking chair and numerous white wooden chairs lined up against the walls. Andrew did not build the white kitchen cupboards until 1952 when he got water for a sink. The black "Favorite" wood stove with its four dampers was the focal point, with a woodbox in the corner. It was replaced by a bigger range in the 1940s. A grate was put in the ceiling to allow heat into the master bedroom.

In the morning, the children grabbed their clothes and hurried downstairs to get dressed by the warmth of the stove. In the early years, Violet kept smooth beach rocks at the back of the stove or in the oven. At bedtime, she wrapped them in a towel and put them at the foot of the bed under the covers for warmth. Cabin boards, smooth varnished pieces of wood put down both sides of the beds on top of the quilts after the youngsters were under the covers, ensured they could not kick off the quilts in their sleep. My sister, Janice, and I remember in later years Nan rubbing the hot iron over the bottom sheets and saying, "Get in fast, cover up and say yer prayers."

The family ate in the Eating Room to the right of the kitchen. The table, with fancy legs, first covered with oil cloth then arborite, was built by Andrew. A busy spot, family and friends gathered round to eat, tell tales, play cards, talk on the telephone and listen to the radio.

Behind the house was Andrew's store. This was not a place to buy goods as the name implies, but rather a small shed. General merchandise was bought at a shop. Andrew's store had two windows, shingles weathered gray and a horseshoe nailed to the right of the door. In the store were barrels of wood, metal and glass, insulators, old telephones, coils of rope and wire, dribs and drabs of anything that could be recycled or salvaged for nothing was thrown away. The place had the oily smell of oakum. At his work bench which stretched the length of the back wall, he made caskets, furniture such as the children's dressers and the Eating room table. Furniture was painted not stained.

Deeann, Beatrice and Violet in front of the store

Andrew made sleds for hauling wood and coal and hand slides for the children. Two wooden runners curved up in the front. Sometimes a metal strip was added to the bottom of the runners for better sliding in winter. Across the runners at right angles were two beams called bunks. The bunks supported a load of wood or two children at play. There were four vertical pieces of wood at each corner called horns. The horns prevented the load from falling off. It also provided a grip for a third child standing on the back of the runners. Runners were not at right angles to the bunks but pitched at an angle. Horns were stabilized on runners with crooked sticks usually cut from the root of a tree. Andrew used few nails. Instead he put wood together with Mortise and Tenon joints.

Behind the store and attached to it, was a two story barn, part of Andrew's father's old house. The barn had electricity and a one seater outhouse. Hay was stored in the second story and in the rafters of the store, providing insulation and warmth for the animals in winter. A solid wall separated the henhouse from open stalls for the horse, sheep and pigs. Andrew kept eight to ten sheep and marked them AS (for Andrew Smith) with green paint, as sheep were allowed to wander. They sold the lambs. Shortly after Verd's wife, Beatrice, had triplet boys, one of Andrew's sheep had three lambs. Andrew considered this a good omen.

Albert and Bob making hay 1977

Making hay for the sheep and horse was hard work. In later years, my father came each summer to help Albert swing the big scythes back and forth. In early morning, the cut grass was spread. At noon, it was turned over to dry. Later in the day, it was raked with a wooden rake into pooks (piles). It had to be perfectly dry before it was stored. The children and grandchildren loved to put the hay in the loft of the stable and shove it out the window in the peak over the henhouse, climbing a ladder made from scraps of horizontal board nailed to studs, left of the door.

Like most people of that time, Andrew and Violet kept a garden. They grew turnip, carrot, cabbage and rhubarb in the front and in the back they grew four different kinds of potatoes, blues, pinks, reds and whites. Andrew fertilized his potatoes with caplin (a small fish) and stable manure from his horse, hens and sheep. The manure was cleaned out every day and put back of (behind) the barn.

Bob and Dulcie on wood-horse

Potatoes, carrot and turnip were covered in thick sawdust in a root cellar on the hill. The cellar prevented them from freezing in winter and kept them cool in summer. It was deep with a permanent ladder and four open bins, one for each color of potato. The dark cellar rose above the ground with a short entry door. The door had a lock, opened with a key. Alma lost the skin on her lips one winter day when the lock was frozen and she blew on it in the hope it might thaw. She liked to have

Verd keep the door ajar for light and stand guard, for she was wary of the horse which inevitably followed looking for a treat. Cabbage was stored in the front yard in a half barrel in a hole with sawdust in the ground. Another half barrel was placed on top, making the site visible and accessible in winter. The frozen cabbage was thawed in cold water before use.

Behind the house, stored upright so they could dry out in summer was a supply of thin trees with the bark removed. Trees were cut in winter and brought out by horse and sled. What was cut one winter was used the next. They were sawed on the wood-horse (X shaped) into junks, short logs to fit in the wood burning stove. A junk was stood on its end on a chopping block and cut into smaller pieces. They were stowed in neat rows. Some were reduced in size again to make splits, to light the fire in the morning. Andrew enjoyed making shavings, lost in his own world, whittling with his knife, down and away so that curls of the wood remained attached to the sides. Violet gathered up pieces of wood chips in her apron from the ground. Heat was later supplemented with coal stored in a locked bin on the other side of the road.

Andrew had a drainage problem. Half way up the hill behind his house was a boggy area. He solved it by digging a long horizontal ditch between the wet area and his house. He then dug a second ditch at right angle to the first to make a T shape. This second ditch flowed down the garden beside his house, into a culvert under the road to the landwash, and out to sea. Before he had indoor plumbing, he dug a third ditch, off the second, and diverted it under the outhouse in the barn to get rid of the waste. As children, we were warned to stay clear of the ditches. They worked well. They just had to be touched up every year. Sadly, the ditches no longer exist; the land is wet and the house beyond repair.

I associate stinging nettles with Dildo. I called them stinging needles for that is how they felt. While they grow in many parts of

North America, I never knew them to exist in Gander, my home town. In Dildo, we had to tread carefully because they were everywhere, in the grass, garden and ditches. Recognizable by the saw tooth edges of the leaves, they would smerte (hurt and sting), leave a rash and cause an itch.

The property was fenced in typical outport style. Posts were eight feet apart. Rails were two inches by three inches and eight feet long. There were two horizontal rails to a post, one on the top and one on the bottom. Palings were nailed vertically to the rails, three inches apart. The fence was usually four feet high. It was painted with a paste of lime and water. Fences defined property lines and kept animals and children out of the gardens, critical for they supplied the year's worth of vegetables and hay. To stop goats from going through fences, wooden yokes were put around their necks. Children knew better than to trespass, especially in summer. Most folk were possessive over their land.

Gloria in the lane between Andrew and Eldred's houses. View is "over around the cove." 1977

THE HOUSEHOLD

Children made an important contribution to the family's well being, participating in the daily chores. They were involved in the garden, planting, plowing with the horse, picking and sorting potatoes, and getting vegetables to and from the cold cellar. They helped with the hay and cut splits. They fed the animals, tended the sheep and collected eggs from the chickens. They lugged water from the well and firewood for the stove. Everything was labour intensive. Most girls knew how to make bread, sew buttons, mend, darn, hem, and knit at an early age. They were taught the value of taking care of things, to waste not, want not.

With more hands to help, there was an advantage to large families. Most fathers made their living as fishermen or loggers or a combination of both. It required them to be away for long periods of time. Even with a job at home, they had little time or energy to help with the numerous tasks after a long day at work. It was left to the mother and children to do what was necessary. It taught them to accept responsibility at an early age. There was little leisure time.

In the spring the house received a facelift. Long winters of wood burning resulted in fine soot everywhere despite their best cleaning efforts. Skirting (baseboards), doors and kitchen chairs were painted as well as the canvas on the kitchen floor. Available from the paper mill in Grand Falls, the canvas was a heavy sail cloth and a durable floor covering. While the paint dried, Andrew laid sturdy planks above and across the floor for walking. The house was in slings for days.

Every room was wallpapered and received new layers. Papering was a task Andrew despised. Violet insisted the borders and patterns line up and match. "An, that's upside down. That leaf shouldn't be there." Andrew just wanted to get the job done. "Dammit, Vi, it looks alright ta me!" They laid out and cut the wallpaper strips on the table, added the paste with a wide brush and hurriedly carried the wet strips to the upstairs bedrooms. The stairs were the most difficult. The challenge was for Andrew to hold the extra long strips while climbing the ladder and install them without tearing the paper. Everyone was relieved when it was done. Violet made the wallpaper paste. She added 1 part flour to 2 parts water, stirred and heated it in an iron pot on the stove until it thickened. Gillett's Lye was added to discourage mold and mites.

Hilda recalls painting the exterior peak of the house. Verd was unable to reach the last two or three boards. A willing Hilda, 10 years old and unafraid of heights, climbed the ladder to the scaffolding. While Verd supported himself by extending his arms and holding the two eaves, she hoisted herself onto his shoulders and finished the job. Watching below, Violet was livid and reprimanded, "An, ya knows damn well they shouldn't be doin' that." He smiled in response, "I wish I had a camera."

There was some routine as to what chores were done on certain days. On Fridays, the emphasis was on the upstairs. Mats were shook, floors washed, stairs scrubbed and furniture dusted. Chamber pots were given a thorough cleaning with Jeye's Fluid. Every Saturday morning, before the children were up, the stove was cleaned with a polish, a process called blackening. It created a fine black powder which spilled over onto the floor. The girls awoke to a kitchen that had to be cleaned.

Saturday night was bath time. Violet put the round galvanized wash tub in the Eating Room on an old blanket and closed the door. Heated water was shared. It was a night's work and required two people to wash each child, starting with the youngest. Rea toweled the younger ones dry and put on their pajamas as Violet washed the next in line. The bigger children sat with their knees to their chins. They bathed once a week. Violet used cakes of Sunlight soap for everything, scrubbing and cleaning, washing dishes and bathing. They used green Halo shampoo. Dulcie's hair was long and thick and she washed it in the kitchen sink. Hilda's short hair was washed in the tub and her mother rinsed it with water from a jug.

Sunday was a day of rest. The children went to the Salvation Army church at 11 AM and 7 PM and to afternoon Sunday School, all rigged out (dressed) in their Sunday best. The girls wore hats and gloves. They were not chastised if they did not go because Andrew and Violet were not regular churchgoers. Still, Violet was very strict that no water used on Maundy Thursday (the day before Good Friday) be thrown out. It was like throwing water in the Savior's face. The family solemnly observed Easter, trying to be the best they could be. Andrew discouraged polishing shoes, using scissors, cutting hair or making splits on Sunday. He shaved on Saturday evenings. They paid their separate churches, Violet was Anglican and Andrew, Salvation Army. The children's religious upbringing was broadminded, not at all typical of the day. Mixed marriages (marrying outside one's faith) were frowned upon, especially between Catholics and Protestants, when the offending children could be disowned by their families

Dulcie, Violet and Lendo with Lendo's
children, Rea and Claude

Most summer afternoons after Sunday School the children played when chores were done. Andrew and Violet went for a walk, sometimes to visit Aunt Evelyn in New Harbour. It was customary for families to take a stroll. Young men and women took the opportunity to check each other out. Aunt Nellie and her family came to visit between church services. Sunday was family time. Hilda remembers going to the back of Dildo Island where there was a nice beach with her parents in Albert Jim's boat. They had a boil up and Andrew caught a fish and cooked it over a fire.

Monday was the big washday. In addition to their clothes, all bed sheets, tablecloths and towels were washed. Water brought from the well in buckets was heated on the stove. In winter, the wash was done in the back porch using a scrub board and the same tub used for bathing. In summer it was done outside, the tub on two chairs facing one another. The whites were done first. There were clotheslines everywhere, inside and out. Their hands ached so badly from holding the frozen clothes when they removed them from the line in winter that sometimes Rea cried. The next day the whites were blued (bleached), rinsed and put back on the line. When dry, they were starched and ironed. The girls shifted the beds (changed the sheets). There was always an oval iron pot on the stove with water and Gillett's Lye for items through the week. Hilda was eight years old when the first wringer washer was installed in the back porch.

The washday Rea dreaded most was the winter quilts. They were heavy because it was easier to patch an old quilt by adding a new layer rather than start a new one. It was done once a year on a sunny day in late spring. They weighed a ton when removed from the tub and were impossible to wring dry. They were hung on the clothesline dripping wet. Sometimes, the line collapsed with the weight.

Violet made many quilts, large squares or rectangles of flannelette or cotton randomly joined together and edged with a border. A worn flannelette sheet was used in the middle as batting. In the 1950s and 60s, summer quilts were made with Crimplene polyester. Violet made quilts for warmth not looks. Quilts were pieced and sewn together by machine in winter. Their weight made it impossible to sleep with feet upright.

Flour came in large fabric sacks. Violet emptied the flour into a barrel in the back room and covered it with a large cloth before adding a wooden cover. The sacks were stamped with a logo, usually Robin Hood, which had to be removed. After scrubbing, they were soaked in Gillett's Lye on the stove. The strong sun in March was considered good bleaching weather when the sacks were hung on fences in the frost under a full moon. They were laid on the grass for days to fade. It was a tedious process but the fabric was free and very durable, almost as valuable as the flour. Violet reused it to make cup towels, aprons, pease pudding bags, and embroidered and crocheted tablecloths, dresser cloths, and pillow cases, which she called fancy work.

When Lendo worked as a cookee in Argentia, she made his cook's cap and apron from sacks. A 100-pound sack measured 19" x 35". Andrew used the fabric for his many poultices and bandages.

Children were not allowed to use Gillett's Lye as it was a corrosive form of sodium hydroxide and could burn their skin. They called it "Jellis" Lye. In the mornings, the contents of the pee pots were put in a slop pail, a white covered pail with a handle, taken to the barn and thrown into the outhouse. Gillett's Lye was used in its concentrated form when thrown in the outhouse toilet. The seat was whitewashed with lime.

Clothing

Violet, in her topper coat, and Alma

Violet had only one coat for many years. Hilda loved it because it was different from the longer darker coats worn by other women. It was a three quarter length in a swag style which Violet called a topper. The sleeves were quite roomy with a cuff. It was collarless, medium slate blue and had a piped yolk with a big brass button. When she replaced it with a more common beige coat in 1973, Hilda was not impressed.

Violet made the children's singlets (undershirts), slips, drawers, pajamas, dresses, pants and shirts. Rea was thrilled when they were able to buy pink, blue, and lemon flannelette for their underwear. Drawers (panties) were not short like modern undies but had long elasticized legs just above the knee. Violet sewed after the children were in bed, working 'til the wee hours of the morning before she fell victim to half a night's sleep. She learned to sew from her mother-in-law, Julia.

Florence and her friend, Martha Cranford, were the first in the harbour to make and wear slacks. She made some for Rea and Alma, brown pants with big legs, bell bottom style. The three sisters marled (strolled) around the cove showing off their pants, giddy with pride. They thought they were somethin' else. Little was known of allergies and wool tore Rea's legs apart. She sneaked Florence's cotton Lisle stockings to wear under her wool. Because heels and toes wore out quickly, Violet kept old stockings to cut up and fashion new heels and toes. Itchy wool stockings would soon be a thing of the past.

Collars of men's shirts were detachable, easy to turn when they became soiled or worn. In time, they were sewn permanently unto shirts. Violet, like many others, painstakingly removed the stitches, reversed the collars and sewed them back in place, extending the life of the shirts. She removed sleeves and seams of wool coats, turning them inside out and sewing them back up. The children thought they looked like new. She added patches to elbows of coats, sweaters and shirts and to the boys' briggs. Briggs or breeks were heavy wool trousers the style of riding breeches ending at the knee.

Knitting

Violet recalled when she was of courting age girls brought knitting when they were in the company of boys. At the end of the evening, the old and new lengths were compared to reassure parents that their daughter's hands had been busy. It was a skill that would hold her in good stead. About those women who did not knit, she said, "When all is said n' done, I dunno how they raise a family."

Violet and Verd

When Violet and Andrew sheared their sheep, they tied the animals' legs together for they would thrash. Then she washed and carded the wool. "No easy task." Sheared wool contained twigs, grass, burr like things and sometimes ticks. Violet washed it in a tub by the door and lodged (laid) it on cut grass to dry. It had to be picked before it was carded with two wooden paddles. She transferred the wool fibers back and forth from one wired paddle to another until the fibers were separate and free of tangles and formed a batt or roll of wool suitable for spinning. Violet never learned to spin, "One less thing I have ta do." Andrew's mother, Julia, was an artist at it, gliding the wool through her hands. Rea's attempts came out in clumps. In later years, Violet sent carded wool to William Condon and Sons in Charlottetown, Prince Edward Island, to be spun. It didn't cost much and she marveled at all the colours she received.

Violet knitting

Violet could carry on a conversation and never look down as she knit, without missing a stitch. Sometimes she fell asleep. Her knitting needles were everywhere. They had no fixed location.

The traditional designs required that she carry stitches using four needles and two balls of wool. It often tangled. She'd sputter as she tried to unwind the black and white wool and, if unsuccessful, the children or grandchildren were called to help. The last resort was to cut the wool.

Trigger mittens (gunner mittens) have the practicality of a glove but the warmth and comfort of a mitten. The forefinger is separate, free to pull a trigger of a gun or jig a cod. These distinctive Newfoundland mitts she knit into her 80's, with an occasional slipped stitch belying her age. She pressed her stash under the mattress of the daybed in the front porch. In her lifetime, she gave away many with no expectation of payment but was delighted if you happened to have a few extra balls of wool. The bulk of her double knit mittens were black and white, with intricate patterns of diamonds or squares on the back of the hands. Granddaughter, Velvet, showed her how to incorporate the carried stitches on the inside so that fingers would not hook in the large loops. Violet pondered, "How come I ne'er figured that out? I been knittin' a lot longer than you!" She knit cabled sweaters with cowl necks, socks, stockings, mufflers (scarves), cuffs (mittens), caps and vamps (ankle high socks). She did not use patterns and sperimented (experimented) with designs. When Bert Vokey came to the house with no socks in his rubber boots, she immediately gave him a pair.

Violet's generosity extended beyond her food, socks and mitts. She was not well to do but her best platters and dishes and the large framed print of the ship, *Lusitania*, disappeared. Sometimes their trust was ill founded. The antique radio which had been such an important part of their lives was broken. A Salvation Army officer who accompanied a youth band from St. John's performing in Dildo, stayed overnight in their home. He promised Andrew he would have it repaired and bring it back. They took him at his word and never saw the radio again. Andrew gave his gun to a friend to be fixed and it was not returned. Andrew believed the best in people and was generous to a fault. He offered his Military Medal to his nephew, Bill Sanger, who admired it. Fortunately, Bill had enough sense not to accept, saying, "Keep it in your family."

Making Mats

Emily, Claude, Violet

Violet hooked rugs. In Newfoundland, it was called making mats and it was winter work. Grandson, Claude, says she came for Sunday supper after Andrew died and Nan and his mother, Emily, chose this time to hook, working on the same mat. They sat across from each other, working on a frame made by Andrew balanced on the backs of chairs. Andrew made hooks from old scidders (scissors). Mats were hooked into brin, burlap from vegetable and feed bags. The design was drawn with charcoal.

The most common was a series of squares or diamonds, filled in with rows of many colours. These striped blocks were called Hit and Miss, squares with horizontal lines alternated with squares with vertical lines, like the Rail Fence quilt design. Occasionally, they did a floral pattern.

Every spring or early summer the mats were washed. Alma was given this difficult job. Andrew's store had several steps to its door. The mats were laid on the upper steps so she could kneel on the lower step and scrub with a brush and soapy water. They were loaded in the wheelbarrow and pushed down to the ocean. Alma hated when the barrow tipped from the weight. She secured the mats in shallow water with heavy beach rocks and swept with a broom to remove the soap. The salt water cleaned but it also shortened the life of the mats. They were put on the beach rock to drain. Sometimes Gerald or Verd helped lift them onto the fishing flakes for further draining before being wheeled back up to Violet who hung them on the fence. They took days to dry.

Rea and Alma

Alma rebelled against the traditional role assumed by daughters. She was not interested in housekeeping. Her sisters, Florence and Rea, took pride in that. She went to the store for groceries, washed mats and got potatoes and vegetables from the root cellar. In wintertime, this was particularly difficult. She put the potatoes in a brin bag on her sleigh. The hill was steep and slippery and she had to hold the bag, walk by the side of the sleigh and guide it at the same time. Sometimes she hit an icy patch or drift and lost control. As she dug in the snow to find the ones she lost, her hands were numb with cold.

Winter also made it difficult to get water. At the time, the well was behind Eli Rowe's house, shared by Andrew and his brother, Eldred. Alma broke the ice by throwing the bucket repeatedly into the well. It was a struggle for the little girl to carry the water home each day, a five gallon bucket in each hand. The snowy conditions caused the water to spill. This got her in trouble with Uncle Eldred and Aunt Mel for the wasted water iced up part of the lane next to their house. It was a bone of contention between the two families. She'd despair to her mother, "I wasted the water agin but I just can't help it."

Cellar on hill behind house. House is not visible.

Andrew and Alma got annoyed with Rea's obsession with cleanliness. Violet said, "She was some particular, in every way." The two girls often got into a row. Alma would sneak away with friends, Irene George and Gladys Moore, whenever possible, disappearing Saturday mornings and not showing up 'til suppertime. It was predictable Saturday bickering, Alma questioning the need to scrub every inch of the house and Rea wanting to please and help their mother. On one occasion Rea scrubbed and waxed the canvas on the kitchen floor and insisted it was Alma's turn to polish. Alma grabbed her by the ankles and wouldn't let go as she pushed and pulled her in circles 'til the floor was shiny. They laughed so hard they were in stitches and Rea peed in her pants!

One Sunday morning, as Rea cleaned while others ate, Andrew took the broom, cracked it in half on his knee and said, "Nuff o' that." He did not condone working on Sunday. It scared them half to death. Alma had only seen him do anything like that once before. He was irate enough at Lendo that Lendo hid under the table. Andrew used the broom handle to try and get him and Lendo, who was quick and strong, grabbed the handle and wouldn't let go. The children were transfixed as they watched the tug of war.

Coronation celebrations. Dildo Hill behind arch.

Dildo celebrated the coronation of King George VI in 1936. Alma and Rea were six and eight years old and rode in the back of a truck in the parade. Later when playing Hide and Seek, they hid in the hen house and came out, their new pink dresses black with hen lice. In 1939, he and his wife, Elizabeth, visited Newfoundland just before the outbreak of World War II.

Alma was to have lice a second time. She persisted in hanging out with people known to have lice. Andrew threatened he'd put a notice on the telephone pole reading, "Alma is lousy."

When her thick fair hair became full of nits and lice, Violet spent hours combing it, pouring basins of water and Jeye's Fluid over her head. Alma's ears were burning and she complained bitterly but got no sympathy from her mother. Her scalp was tender for months. Violet was determined her children would not get the vermin. She sprinkled DDT in their wool caps in winter and everyone put DDT on their windows to kill stouts and mosquitoes in summer.

Dulcie and Hilda

Dulcie and Hilda

Hilda recalls growing up with Dulcie, who was called Delse and Dulce. Dulcie was the lady, the one who was spotless over herself. Hilda was the tomboy who would rather be playing Cowboys and Indians or fishing. They were like chalk and cheese, two totally different personalities, "not handy ta one another." They shared a bed and one dresser, two drawers for Dulcie and one drawer for Hilda. Dulcie was tidy. Hilda was untidy. Dulcie was meticulous like her mother, slow as cold molasses. Hilda did things much faster, like Rea. When Hilda and Dulcie got into it, Albert would say to Hilda, "Ya better run fer it," but she knew she could not outrun Dulcie who was older and had longer legs. She had seen Dulcie running and swinging herself over the gate at the end of their lane!

Hilda was Dulcie's accomplice in sneaking clothing from their mother for Dulcie to wear on weekends. They got away with it until Dulcie lost one of Violet's leather gloves. Dulcie had a habit of losing things like books and mittens because her mind was off in all directions. Violet was furious and they got seriously grounded. However, Dulcie forbade Hilda from borrowing her clothes. She had a fit when she caught Hilda wearing her green Banlon sweater at a high school dance. Hilda shrugged, "I learned it from you!"

Dulcie with Lendo's children,
Rea and Claude

Hilda and Dulcie loved to swim. To get a tan, they popped caramels in their mouths to take away the bad taste of salt water when they jumped off the government wharf. Then they made the trek wearing their wet swim suits to Pinsent's Pond, Trout Rock or Salmon Hole to swim in warmer waters. When they were not allowed to go swimming, they would sneak away, snaking their way through the long grass, thinking how smart they were. One May 24 weekend, they earned their mother's wrath when they went swimming in frigid temperatures. Dulcie got chilled to the bone.

Dulcie was book smart but a little scatterbrained. Living in Virginia with Alma, Dulcie left irons plugged in, refrigerator doors ajar and doors unlocked. She had no sense of direction and often got lost. She was good natured about it and laughed at herself, a big hearty chuckle.

Christmas

Christmas was the best time of the year. In most households, the men left in spring to find work. They came home in droves on December 15, in time to see their children in the school Christmas concerts. The men and boys cut and split enough wood to tide them over the Twelve Days of Christmas. The women and girls baked and cleaned. Work was kept to a minimum. Best dishes and linens were on display. Children did not see the tree decorated until Christmas morning. Decorations were simple, tinsel and crimped paper garland. Cards were hung on a white string in the kitchen. Families stayed home on Christmas day.

The festive mood made it a popular choice for weddings. Andrew and Violet married in Dildo, December 29, 1920 and my paternal grandparents, Herbert and Hilda (Jones) Hellier married on the same date, December 29, 1920, in Little Bay Islands!

Lon or Mervin Smith, Albert Andrew's house in left corner

The General Stores brought in items that might be considered luxuries any other time of the year, tempting those who had saved their pennies for that special gift. Children gawked at the abundance of sweets and candy in the glass jars.

All of Stella Reid's gifts were in her Christmas stocking and invariably included an orange, apple, raisins, candy, a piece of cake and a bit of coal in the toe of the sock. Children were warned they'd get coal in their stockings if they misbehaved. Stella was told it was in the hope she not be cold in the winter months. Rea and Alma did not have stockings but they remember the Christmas Eve they were in bed and heard sleigh bells, no doubt, their father's idea of getting them to settle down and go to sleep.

Andrew's children looked forward to parcels from Aunts Blanche, Violet and Sadie in Grand Falls, which contained wooden pencil cases, book bags, crayons and books. Violet made gifts of clothing such as flannelette leggings but one year the girls were delighted when she ordered a red coat for Alma and a green coat for Rea from Moore's Store. Boys received mouth organs, knives, marbles and games such as checkers and jacks. Eli Rowe gave Alma a beloved sleigh. Albert got his first pair of skates from Albert Jim Rowe.

Andrew's sisters, Blanche, Violet and Sadie

One Christmas Eve, Rea was gravely ill with asthma, her parents frantic she might not live through the night. They propped her upright on the daybed in the kitchen. That night they saw a breakthrough. The coughing subsided and she drifted into a peaceful sleep. When she awoke, a Scottish doll with black hair, wearing a tam and red tartan kilt, had been placed by her head. Later, they told her they thought she was going to make it, but they gave her the doll on Christmas Eve, just in case. She knew why it was a Scottish doll, why she was named Rea.

My father ensured Christmas, 1946, was memorable by showing up at Andrew and Violet's door unexpectedly. Wed in August, he departed in September to study in New Brunswick, to be away one year. Alma first saw him striding up the lane and shouted the news. Violet frantically pulled the hair clips from Rea's pin curls as he walked triumphantly in the door with a huge grin. Andrew ran to his store to get slices of frozen pork to fry up with scrunchions and celebrate the homecoming.

During the Twelve Days of Christmas, December 26 to January 6, the family participated in mummering, a Newfoundland tradition, when people dressed in sheets, long johns and oversized clothing. Cross dressing was popular when men dressed as women and women dressed as men. The goal was to be as ridiculous as possible. They knocked, often with a stick or a cane, asking, "Any janneys in tonight?" or "Any mummers 'loud (allowed) in?" They went door to door to eat, drink and sing for there was often a mouth organ or an accordion. The goal was to guess the mummers' identities by asking questions, trying to trap them in some unguarded reply for they all knew one another. They changed their voices, walk and mannerisms. Alma watched covertly as her father nonchalantly placed his foot on sheets and curtains used in the disguise. One sudden move and a slip of the clothing gave vital clues. If identified, mummers unveiled their faces. She can still hear her father laughing and saying, "Who the hell is that?' and "I knew damn well it was you!" Like most, Violet served syrup and dark fruitcake. It was the highlight of the season. There was no mummering in Dildo during wartime.

Andrew loved Christmas and all it entailed, the singing, dancing, and the storytelling. He was in his element. On Christmas Eve, he and Chester Reid led a group of friends and went door to door to visit and sing carols and the hosts offered all a drink. He was much in demand. His laughter was contagious and he had everyone in stitches. He was a hoot. He was a big kid.

At midnight on Christmas Day, they looked forward to the Watch Night Service at the Army church. The men of the community, even those not regular churchgoers, were invited to the pulpit to sing hymns and carols. It was guaranteed a packed house. Andrew always took part. You could hear a pin drop as the men's strong voices filled the air. It was such a happy time. It was also tradition to shoot guns to bring in the New Year. One such time Rea was with Reg Pretty. Suddenly, there was a gunshot! She thought they were being shot. It was such a relief to see the bright United Towns light over her door. "Serves ya right," her mother said, "fer bein' out so late."

"King Billy" Jack Reid in Orangeman parade

Everyone looked forward to the Orangeman's parade. It started at the Lodge between Dildo and New Harbour. "King William" rode his horse with the flag. Hilda remembers her father leading the parade on Skip, as King Billy, a small man on a big horse, dressed in their orange and gold regalia. Older parade members stepped out to homes along the way to warm up with a cuppa tea and rejoined the parade on its return. Parades were traditionally held on the nearest Monday to July 12. In Newfoundland, because of the demands of fishing in summer, they were held on St. Stephen's Day, December 26, New Years Day or Candlemas Day, (Groundhog Day), February 2.

The Orange Order or Lodge, an organization for Protestant men, was founded in Ireland to commemorate the Battle of the Boyne, 1690. Newfoundland was the most Orange spot in the world in 1920, with 35% of the Protestant male population as members. Violet was a member of the L.O.B.A., Ladies Orange Benevolent Association, founded in 1894, to support the Lodge, its charities and education. L.O.B.A. ladies wore white dresses and white tams on their heads. The Lodge, between Dildo and New Harbour, closed in 1970.

Violet (left) with LOBA

THE FOOD

Every evening after supper, Violet made bread, 12 loaves in Rea and Alma's time, and six in Hilda's. Bread was baked in buns, three to a loaf, not two, which is typical of most cultures. After kneading, Violet wrapped the dough to rise before she went to bed. Andrew was the first up in the morning to light the stove. He often kneaded it to rise again for her to bake in the morning. Sometimes, he cut small pieces to make toutons for breakfast. Flattened and fried, they were delicious smothered with molasses. Children looked forward to coming home to the smell of bread and eating it warm with butter and molasses.

During the Great Depression, the Newfoundland government granted dole to the destitute, designated amounts of flour, fat back pork, beans, corn meal, split peas, molasses and cocoa. Many Newfoundlanders suffered from beriberi, a disease caused by vitamin B thiamine deficiency. Beriberi was most prevalent in March and April, when winter food supplies were depleted. Its victims suffered from exhaustion, constipation and indigestion. Legs were most affected with pain and loss of muscle, making it difficult to walk.

The well intentioned decision was made to substitute brown flour for the traditional white flour in an effort to combat beriberi, for flour was cheaper and easier to transport than vegetables and fruit. Brown flour proved to be more difficult to store and bake, and to Newfoundlanders, whose main diet consisted of bread and tea, the taste was not to their liking. It was an unpopular move and many refused to use the flour. The nutritional value was not understood.

ROBIN HOOD BAKEOFF
Dick Power, Manager of the S.W. Moores Memorial Stadiuim presents 80-year-old Violet Smith of Dildo, Trinity Bay with the first place ribbon and cash prize for the White Bread Category.

Newspaper proof that 80 year old Violet's bread was the best!

When Violet was visiting Carbonear, her bread was entered in the Trinity Conception Fall Fair in Harbour Grace and won first prize. She said to granddaughter, Susan, "Ted Newhook told me I won. I didn't believe him. He's the devil, ya know, a big bluff." When she received her bright yellow ribbon, a stranger said to her, "My bread was as good as yours." Violet replied, "Then why didn't yer bread take the prize instead o' mine? I got her," she said. "That woman was more or less on the jealous side. If I had those feelings, I wouldn't do that sort o' stuff. Everybody's not alike. There's no accountin' fer some people."

Carla asked her grandmother her secret for making bread. Violet replied, "I always had the beautifullest bread come outta the oven. Why, I dunno, yeast, two or three spoonfuls o' sugar, a bit o' salt." Sometimes she added butter or a leftover mashed potato to the barm, a dry yeast cake. "When Beatrice came 'round, she didn't know how. Before she left she was able ta cook fer anyone. She'd tell ya she learned from me." Daughters in law, Beatrice and Emily, gave her credit for teaching them to cook and make bread. It was an important skill because bread was eaten at every meal. Beatrice bought 50 pounds of flour every Saturday to make bread for her large family and she sometimes made it twice a day. Today, she has difficulty making several loaves at a time as the portions seem ridiculously small.

Violet did not bake cookies for they were not filling and were eaten too fast. Instead, she made dumplings, covered with a boiled molasses sauce, a dessert she called molasses coady. Sometimes she added berries. There were steamed puddings and molasses buns. A favorite was figgy duff, a spicy molasses pudding which could be eaten with the main meal or as dessert. A duff was a pudding. A bangbelly was a molasses pudding, cake or pancake done with fat pork. A pie was two layers of cake with jam in the middle and covered with icing, not a pastry pie as we know it. A lemon pie was a tart. Jello was popular, as was stewed fruit or big white dried apple rings, covered with Limoges custard.

Molasses was a staple food. There were two kinds of molasses, baking and spreading. Spreading molasses was thicker and sweeter. In the general stores, molasses was stored in large wooden barrels or kegs. Customers brought their own containers, usually a one gallon crockery jar. Bad tasting medicine was mixed with molasses or kerosene oil to make a toffee substance for coughs and sore throats. It was used to cure cuts. Andrew mixed molasses with rolled oats as a treat for his horses. Some used it as the sweetener in their tea. Every spring and fall, Violet gave her children a spoonful of molasses and sulphur which she premixed in a glass jar to keep their blood clean and discourage disease.

Dulcie and Susan

While cod was a critical part of the diet, the challenge was to preserve it without refrigeration. It was gutted, cured in salt and laid on flakes of tree trunks and branches to dry in the sun, removed at night and in times of rain. It is the basic ingredient of the still popular Newfoundland meal, fish and brewis. Violet had a hankering for cod and enlisted granddaughter Susan's help to go to the wharf on Andrew's bike to buy the fish. Violet cleaned it, cooked it with salt pork and onions, and served it with new potatoes and a tin of corn on the cob. They sat at the dining room table in the front room, a rare occurrence, and laughed and ate 'til they could barely walk.

Albert Jim Rowe and lobsters

Growing up in outport Newfoundland had its advantages. Even with the decline in the fishery, it was not difficult to get fresh fish for supper. Nephew, Reg Downton, remembers Andrew hurrying down the lane on their arrival and returning with a large salmon. Lobsters were plentiful and sometimes used as fertilizer. They were not the luxury food item they are today. When Violet got sick after eating one, the family rarely ate them again. Rea loved mussels and when she was home for a holiday, her mother made sure Albert Jim Rowe had some in a piece of net tied to the wharf. Sunday at noon was the meal everyone looked forward to as Andrew was home. Violet used whatever "fresh" was available, rabbit, birds, pork, mutton, cow or chicken. It was combined with a pastry, pease pudding and Jiggs Dinner. About 10 PM on Sunday evenings, Andrew fried the leftovers in a cast iron fry pan. It was his special treat. They had Jiggs Dinner with greens twice a week. To make greens,

Violet removed the outside leaf of the turnip or the girls cut the leaves of the common dandelion and threw the flower away. It took a lot of dandelion leaves to make a meal. They tasted like chard or spinach.

Corned beef in a can, known as bully beef, and baloney (bologna) can be served cold but Andrew did not like cold plates and salads so Violet baked the bully beef with onions and pastry. Although it was the only meat Andrew had for days during the war, he loved it. Thick slices of baloney were fried crisp and served with fresh eggs, potatoes or hash, a frequent lunch with homemade bread, mustard pickles and tea. A family favorite, it was a quick and inexpensive meal on a busy day.

Lendo had a huge appetite and was not happy when they had company for supper because it meant less for him to eat. He hated to see the United Towns Electric people come for there were no restaurants in the area. Florence and Rea's friend, Florrie Moore, was a frequent guest at mealtimes as she spent a lot of time at their house, helping with chores. Lendo grumbled, "B'ye da Lard jumpin' dyin', is she stayin' fer supper agin?" One breakfast, he was frying eggs he had collected from the henhouse and Violet told him to share with his sisters, "not ta be so covageous" (covetous). Alma laughs when she recalls his reaction. He spit in the fry pan and Alma, predictably, wanted no part of the eggs!

On Friday nights, Violet made pork buns for Andrew's boil ups in the woods. They were made with scrunchions, bits of fried fat back pork. A typical lunch included a tin of bully beef, potted meat or Vienna sausages, cheese, bread, watered fish, caplin or a tomcod. To roast the tomcod, he wrapped it in a wet paper bag before putting it on the fire. He carried his food in his wartime back pack, the same pack he used Monday to Friday for work. He enjoyed going into the woods with his horse and sled on Saturdays in wintertime, limbing out trees for firewood.

Andrew and Violet on a boil up,
with a kettle and a jug.

An oft-told story was the time he was accompanied by Rea's boyfriend, Bob. When Andrew returned from stacking wood, a single slice of buttered bread remained in Violet's lunch. Bob thought Violet's bread next to none and likened store bought bread to fog. Andrew was not impressed and gave the slice to the horse. Albert told my father when he visited, "Now Bob, there's other people in this house besides you who wants that pastry." Violet said of Bob, "Oh, he feed some good. My God, he was able ta eat. He could eat The Funks," (Newfoundland nesting colony for sea birds). Andrew teased when Violet pushed second helpings, "Now Vi, don't feed them too good or they'll be back," but you were always encouraged to fill yer boots (eat well).

A favorite meal was fish and brewis on Friday when the fish, potatoes, softened hard bread and scrunchions were served separately, or fisherman's brewis when they were fried up together, often the next day. Monday was wash day and Violet had little time to fuss with meals so she added an onion to leftover potatoes, turnip and cabbage from Sunday, to make hash. Dinner, the main meal each day, was served at noon. Supper was served at 5 PM. Alma's favorite meal was and still is baked beans. Hilda's was mutton and a dessert of gingerbread and brown sugar sauce. Each night, before bed, they had a lunch. The children had cooked cereal such as cream of wheat, or toast with marmalade, molasses or jam. For visitors, there was a big spread.

The house had no refrigerator until 1960 when they bought a fridge and dining room table set from Eliza "Lizzie" (Shepherd) Pretty when her husband, Arthur, passed away. Prior to that, the pantry or back room was used as a cold storage space. In the pantry, Violet put her bread, cream, milk, butter, jams, partridge berries in bottles of water, fruit for cakes, and her molasses and flour.

Ken George with cod, and Verd

The family occasionally got fresh cow's milk from neighbor, Ellie George, who was also the postmistress. Some families drank goat's milk. Ken and Ellie had a small farm. During the summer, usually on Sunday afternoon, one of the girls went to the George's with a glass jug for milk and a tall drinking glass for the fresh cream which floated on top of the milk when it was scalded. The cream was thick and used on prunes and desserts. Fresh milk was too expensive to buy on a regular basis. Instead, they consumed vast amounts of Carnation tin milk, often diluted with water for drinking. They bought the tins by the case, 24 in a box. In Rea and Alma's time, there was no juice. They rarely drank water. Sometimes they had lemonade. They often had cocoa. Senna Leaves were steeped for constipation. It had a terrible taste, even with a bit of sugar. Much better tasting was the steeped black current tea, with the berries left in the cup, for general good health.

There was always steeped tea on the back of the stove even in summer when there was no fire. They drank cold tea for thirst. There were no tea bags. Loose live tea leaves were used. Strainers were available to prevent the leaves from going into the cup but Violet generally didn't use them. She didn't care if a few made their way into her tea. The trick was to pour slowly. She bought Camp liquid coffee for Uncle Tom because he loved it, a thick rich concentrate with a bitter chicory flavor.

With the milk and cream, they sometimes bought small patties of butter from Ellie George. It was a treat, especially for the main meal on Sunday. Real butter was more expensive and spoiled quickly without refrigeration. The staple in most households was Good Luck margarine. The manufacture of this artificial butter was banned in Canada from 1886 to 1948, except during the rations of World War I. Newfoundland, not yet a province of Canada, had a profitable margarine manufacturing industry, with three large plants, owned by Brehm Manufacturing Company, Harvey and Company and the Newfoundland Butter Company, owned by John C. Crosbie.

They sold their margarine to Canada for half the price of butter. Margarine became a contentious issue in 1949 when Newfoundlanders were voting as to whether or not they would join Canada. They were fearful the manufacture of margarine would be banned in Newfoundland. Term 46 allowed its manufacture but prohibited its sale outside the province.

The family killed a sheep and pig for Christmas. Andrew became attached to his animals and he could not bring himself to kill them. He did not want the animals to suffer and Albert Jim Rowe was a good marksman. Andrew hung the meat to freeze in his store. The boys supplied the family with rabbits. It was Lendo's job to kill and pluck the chickens which Violet called pullets. The laying hens provided the family with fresh eggs, many with double yolks. Violet soaked crusts of bread and fed it to the hens.

In February, on the last day before Lent, they celebrated Pancake Night, an easy meal for Violet and a popular one for the children. The pancakes contained treasures such as buttons, nails and coins. If you got a button, you would be a seamstress or tailor. A nail said you might be a carpenter or marry one. The most coveted pancake contained money. Verd watched his mother like a hawk. He wanted to go to a Times, a community gathering, and the admittance for a child's meal was 10 cents. His perseverance paid off and he got the dime. Pancakes were covered with molasses or Karo corn syrup although some, like neighbor Florence Smith, ate hers with scrunchions.

Children could buy a Jawbreaker candy for a copper. A copper was the name for one cent, as big as today's quarter. These candies, also known as Gobstoppers, were large, hard, glossy balls with a colorful swirl, which were too hard to bite and could take a day to dissolve in your mouth. Attwood Pretty was the first to sell ice cream in his store and he sold a Brookfield Dixie cup for five cents. Rea found a nickel on a shelf in the cupboard under the stairs. She watched it for days. To avoid temptation, she pushed it out of sight. Finally, she succumbed, took the five cents and bought a caramel chocolate bar at Moore's Store. When Lendo saw her with the bar, she told her mother. She was not punished but she never forgot the shame of it.

Andrew had a great sweet tooth. One of his daily treats was a cup of tea with a slice of homemade bread, butter and sugar, drizzled with tin milk and toasted in the oven. For breakfast he loved watered fish, salt fish soaked overnight, boiled in the morning and eaten with toast. His love of sugar was rivaled by his love of salt. He shook liberal doses of salt on his food. He would eat anything, liked everything. The indigestion he suffered after the war plagued him all his life. After every meal, he drank a teaspoon of baking soda dissolved in a glass of water. He couldn't be without it.

When Violet and Andrew were happy, she clapped her hands and he slapped his thighs. She put her hands on either side of her grandchildren's cheeks and squeezed them. To her a thin child meant an unhealthy child. She liked a bit of weight and rosy cheeks. As a tall skinny child, I never got her stamp of approval. She did not have that problem with my brother, Robert. After he wolfed down four slices of her homemade bread, she said, "Ya looks jist like yer father and ya eats jist like him too!" You knew if her bread had just come out of the oven because the smell hit you as you came up the lane, before you entered the house. Her bread was light. It melted in your mouth. It was the best!

UNITED TOWNS ELECTRIC
COMPANY, LTD.

THE JOBS

In the 1930s and 40s, the population of Newfoundland was under 300,000 as compared to 526,000 in 2014. The 50,000 who lived in St John's were called Townies. With the exception of the paper towns of Grand Falls and Corner Brook, and the mining towns of Bell Island, St. Lawrence and Buchans, the remainder lived in 1300 little outport settlements along the coast. Only 100 of these had a population over 500. Fishing, the traditional way of living, was in deep decline. Early fishermen rowed to the fishing grounds, up to 20 miles a day. It was man and his wooden boat against the elements, no engines, no weather reports, no search and rescue.

The 1930s Depression left many families in Newfoundland, and elsewhere, in a state of deep poverty. Living conditions were harsh. However, most people were in the same boat and they did not think of their lives as bleak. As long as they had their health and some food on the table, they deemed themselves fortunate. In order to survive, they became self sufficient, planning for the long cold winters and helping one another. Nothing, even broken, was wasted or thrown away. Without knowing the words, they practiced conservation and recycling.

In 1898, a railway link was completed from Port Aux Basques to St John's, a distance of 547 miles. Labourers worked six days a week for a dollar a day. The Newfoundland Railway had a narrow gauge, 42 inches between the rails, the North American standard, 56-½ inches. The train's first trip across the island took 28 hours. The slow train was nicknamed "The Newfie Bullet." It operated for 71 years until a paved Trans Canada highway meant too few rail passengers. It was a full service passenger train with coaches, diners and sleepers. Each coach sat 50 people. Everyone went to the station to meet the train. It was a social event.

The Newfie Bullet

The highlight of rail travel was eating in the posh dining cars, considered one of the best restaurants in the province. The menu consisted of traditional fare such as fish and brewis, Jiggs Dinner, and bakeapple jam. Fresh fish and game such as char and cod tongues was purchased from locals along the track as the train made its journey. It was served elegantly with real china, silverware, white tablecloths and linens. There was a large Diner staff, including cooks, waiters, pantry man, and chief steward. Service was next to none. A railway job was considered a good job.

The railway made the interior of the island accessible. In 1909, the A.N.D. Company built a pulp and paper mill in Grand Falls, a massive undertaking at the time. The possibility of a Grand Falls job gave hope to many who desperately needed employment. It was a bright spot of prosperity and had a huge economic impact on the island until its closure in 2009. In 1925, a second paper mill opened in Corner Brook.

From its inception until 1961, Grand Falls was a closed company town. Only mill employees and workers from private businesses were allowed to live there and they were not allowed to build houses of their own. Corner Brook, Wabana and Buchans were also company towns. The A.N.D. Company partnered with ASARCO, American Smelting and Refining Company in 1928 to open one of Canada's richest base metal mines in Buchans. It operated 57 years, employing Andrew's three nephews, Walter, Albert and Adolphus (Dolph) Pinsent from Dildo. The company controlled who came and went but those who lived and worked in these towns believed they were fortunate to have jobs and amenities such as hospitals, schools and retail, cultural and sports facilities.

In 1935, the decision was made to clear the forest and construct an airport in central Newfoundland at a site known as Hattie's Camp, an abandoned sawmill operation and railway stop. By 1938, they had completed four long paved runways. It was the largest airport in the world, known as the Newfoundland Airport. It was renamed Gander in 1942. Allied bombers and fighter aircraft used the airport to cross the ocean during World War II. Like Grand Falls, 25 years earlier, Gander attracted many outport Newfoundlanders seeking employment and a good wage, my parents among them. The first residents lived in old barracks on the Canadian Side, American Side and the Army Side, until a new town site was built. Unlike Grand Falls, Gander was not a company town and did not have the smell of sulphur. It did, however, have the frequent roar of airplanes, loud enough to rattle houses, but we barely noticed.

In 1939, half of the Newfoundland workforce was on the dole, government relief of six cents a day. They also depended on the government for necessities such as tea, flour, pork and molasses. World War II brought employment. To aid the war effort, US military bases were constructed in Argentia (NS Argentia), St. John's (Pepperrell AFB) and Stephenville (Ernest Harmon AFB) at a cost of over 100 million dollars. Canadian airports were built in Gander, Torbay and Goose Bay at a cost of 65 million dollars. The Americans provided the railway with locomotives, cars, equipment and rails. Newfoundland was not yet a province of Canada but the Canadian government believed "the integrity of Newfoundland and Labrador was essential to the security of Canada." Canadian and American money bought wartime prosperity to the island. It provided thousands of jobs at relatively high wages. In 1942, the average annual Newfoundland income on the bases was $1500 as compared to $333 in the fishery. The boom employed 20,000 Newfoundlanders who were glad to get the pay although they did not get the same pay for the same job as the Canadians and Americans. The boom left behind a legacy of improved health care, education and communications.

Andrew's Job

Andrew's brother in law, Tim Sanger, was able to get him a part time job in the Grand Falls paper mill. The Sangers had a large family and there was no room for Andrew in their home. Nephew, Andrew Sanger, recalled the store out back used as sleeping quarters by his Uncle Andrew. After the war my grandfather returned to the mill to full time employment. He worked in the Finishing Room where giant cardboard tubes that served as cores for the large rolls of paper were made. Violet said he earned 22 cents an hour and Tim Sanger, as foreman, made 25 cents. Nephew, Reg Downton, discovered in an A.N.D. Co. Ltd. employees work record book that Tim made $276.00 in wages in a three month period in 1922, which equates to $92.00 a month. In Andrew's military file, there is a gratuity check for $70.00 sent to him at 4 Gilbert Street, Grand Falls. This was his sister Violet Sanger's address.

Pay Station sign at Andrew and Violet's house

Andrew developed stomach problems and asthma. Speculation was that it was due to working with sulfur in the mill and from exposure to gas and malnourishment in the trenches. After two years and in poor health, Violet and he returned to Dildo where he began work on his house. United Towns Electric Company, Ltd. was looking to hire somebody in the area. In 1924, when he was 29 years old, they approached him and offered him a job if he successfully wired the house and it passed inspection. Andrew worked for United Towns as electrician, repairman, meter reader and collector of monies owed for the next 40 years. It was a steady job and in Rea's time, he made an impressive $50 a month. He never took it for granted in a time when most jobs were seasonal. By 1930, United Towns supplied electricity to most of the Avalon Peninsula.

Andrew became well known in his area as "the light man." He erected the power line from Whitbourne to New Harbour, a distance of about 13 miles, although he not did personally dig the holes. He wired practically every house. He maintained the lines that brought electricity and telephone service. Andrew and Violet's house in Dildo was one of the first to have electricity, a phone and a radio.

Andrew's phone was in great demand. When it became a nuisance, a pay phone was installed in their home. He received no pay for this but his service was free. During World War II, the phone was busy as people tried to send and receive messages about loved ones overseas. It was an inconvenience having people drop by all hours of the day and night. Rea says, "Mom put up with a lotta public." Eventually, more people got telephones, but Andrew's pay phone continued to be well used. The cost of a call was 25 cents. Some people short changed the phone. The family recognized the deed as each coin made a different sound. The difference came out of Andrew's pocket. Violet once slipped a piece of paper in the slot to catch someone she suspected of cheating.

Andrew and Violet's children delivered messages received. Alma and Hilda went over around the cove and up along shore hundreds of times with messages, in all kinds of weather. There was never a tip. There was often not as much as a thank you as you were a child and you were doing what you were told. Children were expected to be seen and not heard.

The telephone system was known as a party line. Many people shared the same phone line and anyone on your line could eavesdrop if they wished. There was no phone number. There were codes of long and short rings. Andrew and Violet's code was one long and two short. Each phone had two bells. Turning the crank on the phone rang the bells of all the phones sharing the line, including Central, the operator, in New Harbour. It was Andrew's responsibility to fix the switchboard whenever there was a problem. For repairs, he used parts of old phones he kept in his store.

Andrew on the job

For years the only light in the harbour at night was the big light trimmed with blue over Andrew's front door advertising United Towns. The light was so bright that it was possible for people to skate on the harbour ice after supper in the dark. Andrew was on call 24 hours a day, away for power outages, broken lines, fallen poles and fires caused by lightening. Hilda remembers a power outage every Christmas Eve, when people turned on their lights, overloading the system. Violet fretted as Andrew would have had a few drinks and she didn't like him going up the poles to fix the problem in the dark. Sometimes he was late for the midnight service at the Army church.

Part of Andrew's job was to read the meters of houses and businesses with electricity and collect the money owed. He wore a vest with his sleeves rolled up and his salt and pepper cap. He pedaled from home to home on his bicycle, with a shoulder bag for money received, a coil of wire resting on one shoulder going diagonally across his chest, and his khaki war time back pack for his pliers, screwdrivers, hammer, wire cutters and tools of the trade. In winter, he left Dildo on snowshoes for Colinet, to check the lines. A second man left Colinet and they met half way, a distance of about 20 miles.

Alma

Andrew's bicycle was his only means of transportation for work. Few people had cars. All the children learned to ride the bike. They leaned to one side of the crossbar, side saddle style, reaching their leg under it to the other pedal. Rea promised not to let Alma go on her first try but was unable to keep up. Alma lost her balance and crashed, scraping her hand and knee. Most of the spokes in one wheel were broken. The handlebar was bent. The girls put the bike back by the fence and Lendo got the blame. The girls did not own up. Andrew fixed the bike. Dulcie crashed so many times that Violet, tired of bloodied knees, forbade its use. The bike was supposed to be off limits. Andrew grumbled as he depended on it. A flat tire in an emergency was not a good thing.

Andrew kept meticulous records in an exercise book, two columns on each page. He divided the long columns into smaller clusters so the addition was simpler. Violet initially helped him with the division required when he began with the company. He did most of the paperwork on Sunday afternoons. There were sheets and sheets of paper and he hated the repetition of it, filling out the same forms, over and over. Despite their limited educations, Andrew and Violet could read and write well. They learned together.

Andrew was careful not to lose the company money. He hid it in the pockets and lining of his seldom worn Sunday best overcoat. Alma recalls the time she needed to dress for her part in a play and took his good coat. His face dropped when he realized what she had done and that she had left the coat in the cloakroom where young men were hanging out to smoke. Andrew retrieved a wad of bills, about $80, his collection money. Alma still remembers his fear and then relief that it was still there. "Thanks be ta Jesus!" He later put it in a metal moneybox, locked with a key, and hid it under the platform of the newly installed toilet.

Andrew did not like to cut electricity to those who could not afford it. He paid many fees out of his own pocket. Stella Reid remembers her mother telling Andrew she would sell eggs to get the $1.00 monthly fee. Andrew told her not to worry, that it would all come out in the wash. When Stella's father, Owen, killed a lamb or pig, he often gifted Andrew with a quarter.

Lon Smith says Andrew was the only person who could walk into any house or business from Whitbourne to New Harbour without permission. Lon worked with him one summer. Andrew was a likeable and honorable man. There was no reason not to trust him. People looked forward to his visits. He always had a joke for the customers and often shared a cuppa tea.

Lloyd George, a second cousin, friend, neighbor and local historian, said, "I knew Andrew quite well although there was quite an age difference. He was the type of man who was a friend to everyone, the young, middle aged and old. He was of a jovial nature and brought much laughter into the hundreds of homes he visited each month during his forty years of service. I can honestly say that when he passed away, all who knew him felt they had lost a very close friend. We still remember him with great affection. Andrew Smith, a local hero of whom we are very proud." Andrew retired when he was 71 years old.

Violet's Job

In 1956, when Violet was 53 years old, she began working at the South Dildo Fish Plant, the Newfoundland Quick Freeze Limited. It provided work for 300 people. On Carla's tapes, Violet says, "A friend o' mine said I come up now so me and you go get a job up the plant. Andrew didn't know I was goin' up the plant. I asked fer a job fer two women. They said yes, come up tomorrow. We went ta work. If I was there two months, I was put Floor Lady. They fired the other Floor Lady. She done somethin' wrong. I said ta meself I won't be here long now before they fire me. Why they picked me, I dunno." Violet did well. "The girls was nice ta me 'cause I was good ta them. I worked like a son o' a gun. That was a good spell ago," reflects Violet.

The Floor Lady supervised the boning and packing of codfish. She says, "The Floor Lady was o'er the crowd. I showed them what ta do." Labour was divided into tasks. One person removed the guts and the head. Another split the fish. This meant cutting the fish from the head to the tail and removing the back bone. Finally, the fish was filleted, laid in pans lined with paper and put in the freezer.

Violet began with 10 cents an hour which soon increased to 22 cents plus an extra 5 cents for her supervisory role. She said, "I didn't get much money fer plant, but it meant we got unemployment in the winter months. That was somethin' new then. That made a lotta difference." They were expected to pay 25 cents a day to be taken to and from work. It was shift work, one week of days, one week of nights, 7 AM to 7 PM, 12 hour shifts. Violet says, "I get up in the mornin's and went out and sheared sheep before I went ta work. Shear one today and tomorrow mornin', shear another. That's how I done it. I had seven sheep." Violet slept only a few hours during the day when she was on night shift. She worked four to five months of the year, June to October, for five years. Hilda worked at the fish plant for three summers until she was 16. Her starting pay was 45 cents an hour.

Eventually, two of Violet's daughters-in-law, Emily and Beatrice, became Floor Ladies. Beatrice began work in May 1973, working for 18 years until the plant closed. She started at 75 cents an hour and ended at $2.45. She began on the weight scales, weighing individual boxes of fish. Even as Floor Lady, she never used a knife because she was squeamish at the sight of blood. In her time, they handled a variety of fish, cod, herring, capelin, mackerel and squid. They wore white uniforms and aprons, hair nets and gloves. They were on their feet in rubber boots for 12 hour shifts which could become 14, 15, 16, hours if necessary. Beatrice says you had no choice. On their one hour break, they got relief by soaking their feet in warm water. The best part was the people.

Verd's Job

When Verd was young, he helped his father after school and on weekends with United Towns. After graduation, he was offered a job as a surveyor and linesman for United by a Mr. Bartlett who trained him in the use of the transit, a telescopic surveyor tool, mounted on a tripod, used to measure straight lines on land. Verd was responsible as line foreman for constructing power and telephone lines, putting up wires and maintaining the lines. It was strenuous work. Verd was a tall lean man.

Verd 1960

One of his first assignments, in the mid 1950s, was to collect money from those in Old Shop who wished electricity, $10 a household, and erect the poles and do the wiring. One fall evening he told Hilda to go down on the bank. She watched in awe as the lights came on in the dark, one by one for the first time.

On December 1, 1956, Verd left his wife, Beatrice, in labour at Markland Hospital, on a work related emergency. Andrew was at the switchboard and Verd was working on an adjacent telephone pole when a nurse made a collect phone call to Violet to inform her that Beatrice had given birth to triplets. Both men were able to hear the unexpected news but could not take part in the call! Violet sent Hilda to tell friends and neighbors that Beatrice and Verd had two boys. Upon her return Hilda gave Verd a flick and said, "Look at ya. Ya got two boys," to which he replied, "Whatta ya mean, two boys? I got three!" Later, she asked her mother why she said two. Violet shrugged, "I couldn't believe she born three youngsters." She had never heard of a successful triplet birth before. Beatrice's own mother was also skeptical when told of the births.

Verd was told to cut the power to a mother with three preschool children who was in arrears. It was cold. He gave her the weekends reprieve. On his return on Monday, she still did not have the payment. He babysat the children while she managed to borrow the money. Beatrice says he was a sucker for youngsters.

Verd's job often required that he be gone weeks on end, returning home on weekends. Beatrice remembers an ice storm in St. Mary's Bay. He worked in terrible weather for three days with no sleep or change of clothes and no back up. He was digging holes with a pick and shovel. He came home exhausted and soaked to the skin. In local outages, Beatrice said she was usually the last to get her power so there could be no perception of favoritism. Verd died unexpectedly at age 46.

Rea's Job

Young and single women often sought employment outside their communities in the 1920s, 30s and 40s. Outport girls were in demand. Without an education or trade, many looked for work as housekeepers, nursemaids or domestics. They had already acquired their skills at home. Servant girl and lady's maid were not derogatory terms. Girls as young as 10 went in service to people they knew, usually as a babysitter, on weekends or during the summer. The difference in the role as compared to today is that these girls were usually relatives, friends or neighbors of their employers or someone from their hometown, with much in common. They worked for all levels of society, not only the wealthy, ministers and merchants. In Grand Falls, many were employed by mill workers.

Violet's sister, Evelyn, had servant girls help her with housework as she managed her farm in New Harbour. Andrew's sister, Violet, moved as a domestic to Bay Roberts at age 12. Florence, Rea and Alma worked as domestics in St. John's. For each of the sisters, it was their first visit to the city, a bit of a culture shock. Although it was only an hour away, the travel cost and the fact that they had only one day off per week meant they went home only a scattered time.

Rea was hired by Reg and Margaret (Fraser) Knight on 34 Circular Road, St. John's, to look after their daughter, Carolyn. She was referred by her friend, Cassie George, who worked for the Campbells next door. Cassie worked as a nursemaid for Neil and Millicent (Sterling) Campbell's three children, William, Elizabeth and Jill. When Rea settled in, Cassie waved from her window next door. Rea's room was on the third floor, with dark hardwood floors and a fireplace. It was the first time she had her own bedroom. In the time she worked for the Knights, they had two more daughters, Susan and Nancy.

Rea and Cassie

Rea took the babies for a walk in the pram most every day, fed and changed them. She wore a light blue uniform with white collar and cuffs and a white apron. Her starting pay was $25 a month. Rea did light housekeeping, dusting, polishing the silverware and preparing breakfast. With the arrival of the newborns, Rea, who loved to cook, began to prepare meals. Each Sunday she made roast beef and yorkshire pudding and walked up to Rennies Mill Road to get a brick of ice cream. She learned how to make lobster salad from a cook book and hence began her love affair with recipes.

From their windows, the girls watched prisoners working on the grounds of Government House across the street behind a high fence. Cassie was Anglican and both girls took turns going to the Anglican and Salvation Army churches. At a dance at the Caribou Club, chaperoned by the churches, Cassie had a friend who was with my father, Bob Hellier. Both boys were in the Army. That is how my parents met. Rea left the Knights in August, 1946, to marry Bob.

Cassie's older sister, Dorothy, worked for Ches and Jessie (Carnell) Crosbie, a prominent Newfoundland family, who were very good to her. Unfortunately, Cassie developed a serious kidney problem. On August 6, 1945, at the General Hospital, Doctors Joe Murphy and Ian Rusted removed her kidney, an operation she was not expected to survive. When she recovered, Cassie worked at Cohen's in Grand Falls for seven years and married Harry Tait.

Florence's stint as a domestic in St. John's was brief. She was unhappy with her employers. They were skimpy with her food, a restriction of one potato per person, and she was not used to that. She missed her family and as she looked out her window and watched children playing happily in the snow, she broke down and cried. She realized she was homesick and returned to Dildo before Christmas.

After her father, Owen Reid, died of Typhoid Fever, Stella did not continue school as he had asked because, "I didn't want ta give my mother no trouble." At 13, she packed her bags to babysit her mother's sister's five children. After a number of jobs, she worked as a domestic for the Frank Woolridge family in St. John's. They owned a jewelry store and were nice people but she was not treated as well in other domestic positions. Rea and Cassie were fortunate and have fond memories. The Knights, Campbells and Crosbies were good employers.

Alma's Job - Argentia

At the beginning of World War II, the decision was made to build a US military base in Argentia, on the Avalon Peninsula in Newfoundland. In the 1940s, $53 million was spent building a naval base, airfield and extension on the Newfoundland Railway. During the war, Argentia employed 10,000 to 15,000 Newfoundlanders. The promise of good money was irresistible to many locals. Argentia was an hour's drive from Dildo.

Lendo, Hilda, Alma and Skip, the horse.

In the winter of 1948, Tom Newhook promised Alma an Argentia job which would pay her more than the $20.00 a month she earned working for the Suttons in St. John's. Two weeks later, she joined Tom on Llewellyn Thorne's bus. Upon arrival, she was photographed and taken to her room in the barracks which she shared with a girl named Sheila from Bonavista Bay. The toilets and showers were down the hall. A maid cleaned her room every day. They had a midnight curfew.

Alma's first job was cleaning Commander Carter's house, looking after his two preschool daughters and making breakfast and lunch. A bus picked her up at 8:30 and she finished at 2:00. When the Carters left, she worked for Captain Haythorne, his wife and two teenagers, a boy and a girl. When they were transferred, Mrs. Haythorne offered Alma a sea bag full of household items. It was not permitted for employees to take things off base and Alma refused for fear of being caught. As Mrs. Haythorne had to leave her quarters empty, she resorted to smashing the dishes. Alma quickly relented and got the bag safely on the train to her parents. One free weekend, a friend, Eva, asked for her help at the Enlisted Men's Club. They were shorthanded with two or three ships arriving. Alma told the manager, Vic Brooks, that she didn't know one drink from another but he gave her a tray, apron, pencil and paper. She simply had to give the bartender the orders. She made $60 in tips! At the end of the day, she was offered and accepted a full time job. She worked at the club from 4:30 to midnight.

Al and Alma's Wedding

Vic introduced Alma (age 18) to Second Class Boatswain Mate Al Orsak, from Texas. His job was deck crew foreman, assigning and inspecting the tasks of the deck crew, maintaining ropes, knots and sails. In their first conversation, they realized they shared the same birthday. Alma had several serious suitors in Argentia. Two proposed marriage. Both accosted Al, accusing him of taking their girl. One punched Al under the chin, leaving a permanent scar. Alma met Al in November and married him three months later, in the Argentia chapel February 17, 1950. Al was posted to Newport, Rhode Island a couple of months later without Alma as her papers were not ready. She joined him in May.

In Argentia, Alma thought she had it made. She never paid a dime for anything. Her first pay was $35 a month but she had no expenses. There was a large indoor swimming pool, ice skating rink, movie theatre and bowling alley, all free. There was little job turnover as most people thought they had a good situation. Everything was at her fingertips. She often said to herself, "Is this fer real?" She worked in Argentia for one and a half years.

Lendo's Job

"Instead o' goin' back ta school after the Fever," Violet says, "Lendo went ta Argentia and got a job fer the Americans." He was 14 and worked as a cookee, a cook's helper. While swimming, Lendo found a sum of money in a money belt and gave it to the American owner. He was given the man's watch in gratitude.

Lendo then worked as a cook in the Millertown woods camp. Millertown is deep in the interior of Newfoundland, situated on Red Indian Lake. With the decline in the fishery, many Newfoundland men became loggers, to supply the raw materials for the A.N.D. Company pulp and paper mill in Grand Falls and the Bowater's mill in Corner Brook. Loggers worked five to nine months in the camps, ten hour days, and six days a week, away from their families. In 1934, loggers earned 11 cents an hour compared to 30 cents for those who worked in the paper mills. Living conditions were not good. In summer, they struggled with heat and flies and bears. In winter, they struggled with deep snow and bitter cold. Camps were made of logs and seams stuffed with moss. Men slept curled together to try and keep warm. It was a breeding ground for lice. There was no privacy. It was a difficult way to make a living.

Jasper Harnum and Lendo at Vern Brook Dam woods camp

Howard Smith, son of Simeon and Lillian Smith of Dildo, worked in the lumber woods in Millertown in the late 1930s and early 1940s. "I could cut a core o' wood a day by meself with a bucksaw. A core was a wood pile 8 feet long by 4 feet high by 4 feet wide. In 12 days, I would have 18 core cut and I would get $4 a core. Board and food would come outta my cheque."

Food was usually plentiful, although Lendo recalled going hungry, but there was little variety or nutrition. The cook and cookees worked with limited supplies, making do with what was available and subsidizing it with fish and game if possible. On the day before he died, Lendo told daughter, Brenda, of killing a moose when he was 15 in Millertown. Supplies had not arrived. There was no food to prepare. Lendo shot a moose in the water. He stripped to his underwear and dragged the heavy water logged animal to shore and cooked it for dinner. When they got a moose, they ate it for breakfast, dinner and supper. The staples were beans, soup, bread, porridge, salt fish, salt meat, potatoes, turnip, prunes, dried apples and tea. Bread, which was a staple, was a challenge to bake in winter when the inside temperature was almost as cold as the outside. The cooks rose at 4:30 AM to prepare breakfast, porridge, beans, bread and tea. Loggers took a lunch into the woods, typically a tin of bully beef, bread or tea biscuits and jam. Everyone looked forward to supper after a long strenuous day. The cooks banged the iron loop or triangle outside the cookhouse to announce all was ready. The men were ravenous and said little as they wolfed down their meal. They had a lunch before going to bed. They drank tea by the gallons. Occasionally the cook had time to make dessert, a dark cake, gingersnaps or apple pie. As a child, I visited Uncle Lendo at a camp by Gander Lake. He fed us amazing lemon meringue pie, stored in a cold cellar dug in the ground, covered with moss.

Lendo left the woods camps after he recuperated from tuberculosis, and worked on the R.D. Evans, when it operated as a whaling ship. Lendo devoured hundreds of sea sickness pills but he was still wonderful (very) sick and threw up over the rails before going to the kitchen. His last jobs were on the fishery patrol boat, the Arctica, and the smaller inshore patrol boat, the *Goose Bay*. Lendo loved cooking with a full pantry. He retired in 1992.

My husband's paternal grandfather, George Luther Brown, worked as a cook in lumber camps. Before boarding the train to Gambo to go home, he baked gingersnaps. Upon arrival, his seven children waited by the tracks and he tossed them brown paper bags of cookies from the train. It was my father-in-law, Fred's strongest memory of his father who died when Fred was 10. George died while digging a trench in a Bishop's Falls camp, in June, 1937. He was 44 years old. His unexplained death resulted in his body being sent to Grand Falls for an autopsy, a rare thing in those days. It was determined he had pneumonia and drowned in the muddy water in the ditch where he collapsed. The doctor who performed the autopsy was a Dr. Noble, who told the story to Fred's daughter, Marlene, when she became his patient in Toronto in 1972. It was a remarkable discovery for the family.

George Luther Brown

THE FEVER

Andrew and Violet's children recall happy times but their memories all go back to the frightening and tragic events of 1940-41 when Typhoid Fever struck seven of nine members of their immediate family. Three of the children died. Florence, the oldest child, was 19 years old, Gerald was 16 and Larry was 3. Prior to their deaths, Andrew's mother, Julia, died in October, 1940, at the age of 70. The children went next door to their Uncle Eldred's house to visit their ailing grandmother. Laying in her spotless white bed, she gave them each a peppermint knob candy. A Blue Willow wash basin and chamber pot sat on her dresser. Julia had a high fever and Violet expressed concern she had something other than the doctor's diagnosis of old age and gallbladder problems. After the children's visit, it was recognized as Typhoid Fever but it was too late. Violet never forgave him his mistake. It was a life changing and life ending event. In this accounting of their struggle and unimaginable sorrow, I capitalize the words Typhoid Fever, identifying it as the monster it was.

Typhoid Fever is an acute and highly infectious disease, responsible for worldwide epidemics. It spreads when feces or urine comes in contact with food or drinking water. Flying insects feeding on human waste can transfer the bacteria. Today, vaccination, antibiotics, better sanitation and personal hygiene have drastically reduced the number of cases. Like many communities in the early 1900s, the people of Dildo depended on well water and outhouses. There was no outhouse sink to wash hands after a bowel movement. There was no toilet paper. They used pages from catalogues, tore off strips from the large rolls of Grand Falls paper, and saved the soft paper used to wrap oranges!

Symptoms occur 10 to 14 days after infection. They include high fever, headache, severe diarrhea, delirium, chills, sweating, abdominal pain, joint pain and rash like spots on the skin. If the disease causes intestinal hemorrhaging when holes called perforations occur in intestines, it is usually fatal.

While their grandmother was dying, Lendo, age 13, was the first to get sick, followed by Verdun, age 5, and Rea, age 11. All three children had a birthday while they were strickened. Lendo was 14 on November 19, Verd was 6 on November 23 and Rea was 12 on December 11. It was Dr. Gill who correctly diagnosed Typhoid Fever. He told Violet she was in for a hard time. He said of Rea, "The little girl's not gonna live."

Avalon Health sent two nurses, Kirby and Bretton, to look after the family. Alma remembers the day well, a cold snowy Sunday. She was sent to ask Mrs. Moore to open her general store to get hose (stockings) for Julia for her funeral. A car with two women and a man asked for directions to Andrew Smith's house. It was Nurses Kirby and Bretton. They boarded with Dimmy and Susie George, neighbors up over the hill. Kirby's fiancé, Duncan Cameron, from Carbonear, phoned every night to check on her and Andrew and Violet's family. Many times Alma was sent to fetch them.

Immediately a quarantine sign was posted. Only a few brave souls dared come to help. Violet was pregnant and Tom Newhook's mother helped scrub Violet's clothes in the back porch. Neighbors Eli Rowe and his son, Albert Jim, were very much their heroes. They came every day to check on them and see to their needs. Rea remembers their delivering Christmas cards, the only normal thing in that sad, stressful time.

Albert Jim Rowe

Neighbor, Florence Smith, remembers the two nurses coming down over the garden to Andrew and Violet's house every day. The snow was so high that you could see only the tops of their heads for it was an especially brutal winter. They came to the neighboring homes giving vaccinations. At first,

Florence refused the needle. Nurse Kirby said, "Oh yes, my dear, you are, before I leave this house today." Andrew had been told he had immunity as he was in contact with Typhoid Fever in Grand Falls. With the belief he could not get the Fever, he worked tirelessly with the nurses and developed a strong bond with them, especially Kirby. Andrew said there were no words possible he could use to express his gratitude. "I hadden got much ta give ya, but if I could, I'd give ya the world."

In addition to Typhoid Fever, Lendo developed double pneumonia and pleurisy. Dr. McGrath from the Fever Hospital in St. John's gave Andrew heart medicine in a little bottle with strict instructions as to the dosage. He said he wouldn't trust this drug with anyone but Andrew. Violet had Lendo's clothes pressed and Andrew had gathered the wood for Lendo's casket, so convinced they were that he might die.

The children's speech was very affected by the Fever and they could often not be understood. Rea remembers Violet bringing Lendo warm mashed potato with lots of butter. "Gigi, gigi," was his reply and Rea guessed he meant gravy. Lendo's recovery time was longer than Rea's or Verd's because of the pneumonia and pleurisy. His respiratory system weakened and he developed asthma.

Verdun was moved into Rea's bedroom into Florence's single bed. In Verd's delirium, he thrashed more uncontrollably than Lendo and Rea. It may have been because he was younger and stronger or because eventually he passed a worm that would have caused him more pain. Rea was given a stick to bang whenever she felt Verd was a danger to himself and the adults came running up the stairs.

Rea was already sick when Julia died. She remembers dragging herself out of bed and resting her chin on the windowsill when they began singing hymns next door prior to her grandmother's funeral. On December 11, she confided to

Nurse Kirby that it was her 12th birthday. Kirby put Rea's head in her lap when she gave her enemas, which they had every time the children ate. The treatment was to starve the bug. Soft food, like jello, cream of hearts and juice was given for nutrition but enemas whisked it quickly from their bodies so the germ could not thrive. Kirby came back with two red ribbons and tied them in Rea's hair, her only present that day. Rea says of her, "She was born to be a nurse. I would not have survived without her." They wore navy blue uniforms trimmed with white.

That Christmas was very sad. There was no celebration, no gifts, and no tree. The three children were recovering but not well. They lost their hair and looked emaciated. One day a weary Rea asked her mom, "I would like a cuppa tea." Violet said, "Why can't ya make yer own?" Rea replied, "It tastes better when ya do it." Violet smiled and Rea got her tea.

Larry was a beautiful child with blond curly hair. Even at three, he understood he was not to go upstairs where Andrew nursed Lendo, Rea and Verd. He would sit patiently on the bottom step, waiting for his father to come downstairs.

Ken Smith, Roy George and Gerald

Other families in Dildo were quarantined with the Fever. The children of Andrew's brother, Eldred, who lived with their grandmother Julia, survived. Gerald's good friend, Ken Smith, lived but the Fever may have contributed to a crippling arthritic back condition which he believed was caused by a hockey injury. Eugene Pinsent, son of Ralph and Lavinia Pinsent, died while his sister, Amy, survived. Andrew nursed Eugene before it was known he had the Fever.

Andrew's good friend, Owen Reid, was diagnosed three weeks before Christmas. His daughter, Stella, remembers all too well the early morning she jumped up to light the fire because she thought she and her father were going in the woods. She heard him call to her mother, Susanna, because he filled the chamber pot with blood. Dr. McGrath diagnosed him with Typhoid Fever of the bowels, a condition that he would not survive. Susanna was sick with the flu. She never accepted the diagnosis because Owen did not have a fever.

Owen's family was quarantined. They put an empty water bucket outside their fence and neighbors filled it with water for their use. The family was given a chemical to add to the slop bucket to break down its contents and friends threw the pail into the sea. They did not put up a tree and for years, Stella hated Christmas. Owen died on Christmas Eve. He was 51 years old. Andrew made his casket. Stella says she can still "hear" Andrew sobbing as he dressed her father for burial. Owen's son, Lewis, could not find his jacket. Andrew realized he had put the jacket on Owen. Lewis, who was 15, did not go to the funeral.

To everyone's horror, after Christmas, Florence, Gerald, Larry and Andrew became ill with the Fever. At big risk to himself, Colin Pretty drove Andrew to the Fever Hospital in St. John's. In Andrew's delirium, he had hiccups for 21 days. There was no communication between Andrew and his family. The nurses phoned regularly to see how he was, but initially, the news was not good. He did not know until the day he was released that three of his children had died and his wife had given birth to a six and a half month term baby boy. When told the awful news, he insisted on talking to Violet to be convinced the doctors were telling him the truth when they said she was alive. Upon his return Andrew was grief stricken. During the day he and Violet tried to contain their emotions but at night they were heard by their children crying themselves to sleep.

Gerald on his father's bike

Susanna Reid had just buried her husband, Owen, but she instructed their daughter, Stella, to check on Violet who was trying to cope while suffering from morning sickness. They did not know the Fever had struck the family a second time. Understandably, Stella was refused entry at the door. Later, she was shocked to learn that Florence had been taken to Markland Hospital. She ran home to tell her mother who informed her that Florence had just passed away. Stella remembers Florence as a beautiful person who came with Andrew to help her family, brought them fresh milk and stayed over two nights before Owen died.

Alma was terrified to come inside. She was nine years old. She did the outside work in the deep snow, got groceries from the store, wood for the stove, vegetables from the cold cellar and water from the well. She lived in constant fear of getting sick. She ate practically nothing, barely enough to keep a bird alive, for fear of germs. She was skin and bones. She washed her hands 50 times a day. She believed if she spit constantly, she might spit out the germs. Friends crossed to the other side of the road when they saw her as they had been instructed. When Alma went inside, she wrapped a towel around any chair or object she handled. Her mother empathized, "Maid, you'll ne'er go ta hell for you've had yours on earth."

Alma remembers clearly seeing Rea's ghost by her bed when Rea was sick. It was very real, and then faded away. Alma knew her father believed in signs of something unfortunate about to happen, a foreboding. It could be as simple as an unexplained noise. He told stories of ghosts as premonition of death. Alma chose not to tell anyone for years, for fear Rea's death might come true.

When Rea recovered, she assumed the responsibilities inside the home that had been Florence's. It was difficult for the Fever had caused the bones of her ankles to come out of their sockets. She put bottle covers under her heels in her boots to try and keep them in place. She cooked and did the housecleaning and washed Albert's diapers, but it was not that simple. The cooking and eating utensils for Violet and Alma and eventually infant Albert had to be kept separate. She designated a large cream-colored enamel bowl with green trim for their dishes and cup towels. The water used was boiled 20 minutes. She hung the towels on the clothesline no matter how cold the weather with the belief the cold would kill any germs the boiling water did not. She could take no chances. She worked tirelessly to make sure her mother, baby Albert, and Alma did not get the Fever. It was an enormous responsibility for a child. There was no respite.

Larry and Gerald's condition deteriorated and Violet dressed them in their best clothes to be taken to the hospital. They sat waiting by the kitchen stove, but a vicious snowstorm prevented the nurses from coming. Gerald confided in Alma that he put a pouch of tobacco behind the clock on the wall for when he got back home. Back in his bed, Rea noticed a change in Larry's breathing and told her mother who rushed upstairs. Alma ran for the nurses. Larry died that day. It was January 22. Five days later on January 27, the nurses helped Violet give premature birth to Albert. Alma was asleep on the couch in the kitchen and was awakened by her mother's distress. Lendo, Rea, Verd and Alma listened to the sounds of her labour.

Rea remembers her last conversation with Florence, who was in bed, her thick hair across the pillow. The conversation was something like this: "Whatcha doin', Rea? I'm cookin' supper. Whatcha cookin'? Fish. My darlin', ya dunno how ta do that. Well, I am." When Rea told Florence how she made the meal, Florence smiled. Later Florence was taken to Markland Hospital in Whitbourne, 20 minutes away.

Before Albert was born, Alma slept with her mother. Rea remembers crying to be allowed to lie down on the foot of her mother's bed, to get comfort from her and to be allowed to sleep with her too. The nurses would not permit it as Violet and Albert had to be isolated as much as possible. Rea believes this was the night they took Florence. She has no memory of Florence leaving and she is puzzled by this.

Gerald's casket

Violet felt helpless. She had lost a child. She did not know the condition of Florence or Andrew in hospital. She had an infant not expected to survive. She despaired as she heard Gerald's arms hitting Florence's iron bed frame in delirium and asked that someone pad the frame. On February 3, Gerald died at home. When they took his body, Violet cried in her misery, "Have they got that poor boy put out in that cold store?" Alma was put in her mother's bedroom with the door closed the night Gerald died as Violet tried to shield her. Alma still remembers the sound of the men's rubber boots on the stairs as they came for his body.

The next day, on February 4, Florence died at Markland Hospital. Violet and her children did not go to the funerals. The children were buried down the side of a hill. Neighbor, Florence Smith, attended but she can't remember much as "it was too sad ta have memories of. They were just like family." We do not know who made their caskets although we have a photo of Gerald's white wooden casket on a sled. Florence Smith is in the middle of the photo, the lady on the right.

After the funerals, Violet screamed and screamed and cursed her God vehemently. Alma felt sick. The other children began to cry, devastated that it might start all over again but Alma was simply exhausted. When Violet said she wished her life had ended too with the death of her children, the nurses took her words seriously. Alma overheard her say she wanted the bottle of rubbing alcohol to drink. The nurses removed it and all other medication from the house. Violet was bedridden for a long time as her varicose veins were in danger of breaking. Rea was so relieved when her mother finally came down the stairs again even though she looked like a ghost with huge eyes. Rea could not get her to eat. Rea remembers her saying as she grieved, "Ya can't die when ya wants ta."

For years, the belief was that Grandmother, Julia, got the Fever from drinking tainted water while berry picking. Stella was told her father got the Fever from drinking water from a well that was poisoned from the remains of a horse buried nearby. Violet believed Julia got infected from visiting the grandmother of Eugene and Amy Pinsent before it was commonly known they had the Fever. There was much speculation. The cause was never determined.

Alma remembers two men from the Department of Health getting water samples from the shared well on the hill, next to Florence and Gordon Smith. The hill was very slippery and the larger man fell down. Alma found a number of coins where he had fallen, apparently come out of his pocket. She thought she had a fortune. The well was forever closed and they were told to boil their drinking water which was set in the snow to cool.

Violet blamed herself for the rest of her life. Andrew always had a habit of double dipping the spoon, licking it and putting it back in the jam. "Andrew always had that fashion and ya could kill him and he still wouldn't quit." Violet's guilt was that she was not more careful and had not thrown out the jam when the Fever struck her family. "I said ta Florence, don't touch that jam 'cause yer father licked the spoon. I was busy lookin' after Rea, who was sick. She never listened. Alma said ta Florence, Mom told ya not ta touch that jam, and Alma didn't touch it." Violet had been such a stickler for cleanliness. There was always a white enamel pan on a stand with water and a bar of soap in the back porch. Rea can still hear her mother say, "Andrew, have ya washed yer hands?" Alma still washes her hands 10 times an hour. A paper towel is her best friend.

The house had to be thoroughly sanitized. The canvas on the floor was torn up and burned on the beach, along with the children's clothing and bedding. That which was salvageable was boiled in disinfectant on the stove. Rooms were painted and wallpapered. It is hard to imagine but Violet never went outside the house for years, and when she did venture outside, she did not go past the gate. "Nobody hardly e'er laid eyes on her." Dulcie was born two years later in 1943 and Hilda in 1945. Albert's premature birth left him frail and developmentally delayed. Violet's reserves had been exhausted.

Florence's boyfriend, Pete Pretty, was devastated and went through a hard time. He did not go to her funeral. He came to the gate at the bottom of the lane and stood, looking up at the house many times after Florence died. A frequent visitor to the house before, it was 10 years before he could bring himself to enter again when he showed my father a picture of Florence which he still carried in his wallet.

Years later, Hilda asked her mother why her father's legs and arms were hairless and she replied the Fever caused the loss of body hair and his simply did not grow back. Prior to the Fever, Rea's hair was straight. When it grew back, she had curls. She has one nice memory shortly after the Fever. Her father got her first pair of little high heels and a pair of black fur top boots to fit over them.

For a long time, by some unspoken agreement, nobody talked about the Fever. Only once during the crisis did a minister come to the house. Violet was in bed with newborn Albert. The Army officer advised her of Florence's death in hospital. Violet recalled that he stood there and trembled and left. The loss of Andrew's mother and three of his children was shocking. People didn't know what to say. Few people dropped by and Violet was in no state to receive visitors.

In 2012, Hilda and her husband, Jim, discovered a single white headboard and footboard lying in the attic of the old home, easily missed under the eave. As I fished it out of the insulation, I realized that it might have belonged to Florence, the frame admired by my mother who had often wondered what had happened to it. It was also the bed used by Verd and Gerald when bedridden with the Fever. Mom confirmed its identity. Nobody knew it was there. One can only speculate that they could not bear to part with it. We had something tangible of that awful time and as we gazed almost reverently at it, the Fever became very real.

THE CHILDREN

Annie Florence

Florence was a second mother to all, cooking, cleaning and looking after the little ones. Vida (George) Trickett was a childhood friend. She had a small table and chairs in her garden where she and Florence had afternoon teas. Florence was frequently called home by Violet. Vida said, "Florence was grown up at an early age, motherly like. She was an extension of her mother's arm." Florence did what was expected of the oldest daughter of large families. She assumed the extra responsibilities and Violet depended on her. She did not begrudge her role. Mature beyond her years, she carried the load without question. Her brothers and sisters knew who to go to, especially when their mother was ill during pregnancy. Florence could do anything, everything. Old enough to do the job and young enough to relate to her siblings, she was always there for them. Patient and caring, they were quite content to have her look after them, wipe their tears and put them to bed.

Florence Smith, Maisie Thorne,
"Our" Florence, in fur top boots

Rea and Alma looked up to their big sister, Florence, and shared a bedroom with her. They were fascinated with her top drawer in their dresser, the perfume, face powder, lipstick and nail polish. They watched as she applied makeup in front of the kitchen mirror and put polish on their fingernails. Florence had thick hair like Violet, Alma and Dulcie. Her best friends were her cousin, Maisie Thorne, Amy Pinsent, Jean and Pearl Cooper and Martha Cranford.

Violet was dead set against Florence's first serious relationship with Jim Newhook. Florence was seeing Pete Pretty when she died. She would take him by the face and say, "Bless yer beal," (a beal is a mouth). It was her favorite term of endearment. When Florence helped Ruth Reid make baby clothes, Florence talked of marriage to Pete. When Florence died, Ruth said she not only lost Florence, she lost Pete too.

When Florence was taken to Markland Hospital, there was no time for her family to say goodbye. When she died at 19 of Typhoid Fever, Violet said it was like losing her best friend. She said, "Rea picked up from Florence, that there were ne'er two born any better housekeepers."

We had no photo of Florence until 2010 when a grainy old picture of Gertie Thorne's caught Hilda's attention because she recognized her friend, Florence Smith. Imagine our surprise when Florence viewed it and said, "Ya recognize me but ya don't recognize yer own sister!" Hilda had never seen her sister, Florence, who died before Hilda was born. It was an exciting day!

Gerald Silas

Gerald and Verd were both slim with dark wavy hair, but Gerald was shorter. Both had striking eyes with long lashes. Alma remembers Gerald's eyes, kind and almost sad but with a twinkle. Gerald was a gentle soul, quiet, a really nice guy. Ed George says he was carefree and happy with a perpetual grin on his face.

Gerald loved to bike and there was sometimes a racket between Gerald and his father who was protective of the bike. Gerald was finishing grade 11 and planned to work with his father. Gerald's friends were Roy and Ed George, Ken and Selby Smith, Rex and Jack Moore. Lizzie Smith, a girlfriend and daughter of Phil Smith, made a floral arrangement for his casket when he died of the Fever at age 16. Lizzie remembers him as a sweet boy, a gentleman. They danced in her kitchen to the music of her father's radio.

Recently, in a strange twist of fate, Hilda was visiting his gravesite when an older lady, a Mrs. Cranford, approached her and said, "I used ta go out with Gerald." In hindsight, Hilda wishes she asked for more information.

Orlando Maxwell (Lendo)

As a boy, says Violet, Lendo wasn't 'fraid o' nothin' or nobody." He was a hard ticket, rough as the devil. He was checked (verbally chastised) by Andrew more than the other children, "Git up those stairs, into yer room, shut the door and don't come out 'til I say so!" But Lendo was bold enough to sneak out, down the fire ladder. He was not to be contained. Florence Smith says he was a scalliwag, she never knew what he was up to. He was a scrapper, strong as a horse.

He left home after the Fever, despite his mother's objection, at age 14. His work as a cook required him to be away from his family for months and years on end. Despite asthma, he worked hard all his life. His son, Claude, says he did not get to know his dad until he worked on the fishery boats closer to home.

Lendo may have had a rough exterior, but his sisters remember special gifts. When he first went to work, he surprised Alma with a brown pleated dress with white collar and cuffs. When Hilda was a teenager at St. George's High School, he gave her a pair of leather boots with sealskin tops. He made her six lemon meringue pies for her 15th birthday. He baked cherry cakes and bread and gave them away until the year he died. He picked berries and made his own preserves. When nephew, Randy, went moose hunting with him, Lendo talked too loud to ever get a moose. They got lots of rabbits instead.

Lendo loved cards and he loved to win. When he and his wife, Emily, played with Verd and Beatrice, the games were lively. The wives grumbled as the men were adept at cheating, which they said was part of the game. When his daughters taught him new games like Canasta and Skip Bo, he would say, "Take 'er easy now b'ye, I'm green," but he was a smart cookie when it came to cards. When he was concentrating or distracted, he pressed his tongue against the front teeth of his upper plate. The teeth dropped down and Lendo flicked them around in his mouth!

He married Emily (Cooper) from Spreadeagle on December 26, 1949. Emily loved to cook and bake and was so clean you could eat off her floor. She was as small as a mite but she ruled with an iron fist with Lendo working away from home. After a successful moose hunt with Lendo, Verd and Beatrice, Verd gave her the head to lug through the woods. She was so tiny, she fell into a bog hole and had to be rescued!

Lendo and Emily raised five children, Rea (Robert Hendry), Joy (Bill Pryce), Claude (Joan Osbourne), Brenda (Earl Russell) and Lorraine (Terry Young). Lendo looked after Emily for 10 years before she died on November 20, 2005. She suffered many mini strokes known as TIAs. Fifteen months later, on February 5, 2007, he died suddenly of a heart attack. He was 80 years old.

Rea Edna

Violet believed Rea had her first asthma attack when she was four months old. Although most of the children and Andrew eventually suffered from asthma, Rea was the only one who had it from infancy. Her life was shaped by it. She was protected from the elements, not allowed to swim or skate. She was afraid to get cold; terrified she would not be able to breathe. She missed a lot of school. She has lived far longer than her parents would have predicted, thanks to modern medicine, "Thanks be to God." Although she is not particularly zealous about religion, she adds, "God willing," "Please God," "As God would have it" and "God forbid" (that anything bad should happen) to most things she says.

She is a natural cook, continuing her mom's legacy of wonderful bread. She was fastidious, a great help to her mother. Violet would say, "Ya knows yeself, Rea could do in an hour what would take me all day ta do. She was one o' those that never stopped." Rea is curious, thoughtful and determined. She always needs to be doing something and she never has to be told what needs to be done. She enjoys the challenge of Find a Word and game shows, watching the news and reading newspapers. One of her favorite pastimes is knitting, especially Kroy socks, a valued gift for her children, grandchildren and great grandchildren, who call her Nanny Rea. She loves a bargain! She takes pride in her appearance, clothes and jewelry.

She has an amazing memory. My father said, "She can remember back before she was born!" She appreciates old things. I depended on her for much of this history and it was important to her that it be recorded. I am indebted to her for her support. Without her, this would not have been possible.

Rea married Robert (Bob) Hellier from Little Bay Islands. Bob attended Memorial College at 15 and had careers as a teacher and a purser before working for Aeradio and The Co-Operators. As a young man, he played competitive soccer. After retirement, he walked every day, whatever the weather. He loved a game of cards. He was involved with The Legion and Gander School Board but his passion was the Masonic Lodge.

Rea and Bob had five children, Gloria (Carl Brown), Janice (Keith Wallace), Debbie (Kevin Pike), Robert (1. Sheila Mortell 2. Caroline Urbanksi), and Tammy. Bob died December 16,

2002 of kidney cancer. Rea left Gander in 2009 and moved to Nova Scotia to be near Gloria and Debbie and their families.

Alma Mary

Hilda calls Alma the roadrunner because she is never home. Alma was always on the go. She was a tomboy, an outdoors person, with no interest in housework or cooking. Today her fridge is mostly empty but her pantry is well stocked with tins of baked beans! Her house is immaculate. She fusses with the landscaping. Violet said, "Alma was different from all the rest. Alma wanted nothin' ta do with housework. All Alma wanted was ta be goin'."

Everyone liked Alma. She had a wide crowd of friends. Some things are the same. Today, her phone never stops ringing. At 18, she met and married an American serviceman, Al Orsak. They had three children, Barbara (Brad Hunt), Ivan (1. Blanche Osborne, 2. Jane Adkins, 3. Molly Kelly), and Darrell (Kim Freeman). She lived in Rhode Island, Florida and Virginia. She married a second time to Harold Varvel. Both husbands and her son, Ivan, have predeceased her.

Alma is young for her years, upbeat, and does not look or act her age. She has a contagious positive outlook and a wonderful laugh. She looks more like Violet than anyone. She feels she lost contact with her family. In recent years, this has improved and it makes her happy.

Alma was a supervisor at JC Penney's for 25 years but she does not like to shop. She rarely dresses up. Her style is definitely casual. When she buys, she gives most of it away, kind and generous to a fault. Despite asthma and more recently a stroke from which she has recovered, Alma continues to work in her 80s, traveling on a daily basis for Don Clark's Trucking Service, picking up and delivering heavy equipment! She seems to thrive on working. She says it keeps her young. She lives in Norfolk, Virginia.

Andrew Verdun

Verd, like Andrew, could outrun anybody. He gave Hilda a head start and still beat her, grabbing her by the scruff (back) of the neck if she got too close. Violet had the devil's own job to get him up in the morning and still he'd pass everyone who had left earlier on their way to school. He was an excellent swimmer and taught Hilda and Dulcie to swim. With their tall frames and long strides, Violet had no difficulty picking Verd and Dulcie out while they skated on the harbour ice.

Like his father, Verd was not a fighter and did not like confrontation, although Verd could be very stubborn when he had a mind to. Whatever the situation, they tried to turn it into a laughing matter or diffuse a tense situation with a joke or a smile. They worked together for many years with United Towns Electric and made a good team.

Lendo's son, Claude, says Verd taught him everything he knows about being in the woods. Verd was a good hunter. He got many legal and illegal moose! Verd's passion was hunting black ducks. As a child, he loved fishing for trout, mussels and scallops. He used a square glass-bottomed box on a pole in order to better view the bottom and another long pole with a net to rake up the mussels.

Verd married Beatrice (Piercey) from Normans Cove on August 30, 1956. They had 14 children, including a set of triplets and a set of twins, Randy (Chryl Newhook), Roger (Theresa Hartery), Ricky (Barb Rowe), Gail (Steve Mason), Robin (Melvin Green), Tina (Paul Fifield), Velvet (Dennis March), Veona (Perry Oliver), Dackenic (Wade Drover), Roxanne (Ed Newhook), Deeann (Bern Hartery), Rocky, Holly (Gaby Casseus) and Dana (Chantel Gaulin). She can turn out large amounts of food for any occasion with seeming ease. Hilda says, "Beatrice was always the one way, very jolly."

Like his father, Verd loved children. In April, 1981, he told Beatrice he would have brought her, if he could, a little girl he befriended on a bus from Corner Brook. The child, about three years old, was being taken to an orphanage in St John's. It broke his heart. Verd and Beatrice still had seven children living at home. Three months later, on July 23, 1981, he died unexpectedly in his sleep at age 46. Beatrice was devastated.

When Verd died, Violet said, "I don't understand why He's takin' these children o' mine and not me." She believed you lived on borrowed time after three score years and 10, (age 70), and she was not comfortable with the idea she may have been living the lost years of the children who predeceased her. Including the miscarriage of twins, she outlived seven of her children, more than half, and she grieved them and talked about them the rest of her life.

Lawrence George

Larry was 3 years 9 months old when he died of Typhoid Fever. He loved Andrew, his poppy. He was a sweet little boy, with blonde curly hair. He adored Florence. They seemed to be joined at the hip. He couldn't say Florence so he called her "Poshy." There was only two and a half year difference in age between Verd and Larry. They were playmates. Larry called Verd,"Audie," a name that stuck to him for years. Larry cried to go to Verd when Verd had the Fever and Verd often wondered aloud what Larry would have been like had he lived.

Shortly before he died, Alma and Beryl George took Larry on a ride in the sleigh. Despite layers of clothing, he was cold and wanted to go home. Alma sat behind him, holding him in her arms to make him warm while Beryl pulled the sleigh. Alma feared then he had the Fever. Violet was convinced when later, Florence tried to take him and he said, "I doan wanna go with Poshy today." We have no photograph of Larry.

Edward Albert

Albert was born premature, a six and a half month pregnancy, brought on by his mother's stress and grief when her family had the Fever. He was not expected to survive. When he did, doctors told his parents he may not live past six or seven years.

For several years, Albert did not let a leg harness and crutches slow him down. He climbed ladders and played on rocky beaches. Merv Smith said that with two good legs he could not run as fast as Albert could on crutches. He was like a whirlwind. He was a good looking and happy little boy. School was a turning point in Albert's life. He was unable to keep up with his friends and was left behind. The difference, which was not apparent as a small child, became evident as he grew older. It was a difficult adjustment for all.

Albert's longevity surprised everyone. He can be opinionated and stubborn as a mule. His idea of communicating is to argue and grumble but it is probably his way of trying to exert control over his life. He has no trade. He cannot read but Lon Smith says he probably knows more about the local people and past events than most people give him credit. Nephew, Randy, says you cannot watch TV with Uncle Albert. He flicks the channels and talks too much.

He wanted to live his life his own way but did not have the skills or good health to do so. Despite his limitations, he lived by himself for 16 years in Andrew and Violet's old house with help from friends, especially Max Reid, and Hilda and Jim. In 2012, he left the only house he had known and moved into a Personal Care Home.

Dulcie Violet

Dulcie was a fair baby, tall for her age like the Higdons. I have been told I resemble her. She was determined. If things did not come naturally such as sewing or riding a bike, she got mad as the devil, and did not give up until she had mastered it. She was a good student and never had to be told to do homework.

Dulcie was particular. She separated her white bobby socks from Hilda's by sewing black thread in the toes of Hilda's socks. Her white buck shoes and laces were always whiter than her friends. Violet and Hilda were not allowed to wash her clothes. She liked nice things and took pride in her long hair. She was Violet's girl.

She married Weldon Mercer from Blaketown. They had three children, Susan (Ivan Jerrett), Paul and Andy. When the marriage failed, she moved to Carbonear, Alberta and Virginia where she lived near Alma for eight years.

Alma says Dulcie was the hardest working woman you ever met, that she worked like a Trojan. She tackled any job however daunting. She renovated a neglected two story house with the help of her best friend, Arnie Denton, and Alma. She delighted in the opportunity to make a new life, try new things and travel in the US to the Carolinas, Florida and New Orleans. Adventurous, she climbed to the bottom of the Grand Canyon and back up in one day. She loved to sing and dance and shop. She was great with kids and had empathy for the young and old. She was animated and talked with her hands. She was open and warm, a vibrant woman, with a big heart.

In May, 1993, Brownie and I made an impulsive decision to visit Dulcie and Alma in Virginia. Dulcie believed she was suffering from a bleeding ulcer. In July, Alma took her to Alberta where she was diagnosed with bone cancer. Dulcie made a video for her mom which Violet could never bring herself to view. In it, she tried to reassure Violet that the 8 years she lived "in America" were happy years. Stunned by this unexpected turn of events, she showed no anger and was grateful for the love of her family. She died August 22, 1993, 23 days after being diagnosed. She was 50 years old.

Hilda Joy

Hilda was an outdoors girl, a tomboy like Alma. She loved to be active, swimming, biking and skating. She was Andrew's girl. He encouraged her to dance and sing and she excelled at it. He had her sing to his friends. The home was a gathering place and her efforts earned her enough money from her audience one Christmas to buy a new red sleigh from Pretty's Store.

Hilda and Violet sometimes clashed for both were strong willed and headstrong. Violet would be the first to say though that Hilda could do anything she set her mind to. Self-taught, she has decorated wedding cakes and designed and sewn wedding and prom dresses. Now her passion is quilting. She has a wonderful sense of color and uses every little piece of fabric. Her quilts are works of art. Her mother said, "What she can put outta her hands, you wouldn't believe." She was very much a Smith, a small freckled faced girl with dark hair.

Like all the children, she is a hard worker with a no nonsense approach. She has an excellent relationship with her nieces and nephews. She has been extremely helpful to me with my research for this book and I have valued her insight and opinions.

I delight in the Newfoundland expressions that frequent her speech. Like many dialects worldwide, the Newfie accent was perceived as a corruption of proper English. Today, its uniqueness, and hence its value, is being recognized as the language spoken by the original emigrants to Newfoundland from Europe, mostly unchanged in isolated outports. Hilda's expressions include: "Mind the time, My dyin', Make no wonder, Had a mind ta, Hear tell, The once, Fer pity's sake, O me nerves, Got me drove off the head, Perish the thought, Be after doin' somethin', some squish (uneven), scarce as hen's teeth (have none), I dies at ya (you make me laugh) and It's a funny situation."

Hilda married Jim Barrett from Tack's Beach, November 27, 1964. Jim was a mild mannered, kind, hard working man with a big smile and a green thumb. He loved flowers, birds and Pomeranian dogs. His huge hands belied his gentle nature. He had sheds full of stuff he was always recycling. He was a gem of a man, a wonderful dad. He died unexpectedly of a heart attack April 20, 2013. He was 70.

Always pragmatic, Hilda focused her attention on the tasks formerly done by Jim that were heaped on her plate. She set priorities and concentrated on one task at a time. Her philosophy is that she and those she loves will be stronger if she does not wallow in self pity. She is realistic. She has her moments but she is determined to be independent. "It is what it is."

Hilda and Jim were a good team. They had two children, Denise, (1. Terry Gilbert 2. Don Michaud) and Brian, (Irene White). In July, 1988, Hilda gave one of her kidneys to her daughter, Denise who was 23 years old at the time of the transplant. Hilda lives in Blaketown, Trinity Bay.

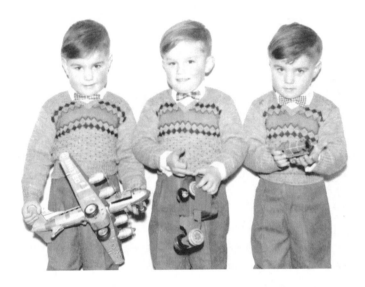

THE GRANDCHILDREN

Andrew and Violet had 32 grandchildren, 20 granddaughters and 12 grandsons. I am the oldest. We have precious few memories of our grandfather, who died in 1970. We have more memories of our grandmother, who died in 2002. While we all called Violet "Nan," most called Andrew "Pop." Some of us called him "Grandpa."

Joy, Hilda and Rea with the triplets

One of the highlights of Andrew and Violet's lives was the birth of triplet grandsons, Randy, Roger and Ricky, the first of 14 children to their son, Verd, and his wife, Beatrice. Andrew was 62 years old when they were born. He marveled at their birth and was hands on with their care. He doted on them. Randy says, "If anybody come in, no sir, Grandfather wouldn't 'low (allow) 'em ta touch us. Even the dog, Toby, used ta sit down by the end o' the table and bark if anybody come near us." Nan added, "If the dog seen yas comin', he'd take ya holt be the pants or hand and lead yas up the lane."

Every birthday, the triplets had their photo taken for The *Compass* and the provincial newspaper, The *Evening Telegram*. They were celebrities. When Andrew was dying, they were 13 years old. They did not know what to expect when he asked to see them and broke into tears. Their mother recalls their grandfather smiled, told them to be good, and promised to look out for them. Other grandchildren were not allowed in the house. The children were not permitted to walk on the road in front of the house the week of his death out of respect. Instead they walked on the beach, parallel to the road, to reach their destination.

The triplets were three years old when their third sister, Tina, was born. A snow storm prevented their father from returning from Marystown and their mother from getting to Markland Hospital. Andrew brought Beatrice and the five children to his home to prepare for the birth. Violet helped midwife, Clara Pinsent, with the delivery. Tina was born with the cord around her neck. A proud Andrew said to Beatrice, "By God, ya ne'er made a sound!" After the birth, Hilda watched her father celebrate by helping the boys drag their grandmother into the tub with them. Violet said of the triplets, "Andrew would get 'em holt and wash 'em. He loved 'em." The boys could turn their grandparents inside out.

Andrew and Rocky

After the triplets and eight daughters, Verd and Beatrice had a fourth son, Rocky. They now had 12 children in nine years! Beatrice was only 28 years old. Five and seven years later, Holly and a fifth son, Dana were born. Beatrice recalls, "After each o' 'em was born, Pop would come down ta the house, take the crib, pack us all up and bring us ta his house fer awhile so him and Nan could help. Nan washed a good many cloth diapers out fer me. They were the best people in the world. I couldn't have gotten any better support or care anywhere."

Dana and Holly

Back; Randy, Ricky, Roger, Gail, Tina
Front: Robin, Dackenic, Roxanne, Deeann,
Velvet, Veona

Hilda was a babysitter for Verd and Beatrice's large family. For lunch, she fried two dozen eggs, a full bologna and sliced three loaves of homemade bread. She made them flannelette pajamas, with simple draw string tops and bottoms. She washed them in the kitchen sink before they went to bed. A bedtime snack consumed a bag of apples. Hilda was impressed they were asleep by 8 PM but that also meant 6 AM risings!

Five of Andrew and Violet's children settled in Dildo and Blaketown, home for 24 grandchildren. Rea and Alma moved away. Alma's children in the United States were cousins in pictures only. We made the trek to Dildo from Gander once a year for a week's vacation. Only three times did our grandparents visit us, by train. Travel was difficult at best.

In 1960, Alma, her husband, Al, and three children drove from Virginia to Dildo. Newfoundland roads were deplorable, flat tires inevitable, the dust inescapable. Al was unhappy. It was his first and last drive to Newfoundland.

Ivan, Darrell and Barbara

Barbara, Ivan and Darrell remember little of the visit but they were fascinated with Nan's wringer washer. They shouted, "Mommy, come and see. The washer is pressing the clothes!"

This trip by Alma made possible the only family reunion for Andrew and Violet. On a sunny day, 16 grandchildren and their parents gathered at Holiday Hill, a popular park in Blaketown, with covered picnic tables, fire pits and a jute box in the snack bar. We snacked on sandwiches, sweets, juice and soft drinks. It was the first week of July. Given our young ages, we have few memories and fewer photos but Andrew was wearing a dress shirt and tie so it is likely it was a Sunday.

Violet and Janice

Every road trip from Gander to Dildo was an adventure due to poor conditions and lack of facilities. My sister, Janice, recalls the summer the headlights of our car gave out at the Dildo turnoff. It was evening and pitch black. A wrong turn to the left and we would be over the bank and into the sea. How thankful we were when a stranger guided us to our grandparents' house. Dad was white knuckled as he followed the man's tail lights in the dust.

Janice, the more sociable of us, did not always stay within Mom's boundaries which were well intentioned, imposed so that our short visits would not be a worry to her own Mom. Janice spent a lot of time with Uncle Verd and Aunt Beatrice. Verd treated her like a princess. She remembers the buildup of excitement every weekend when he came home. He put his arm around Beatrice and she giggled like a little girl. They sat holding the babies and the rest of the children squished on the floor around them, waiting to hear what their father had to say.

Andrew and Debbie

When Janice was 13, she had her first kiss and told Nan. The next morning, Nan woke her and said," Yer young man has been at the bottom o' the lane fer half an hour. Go put him outta his misery. Tell him you'll have yer breakfast and you'll see him later." Nan's idea about birth control to Janice was, "There's no rush. It's not all fireworks like in the books."

Janice says of her grandfather, "I picture him in his old gray tweed cap in the yard or working in his store. He was not a man of many words or imposing size but you felt safe with him. He knew what he was about." She watched him clean his gun, a .303, the British Army's standard rifle. It was shiny and the wood polished. He cocked it swiftly and effortlessly. She tried but was unable. She asked what was in the canvas. He put it on the end of the rifle and said it was a bayonet. She asked its purpose. He stopped talking, wrapped it and took it away. In retrospect, she realizes why he left her puzzled and alone.

Robert and Debbie

Nan gave my sister, Debbie, a baby bottle to feed a lamb, and advised, "Be careful and hold on tight. He's strong." The lamb just about tore Debbie's arm out of the socket! The mother sheep had twins. Sometimes the second lamb was ignored and died within hours without milk. Violet wrapped these orphaned lambs in an old towel and put them on the oven door for warmth. They needed to be bottle fed and, in time, came daily to the back door for milk.

My brother, Robert, was a quiet boy who pestered his grandfather with wartime questions. Andrew probably didn't know how to respond. It was easier to deal with grandson, Claude, an active little boy who always had to be doing something. Andrew gave him a hammer and the steps to the store soon became riddled with nails. Nan knew how to make them all happy. Feed them her homemade bread!

Andy, Paul and Susan

Pop loved the grandchildren fiddling with his hair. He laid on the day bed in the kitchen while they combed, rubbed in hair tonic and even added bobby pins. He did not care what they did! He would say, "If I goes ta sleep when you're combin' my hair, doan wake me. I'll pay ya when I gets up." And pay he did, five cents or whatever he had.

Brian, Tammy and Denise

When I think of Nan, I think of colorful phrases which punctuated her speech. The one which I associate most with her is, "I have the impression ta think..." Others are "Won(d)erful way ta be" or "Wonerful thing, Have it this way, In (re)guards of, I garntee (guarantee) that, Imagine, Ya talk about, My gracious, Oh my blessed goodness, and In all me born days." She said afeared (afraid), afore (before), apast (past) and disremember (forget). You pulled the door to and it "scroped" (scraped) the floor. My favorite, which defies explanation, is duflicky, chummy jigger, chummy thing and thingabob or thingamabob, used for anything that one cannot remember the proper name for! An unknown person was a "chummy." She did a multitude of tasks quickly "in three shakes o' a lamb's tail" and "between the jigs and the reels." If housework was frequently interrupted, it was done in "dribs and drabs" (little by little). I recall, as a child, telling her that her bibbed apron was inside out. She laughed and said it was "hinder part before" or "back formas" (backwards). These sayings transport me back in time.

Lendo's children Joy, Rea and Claude with Andrew

As the oldest grandchild, I was between my aunts and cousins. If I felt a little out of my element, a "come from away," I sought refuge with Hilda. She is my aunt but she is less than four years older. I tagged along whether she liked it or not. Sometimes she avoided me. Sometimes she enjoyed or tolerated my company. I was in awe of her singing and that she knew the words to so many songs. I still know every word to Ricky Nelson's song "Travellin' Man." I opened her turquoise music box and listened to Patti Page sing "The Tennessee Waltz." We went swimming. She told me about her boyfriend. She didn't take flak from anyone. Undaunted, she was game for anything. I hadn't known anyone like her. She made me feel grown up.

Violet and Gloria

At university, Brownie had a small 75cc Yamaha motorcycle prone to piston problems and flat tires. When we travelled, we were never sure we'd reach our destination! We took it on weekends to Dildo and stayed with Hilda and Jim or Dulcie and Weldon. The motorcycle was a big hit with their kids. We went to Saturday night dances. They made us lemon meringue and coconut cream pies. Hilda's cat peed in my suitcase. We laughed as Jim tried to coax the trout onto Brownie's line at a fish farm. We learned about mink and their baby kits at the ranch where Jim worked. It was a turning point, the beginning of an adult relationship with my mother's sisters. The age difference disappeared.

Dildo did not seem to change and neither did my grandparents. Their love was unconditional although not expressed in words. As I grew into adulthood and continued the annual visit with my three children, Nan was still sitting on the bridge (front steps), with a big smile awaiting our arrival. I observed the same joyful welcome, hugs, tweaking of cheeks and pronouncements about how they'd grown and who this one and that one looked like. My children were, in effect, little strangers, much the same as I was with my siblings long ago. She treated them the same as she did me and she had over 80 grandchildren and great grandchildren. She was up for the task. I could count on her.

Brenda and Lorraine

THE SEA

Dildo began as a fishing community and families continued to catch and salt fish for their own use when the industry could no longer support them. There was nothing better than being wakened by the little putt putt boats on a cam (calm) day. Life revolved around the sea.

In June and July, the water turned black with the arrival of large schools of caplin, small silvery fish like smelt. Capelin (spelled caplin in Newfoundland), came to shore to spawn. They were easy to catch and families looked forward to the sport. From the shore, they cast small circular nets or waded into the water with their white salt beef buckets. The gulls were ravenous.

Andrew filled his box cart, a large box on wheels, with caplin to cover his newly sprouted potatoes. The remainder was dried and salted for winter use or used as bait. Fried caplin was delicious. When Hilda worked in the fish plant, boats waited in line to sell their caplin and squid. The plant operated three shifts a day, eight hours each, to meet the demand. Half the dicks, the male caplin, were thrown away. They wanted the hens, the females, which were full of spawn. In less than 10 years, due to overfishing, the caplin had to be trucked in.

Ed George jigged squid to earn a few extra dollars. Squid was sold as bait to schooners fishing for cod on the Grand Banks. Jigging was the traditional way to catch fish. A line, attached to a hook and a lure, molded to resemble a small fish, was jigged, or moved up and down. The repetitive hand over hand action was labourious. The boys came home with aching arms and shoulders, bloodied hands, and oilskins and caps covered with squid juice. When disturbed, squid squirts out a black inky liquid as a defense mechanism. About 20 per cent of all giant squid found in the world have been in Newfoundland. In 1878, the largest ever recorded by Guinness Book of Records was in Thimble Tickle Bay, now called Glover's Harbour, Newfoundland. It measured 55 feet (16.7 meters) in length and weighed over two tons. In 1933, a 30 foot long giant squid was caught in Dildo by Reuben Reid and Richard Gosse.

Gerald, Munn George, Gordon Smith, Unknown

Ed George was part of a group of boys including his brothers Roy and Munn, who hung out with Andrew and Violet's son, Gerald, in the 1920s and 30s. Life centered on the wharves where they caught conners, small blue perch fish used as fertilizer, and occasionally jumped off the boats moored close to shore. The ocean was usually too cold for swimming. They swam off Dildo Island, Anderson's Cove and New Harbour Pond. It was a happy childhood.

After the Second World War boom, the fishery continued its decline. From 1954 to 1974, resettlement became a government program. 300 remote communities disappeared and nearly 30,000 people were moved to find work. Many refused to abandon their houses and floated them on skids buoyed by drums in the ocean to their new home. Premier Joey Smallwood promised two jobs for every man, woman and child. Dildo probably survived because of its proximity to St. John's. Resettlement proved to be one of the most controversial events in Newfoundland history. Unemployment rates continued to be high. Although a need for conservation was recognized in the 1970s, the unthinkable happened. The Atlantic cod, king of the global fish market, was fished to the brink of extinction. In 1992, the Canadian government put an end to the inshore cod fishery due to dwindling stocks and ended a 500 year old way of life. It was the largest single mass lay off in Canadian history. The question is still, "Will the cod come back?"

The Potheads

At various times since 1898, Dildo has been an important whaling centre. The pothead, a long finned pilot whale, came into the bay feeding on squid. It travelled in pods, by the hundreds. The shallow waters of New Harbour and Chapel Arm were ideal. Dildo's water was too deep. The industry reopened in 1947. It was seasonal, an income supplement to the locals.

It is my most vivid memory of a summer vacation. I was six years old. I travelled by train under the care of a family friend, Jim Parrott. Verd and Hilda met me at the station in his truck, eager to surprise me. It was July for my birthday was in a few days. We were to witness a Pothead drive.

It was a spectacle, a day of excitement. With news of a pothead sighting, families came from all around. Boats were sometimes damaged by the whales in their dying fits. The sea was red with blood, the noise deafening. I was overwhelmed, but to the crowd, it was not cruel. By today's standards, it appears so but at that time it was an honest way to make a living. I will never forget it.

The harvesting of the potheads was done in a simple manner. Men in small boats went outside the pod and formed a semicircle. They advanced to shore, making as much noise as possible, yelling, rattling cans, throwing rocks and beating on the sides of the boats to confuse the whales. Men grabbed their fins as they beached and used broom handles sharpened to a point to lance them. The dead were hauled to shore by cable and winch from a power truck. When Lon Smith was 16, his job was to help drive the potheads towards the beach and when they beached, to cut them up. That summer they did over 100 potheads. He got $20 to $25 a day.

The foul smell of boiling blubber permeated everything in the South Dildo plants operated by Arctic Fishery Products Co. Ltd. and Newfoundland Quick Freeze Ltd. One whiff and all car windows were shut. Still, the curious swarmed the wharf to view the whales where oil was rendered from their fat, cooked by steam and stored in large tanks. When he was 15 and 16, my sister's father in law, Cyril Pike from South Dildo, shoveled coal into the boilers for two summers. It was hot sweaty work for 50 cents an hour. The plant now has limited use.

In 1954, mink farming was introduced to the area to take advantage of cheap whale meat as feed. This industry declined with the fall of fur prices and government legislation in 1972 to end more than 400 years of whaling in Newfoundland. Hilda and her husband, Jim, worked two years for Trinity Mink. Jim had just served three years in the navy. From 1965 to 1981, Jim and his brother in law, Jimmy McEntegart, operated Dildo Boat Yard. Jim and Jimmy Mac constructed 80 long liner wooden fishing boats, 35 to 54 feet long. It closed due to the arrival of fiberglass boats and the downturn in the fishery. The danger of working with fiberglass was unknown and Jim was diagnosed with COPD, chronic obstructive pulmonary disease, in 1992.

Close Calls

I got homesick that summer. Nan wanted her children and grandchildren away from the water. She was a worrier and fretted to no end about their safety, wanting them within calling distance at all times. It was a constant fear. There were many close calls.

Albert with Sunfish

Albert saved Mervin Smith's life. Albert, Mervin and his brother, Lon, were playing on a wharf. It was springes, a time of high tides and water was creeping over the wharf. Merv fell in. None could swim. They panicked and froze. Albert grabbed a long pole and pulled Merv to the safety of the locker, the wooden supports under wharves and stages filled with rocks. He was the smallest and the youngest, but he acted quickly. Springes (springtides), and neaps, the lowest high tides, occur twice a month. During springes, the sea level is 20 per cent higher than normal.

Beatrice and her children were on the Government wharf watching Verd in Charlie Smith's boat looking for lobsters. The kids were throwing rocks. When Verd heard a splash, he thought nothing of it until he heard screaming. Robin had fallen into the water. Verd used a gaff to hook her by the sole of her boot and hauled her aboard. A gaff is a pole with a sharp hook on its end used to kill or stun a seal. It was also used as a walking stick on ice pans.

In the weeks following Andrew's death, Hilda left her house in Blaketown to stay with her mom and Albert. Her daughter, Denise, was five years old and playing with cousins when she fell off the wharf into the water. Verd's daughter, Velvet, who was nine, got into the locker and grabbed Denise by her hair when she bobbed to the surface. Verd and Beatrice dressed Denise in dry clothes and said to Hilda, "Don't go off yer head. She got a big enough fright." Denise was told, "You're a lucky little girl. We could be buryin' ya with Pop."

My brother, Robert, was three years younger than the triplets. Growing up in Gander, he knew nothing about boats and fish. During his summer vacations, he was dutifully included in their play. He enjoyed the adventure but recognized he was the butt of their teasing. They showed him how to catch seagulls by attaching a cod liver to fishing line and throwing it in the air. Once they caught a sunfish and told him it was a shark to scare him. "Step on the fish right here," they said. It peed all over Rob's foot. On another occasion, they caught a cod as tall as Rob, put their thumbs behind the cod's eyes, popped them out and put them in Rob's hand. Rick recalls his father's stern warnings to stay away from the wharf. Despite the fact that Verd could see Charlie Smith's wharf from their house, the triplets went there whenever they could, especially when their father was away. The scariest time was when they decided to go out in boat during Hurricane Blanche in August, 1969. Rob was nine years old. Waves were crashing over the wharves. They quickly turned back. They had to time the rise of the bow of the boat to the top of the wharf to allow each to jump off, one at a time. Someone reported the boys out in the boat but Rob never owned up that he knew anything about it.

Winter

In winter, the harbour usually froze. Men took horses and sleds onto the ice to bring their wood home. In the spring, when the ice started to melt, it was important not to take chances. If Andrew saw a crack, he shouted in a very loud voice to hurry ashore to those still on the ice. It no longer freezes over.

The children's winter games are familiar. They sledded, made snowmen, snowballs and snow forts. They skated and played hockey on the harbour although Lendo's first skates were blades strapped to his boots. Stella and Gwen Reid played goalie for Lendo. The girls knelt on brin bags and were given a piece of board to block the wooden puck. Alma was left shaken when a puck hit her in the neck. She skated as long as she could on the pond near Pretty's Ice House, to postpone the inevitable household chore at home. Her feet were numb and her father rubbed them vigorously to bring them back to life. When Verd taught Hilda and Dulcie to skate, he brought homemade bread in his pocket. He could get more skating time if they had a snack.

The children slid from the top of the hill, down the lane, onto the road. Lon Smith says the steep hill which made up the garden of the two families was a Winter Wonderland with icy snow for sliding. It was amazing they didn't get killed as they sped down to the bank on pieces of Grand Falls canvas if they didn't have a sled. They wore out the knees of their pants and the soles of their boots as they slid to their stops.

One day Lendo went sliding alone after supper in the dark. He was 11 or 12. He overshot the road and went over the bank into the harbour. When he made it home he told his mom that he survived because he remembered advice from Joey Smallwood's radio program, The Barrelman, to kick, pull and roll. He broke the soft ice repeatedly until he finally reached hard ice and with difficulty he was able to kick his feet and swim his way out, rolling and crawling to safety. Frozen and soaked to the skin, it was a wonder he survived the cold and the weight of his coat, sweater, boots and woolen briggs. Violet's upset as she peeled off his wet clothes soon turned into anger as a pack of Bugle tobacco fell from his pocket.

For generations of Newfoundland boys, a popular but dangerous pastime was copying. As soon as school was out, they were copyin' the pans. It meant jumping from one floating pan of ice to another, which could sink under their weight. The goal was to move so quickly they would not fall into the water. They often used sticks as aids like the sealers' gaffs. The rivalry sometimes caused them to take risks, venturing far from shore. Copying developed as training for swiling or swoiling (sealing), a job coveted by many despite its danger and hardship. For over 200 years, sealers trudged miles on treacherous shifting ice in Northern Newfoundland and Labrador at the mercy of sudden blinding snow storms. It was called a wild death dance. In March of 1914, 252 men died in two separate incidents from the *SS Newfoundland* and the *SS Stephano*.

Girls were less likely to partake in copying but Rea, Alma, Rea's friend Cassie George and her sister, Irene, thought they were safe if they copied the pans close to shore where the water was not over their heads. Alma and Irene fell in and got soaked. Rea's legs and stockings were wet. They went to Lenie Newhook's, the nearest house, to dry by the wood stove as they were too cold to walk home. At dusk, Cassie rolled Irene in the snow to make it appear she got wet from playing in the snow. Rea and Alma had been warned many times not to go on the ice. Their mother would be furious and they were afraid so they went to neighbor, Eli Rowe who fed them rice soup. Eli felt sorry for them and took them home. While Alma hovered behind Eli, frightened to death and clutching his leg, Eli spoke sternly, "Now Violet, doan say a word. They're all right," and the girls were spared their mother's wrath.

Horse Mackerel (Tuna)

Andrew stored his guns and powder horn in a corner of the pantry. He used a long barreled gun called a muzzleloader. Although he was never one for hunting in the woods, he did use his guns in the boat, usually on a Saturday. Like many men in the community, he shot seals and salt water birds such as ducks, turrs and puffins.

While Andrew did not fish for a living or own a boat, he was well known for his accuracy in harpooning the blue fin tuna. One day there was a surprise knock on the front door. It was Lee Wulff, a world-renowned American sports man and conservationist. In 1938, he was commissioned by the Newfoundland government to investigate sports fishing as a tourist attraction. During the late 1930s and early 40s, he looked into the possibility of a recreational tuna fishery. Wulff heard of Andrew's extraordinary success in catching tuna, which the local people called horse mackerel, and was curious as to Andrew's technique. Wolfe was surprised that Andrew used only a harpoon he made for himself and a coil of rope. It took great skill for Andrew to aim and throw the harpoon, holding unto the rope and letting the coil run its course as he played out the tuna which would fight for hours. Andrew's hands were thick and strong. It was said he had hands like paws.

Andrew fishing for tuna

Ed George remembers Andrew "standing in the bow of the boat, harpoon in hand, with only seconds to aim and throw the harpoon, often in choppy waters and able to hit and capture a fleeting target." Some of the tuna were as big as the boat itself. Ed says Andrew held the record for capturing the most tuna in the area. "His record was uncanny. Maybe it was due to his army training in the Royal Newfoundland Regiment that made him so accurate."

The shaft of the harpoon was wooden, usually spruce. At one end of the shaft was a metal point fitted into the head of an iron dart and held in place by a rope. The dart was not permanently attached to the shaft and had an extra barb to prevent it from pulling out of the tuna. The dart had a hole. In this hole was a metal loop or piece of cable, necessary because a rope could chafe against the dart and break with the weight of the tuna. Sometimes it did not work. Rea remembers her father shouting from the boat, "Tuna for ya tonight, Bob by'e," but it got away.

A strong thin nylon rope was tied onto the loop and ran the length of the shaft. The rope continued into a coil on the bottom of the boat, between Andrew's legs. Great care was taken that the rope was coiled properly so it did not tangle around his legs. He carried an axe to cut the rope in case that happened. When the tuna tried to flee, the rope uncoiled at a rapid rate. The chucker held the shaft and rope when he threw the harpoon. When the harpoon found its mark, the shaft separated from the dart and the dart stayed in the tuna. The rope was attached to a barrel which was thrown out when the rope had run its course. The barrel was chased until it stopped, indicative that the tuna had died. The barrel also provided drag. The men were better able to protect their boat from being swamped by watching the barrel's movements. Wes Pretty often went in his boat with Andrew. They manually pulled in tuna which could weigh up to 600 pounds.

A picture etched in Lon Smith's memory is that of Andrew and his brother, Eldred, standing on the road for what seemed like hours scanning the horizon for horse mackerel. The boat was in position, the rope neatly coiled. They were ready to go. On a calm summer day between July and September, when the tuna were seen on the surface, Andrew's voice could be heard yelling, "They're comin'!" If he was not watching, Rea can still hear people yelling from across the harbour, "Andrew, Andrew, there's tuna in the bay!" Word spread like wildfire. Her father's boat was dragged at high speed around the harbour. Few hunted the tuna because of the danger. On one occasion, the boat looked dangerously low, gunnels barely clearing the water for he had a tuna on each side. In minutes word spread and crowds gathered as a proud Andrew divvied up (shared) his good fortune. Tuna no longer comes into the harbour.

THE SCHOOL

Prior to 1934, Newfoundland schools were in an appalling state. Buildings were dilapidated and overcrowded and 85% did not have a single book. Some students were reduced to writing on brown paper bags. Teachers were poorly trained, underpaid and lived in poverty. Attendance was erratic, enrollment low. The Commission of Government mandated changes. It reopened a one year program and a five week summer program at Memorial College. My father, Bob Hellier, completed the one year program in 1942. In 1939, the annual teacher's salary doubled to $450. By 1945, it had increased to $992. Despite the effort, more than half the schools were still one room, many with no water or electricity. Only 57 of the 2,375 teachers had degrees.

The education system was denominational. Each religion had its own schools. All Saints Anglican, the first church in Dildo, was built in 1878. The population of Dildo was 337. By 1921, the population had grown to 525, of which 289 were Anglican and 168, Salvation Army. Families were often divided. This was true for Andrew and Violet. Violet never lost her Anglican roots, but married into Andrew's faith. The children were Army but they attended the Anglican school. The first Anglican school was replaced by a second, built in 1904, (later Society of United Fishermen Lodge) and a third, in1931.

This school was closer to Andrew's home than the Army school. He volunteered the use of his horse to go into the woods for lumber, with the understanding that his children would be able to attend the school. On her second day of school, Hilda and her cousin, Phyllis, were sent home because they were Army. Hilda was allowed to return but Phyllis was not. The Anglican school was one room, Grades 1-11 until 1939. As the number of students increased, a folding accordion wall enabled it to become a two room school, grades 1 to 5 and grades 6-11. It had an outhouse and no running water.

When Rea began school in 1935, her teacher was William Kelloway. Rea and Alma had mixed feelings about him. He was stern and did not smile. Teachers expected unquestioning obedience from their students. Maybe he was typical of a teacher of that time? Maybe her memories are tainted by the strapping of her sister, Alma.

Alma remembers the day well. She was 10 years old. Edna Smith punched her in the back to show her a picture of a monkey and mistakenly whispered, "Smonkey." Alma laughed out loud, a short burst of laugher as she quickly put her hand over her mouth. Kelloway instructed her to put out her hand. The shock of the strap caused her to bend over as she tried not to pee in her pants. The second strap was harder. Alma burst into tears.

Violet thought Alma must have done something to deserve the strapping but Eli Rowe would have none of that. He wrote a note to Kelloway which Alma delivered but was instructed not to read. Eli came to the school that afternoon. The girls do not know what was said but Kelloway never spoke to them out of turn again. In 1944, after 10 years, Mr. Kelloway left Dildo and taught in Whitbourne. He was replaced by Mr. Walter Martin. The strapping ruined school for Alma. She tried to convince her parents to let her go to the Army school with her friends. Two years later, they relented.

Strappings were not commonplace but Rea's friend, Cassie George, recalls splashing boughs with friends in the brook which ran by the school. They were not hurting one another but by Mr. Kelloway's reasoning, they deserved the strap. Boys were targeted more often than girls. Andrew's nephew, Norm Sanger, was strapped in Grand Falls when he was in Primmer, his first year of school. He forgot to remove his cap during prayers, which were said at the beginning of each day. In Grade 7, when Hilda reacted to the boy behind her poking her three times with a pencil, she was strapped by her teacher, Leonard Way. She did not cry or tell her mother. After school, she nailed (hit) the boy who got her in trouble. In later years, Leonard and Hilda were friends. He had regrets, "That was not a good day."

The highlight of the day for Rea, Alma and Cassie, was drinking cocomalt. It was a government sponsored program to improve child nutrition, started in 1936. At recess, cocomalt, high in calcium, carbohydrates and Vitamin D, was made on the pot bellied stove. To keep the stove burning, students brought a junk of wood, one to two feet long, to school every day. The older boys took turns coming early to light the stove. On Fridays, the older girls swept the floors with Dustbane and cleaned the desks and windows. Regularly, mothers did a more thorough cleaning of the church and school, on their hands and knees, using a scrubbing brush on the wooden floors.

The emphasis was on the 3 R's, Reading, 'Riting and 'Rithmetic. Red hard cover books, The Royal Readers, were introduced to Newfoundland schools in the 1870s. Published in Britain, with elabourate illustrations, there were eight books in the series, the Infant Reader and the School Primer, followed by Readers 1 to 6. Students did not always think of themselves as in grades 3 or 4 but rather "in the Number 3 Book." Progress was charted not by grade but on which level Royal Reader was completed.

Children were expected to memorize poems in The Royal Readers, many of which were tragic and foreboding, and had multiple verses. Even the simplest poems and stories promoted values such as perseverance, thriftiness and honesty. These qualities became entrenched in generations of Newfoundland children whose only textbooks were The Royal Readers.
"A noble lesson this should teach
Dear children unto you
Do unto others as you would
That they to you should do."

Bill Smith, Len George, Wilmore
Pretty, Verd

There was lots of homework. Violet tried to make sure they did their lessons. This was difficult when Andrew had his friends over. Violet showed her frustration and Alma recalls her mother saying in resignation, "Why do I bother? You'll be just like the rest o' us, get married and have youngsters." They were bright and capable but, like many girls of that time, her daughters did not finish school. If Andrew and Violet had a better education, would they have made it more of a priority? Until 1943, children were not required by law to attend school.

The Christmas school concert was a big deal. Everyone worked hard in preparation, practicing their parts and preparing the props. The stage was the elevated platform on which the teacher's desk sat year round. There were recitations of poems, skits (plays), dances, singing and puppet shows. Students wore their best fit out o' clothes. They wanted to do well. For some it was a chance to shine, to have a moment of glory, talked about for days afterwards. The teacher(s) chose the pieces, tutored the youngsters and heaved a great sigh of relief when all was said and done.

Gerald and his friend, Munn George, worked the puppets behind the screen, for that was the older boys' job. Alma and Cassie George recall putting their faces in holes cut in cardboard. Around each hole were painted yellow petals and green leaves and stems. Their faces became the flower centers. Hilda's favorite part was singing carols in the choir. The young looked forward to Santa making his appearance at the end of the evening.

One concert stands out in Rea's memory. Uncle Eldred and Aunt Mel's son, Billy, (Bill) was alone on stage. He was a talented little boy, a comedian, singer, dancer and actor. He could play the mouth organ and the guitar. He had everyone in stitches as he dressed like a fisherman and sang all the traditional Newfoundland songs.

Rea missed a lot of school. Her asthma made it difficult, especially on bad weather days. Cassie remembers snow being so deep they walked on the tops of fences! Rea hated depending on her siblings. Lendo pulled her on a sleigh. Alma tried protecting her from blowing snow by walking sideways or even backwards, hands on each other's shoulders, heads down in their coats. When Rea struggled to breathe, they would have to return home.

During recess and after school, boys and girls played marbles, jacks and cat's cradle (a string game). Girls enjoyed hopscotch circle tag, Ring Around the Rosy, Hide and Seek and the favorite flower game, "He loves me. He loves me not." Alma loved skipping and jump rope. Boys played Cowboys and Indians, kicked balls made from pig bladders, and rolled barrel hoops with a stick. Lendo whittled flutes with his knife and made catapults to fling rocks which sometimes got him in trouble. Boys and girls played on the wharves.

The school was a location of a popular community event known as The Times. In fact, a Time was any social occasion, big or small, a dance, concert or church supper or a simple game of cards. The folding wall separating the two classrooms was removed for the Times, usually in the fall and winter months, which was a Church of England (Anglican) fundraiser.

Rev. and Mrs. Cracknell

The Anglican Minister, Rev. William. E. R. Cracknell thanked everyone for coming and said grace. He was the minister for 31 years from 1927 to 1958. He had the only car Rea remembers in Dildo for years, a little black coupe. Rev. Cracknell was from England and served as a Chaplain during World War I from 1916 to 1918. Andrew described him as a proper Englishman. Although Andrew was Army, they had a good relationship. Cracknell would say, "I'm some glad you're here, Andrew, b'ye," as he depended on him to keep the peace during the Times. He knew the troublemakers would be controlled or taken home in Attwood Pretty's car. Andrew also auctioned off the left over food. He had a loud voice and was a good auctioneer, successful at getting high bids by happily cajoling the bidders.

Everyone paid to eat at The Times, (as in a good time), at the school and the Fisherman's Hall. Rea remembers 10 cents a child and 25 cents an adult. Families donated sandwiches, preserves, bread, cake and dessert. The meat was bully beef from a can. Eventually, with electricity, the scoff became a hot meal, usually a salt meat and cabbage dinner. After the auction, there was a scuff (dance) to the music of an accordion and mouth organ.

The popular square dance was The Lancers. There was no caller. Andrew taught his daughters and their friends the steps. Vida George was breathless when they finished and says Andrew danced all night with young and old alike. Stella Reid, recalls, "Nobody could dance like Andrew." Mary Pretty remembers the men swung the women round and round 'til they were off their feet. When they stopped to take a spell, the women were dizzy and unsteady. As little children, they conspired under the tables to see under the women's skirts! It was a fun time.

When Hilda began school in 1951, the first year combined Primmer and Grade 1. She was six years old. Each student was given a blue bottle of cod liver oil to bring home and take daily. Many threw it on the beach to become sea glass. Albert was four years older than Hilda. He was hyper and disruptive and found it difficult to focus. This did not bode well in school. He was always talking and couldn't stay still. He missed a lot of school in winter as his crutches made walking in the snow difficult. Eventually, the teacher, Doris (Warren) Newhook, encouraged Violet to keep him home. The system was not geared to deal with learning and/or physical difficulties.

Verd and Dulcie attended school with Hilda. Dulcie hung around with Eileen Martin (her teacher's daughter), Rosalie Smith, Joan Newhook and Mervin Smith. Mervin came down over the garden each morning to walk to school and compare homework. When she was 14, Dulcie went to school in Gander for a year, and lived with her sister, Rea, and family. I was seven years old and I remember her refusal to wear a cap in winter despite Mom's protests. Hilda can still see Dulcie, after her train trip from Gander, "this tall person stridin' up the lane, dressed in a cool yellow jacket with a brown collar and a brown cinch belt, suitcase in hand, and long wavy hair flyin' in the wind."

To his credit, Verd completed his Grade 11, the only one of Andrew and Violet's children to do so. Verd was not a morning person. A story that made Violet chuckle and that she loved to retell was the day she was going to teach him a lesson for not getting up 'til the last minute. Getting Verd out of bed for school was always a big racket. She was having no success and in a huff, getting madder by the minute. She got a piece of rope from the store which she tied around his bedroom doorknob and secured to the stair post. She smiled at her cleverness but Verd had done one better. He had gone unnoticed upstairs to Albert's room while she was away. Beatrice also had a devil of a time getting Verd out of bed. The only time he got up early was if he wanted to check his rabbit snares!

David Moore, Len George and
Verd in front of Orange Lodge

In 1959, the two room school closed. Hilda moved to St. Georges, a new high school mid way between Dildo and New Harbour. She was in Grade 8. It was very different from the old school. There was one classroom per grade and subject teachers, and for the first time a gym, Phys Ed classes, assemblies and indoor toilets! There were High School dances. Hilda could dance the jive and the lancers all night long. She would be so tired that she literally crawled up the stairs when she got home. Her mother would say, "Good. Now I know ya was dancin' and not out gallivantin' around." St. Georges became the new high school for all the local Protestant religions. It was the beginning of a new era.

THE BLUEBERRIES

In Newfoundland, many families subsidized their income by picking blueberries to sell to local merchants. It was an important cash crop, especially in the 1930s during the Great Depression. They picked blueberries, partridgeberries, raspberries and bakeapples for their own use. Partridgeberries and bakeapples were stored in water in a jar. Blueberries and raspberries were made into jams and jellies.

Bakeapples are tart orange yellow berries with large seeds found in Newfoundland and Labrador, Northern Quebec and Alaska. They also grow in Scandinavian countries, Russia, parts of the United Kingdom and are called cloudberries. Stooping to pick the bakeapple in late summer is back breaking work. They grow in boggy, insect infested areas, low to the ground. They are considered a delicacy in Newfoundland.

Andrew's family sold their blueberries to merchant, Arthur Moore and his wife, Molly (Higdon). Their middle man in the 1930s was Eli Rowe who set up a station in the berry grounds. Molly (Mary Kate) and Violet were first cousins, their fathers were brothers. Andrew and Violet frequented Moore's General Store most every day. No money was exchanged. The purchases were on the account or as they would say to Molly, "Mark it down." Andrew straightened out (paid his bill) once a month when he got his cheque. The odd time, Molly gave him a bag of peppermint knob candy for the children. The general stores carried food, fabric, clothing, and hardware.

When Molly's son, Rex, and his wife, Pearl, took over the business, he eliminated the middle man and took the job himself. Rex started around the cove at 7 AM and picked up the berry pickers, standing room only, in his GMC stake body truck. Hilda could hardly see over the wooden sides. She sat on the tailgate, legs dangling. Rex took them to Broad Cove Road. The morning drive was quiet. However, the 6 PM return was noisy, the pickers singing, waving and hollering at everybody they passed so glad to be going home. If the weather was good, they went Monday to Saturday, for two weeks in August. Before Rex provided transportation, they walked to the berries. They were bent over for hours, climbing over stumps and warding off stouts, hornets and ants nests. Alma says the nippers (mosquitoes) and sand flies ate you alive. Every evening, hair sticky with blood had to be washed despite the kerchiefs and bandanas the women and girls wore on their heads. It was hard work especially for children as young as 8 years old.

The men carried five gallon wooden boxes strapped to their backs like packsacks with rope loops. They were too heavy for the women and children, who carried enamel pails, galvanized buckets and plastic beef buckets. Hilda used a two gallon boiler, Violet's old pot. They carried small enamel dippers (saucepans) which they filled with berries to put into their pails. Andrew put a wire handle on an old fruit can for Hilda.

At 5 PM, Rex returned, measured their berries in one gallon, half gallon and one quart tins and gave each a berry note. This recorded the quantity of berries picked, the current price per gallon and the amount of money earned. The note was redeemable at his store. In the 1930s, a picker could earn 10 cents a gallon, for a total of one to two dollars a day. This seemed like a fortune to those families who were receiving the dole, six cents a day per person. In September, children skipped school, so critical was their contribution to the family income.

Arthur Moore and Son and S.J. Pretty were the two biggest merchants in Dildo. Berries were shipped by train and truck to St. John's. About the same time the berries were ripe in August and September, Moore and Pretty were also shipping two million pounds of squid a season in a second lucrative business.

S. J. Pretty's granddaughters, Mary (known as Lee) and Evelyn (known as Chattie), daughters of Arthur and Lizzie, rode in their Uncle Boyd's truck to the blueberry grounds. The road was the old railway track, with lots of potholes, wide enough for one vehicle. Lee remembers Lloyd George in the truck, his long dark eyelashes white with dust.

Her poppy looked the part of the merchant. He wore a black suit and round derby hat with a gold fob chain watch and a brass handled cane. He came from Chard, England. At the beginning, much of his business was based on barter, when the merchant supplied the fishermen with food and supplies and took their fish in payment. Fishermen rarely saw cash. At Christmas, Mary and Evelyn helped fill empty brin bags with toys and canned food from the family business to deliver to families unfortunate enough to be on the dole.

Sam Pretty was father to Arthur. Arthur and his wife, Lizzie, were friends of my parents and lived in Gander. Arthur's hobby was painting and I looked forward to his visits because he encouraged me to draw. I owe him a debt of gratitude for nurturing in such a small child a love of art. I am the proud owner of one of his lighthouse paintings, an unexpected Christmas gift to my parents.

Painting by Arthur Pretty

Sometimes Violet picked berries, a chance to get outside in the fresh air. While many pickers scattered, she stuck to one big patch, collecting the berries in her apron until she had enough to fill her bucket. Because of her asthma, Rea stayed home, babysat the younger children and made supper. Alma and Hilda say they were not good pickers. Alma was too particular. She picked one or two at a time so her berries would be clean, with no leaves or stems. Hilda picked 'til lunch, enough to fill her two gallon pail. After lunch, she went swimming at the cribbin' (cribbing), an underground railway trestle made of slate. Lendo was a strong picker, able to pull berries off the bush by the fistful without much debris. Sometimes he stayed overnight in a log shack with a bunk so he would get the best picking in the morning. The bunk was a primitive wooden frame on the floor filled with boughs, covered with an old quilt.

Hilda

In addition to buckets and pails, the pickers carried lunch. Alma's lunch was a tin of beans, bologna, homemade bread and a kettle to make tea. She often picked with Lendo and Emily and they had boil ups, taking care to dout (douse, put out) the fire when they were finished. They made Jiggs Dinner with salt beef, potatoes, turnip and cabbage. In Hilda's time, fires were not allowed. She brought a tin of Vienna sausages, bread, buttered crackers, cheese, cookies and a drink.

The money received from the berries was designated mostly for school supplies, scribblers, book bags, pencil cases, and pencils. Hilda says sometimes she might get a pair of socks and a chocolate bar. Lendo once bought a pair of short red rubber boots for Larry with some of his berry money. After Larry died, it broke Rea's heart to see those little boots.

Alma reflects on those times. She can hardly believe the changes in her lifetime. However blueberries continue to grow and it is as popular a food as ever. Blueberries, partridgeberries and bakeapples continue to be a source of income today for many along the highways of Newfoundland with the berries for sale displayed on the hoods of their cars.

There is a new kid on the block. The high bush blueberry can be grown in more climates and it therefore more plentiful, can be harvested earlier, and visually, it is bigger and plumper. The low bush wild blueberry, found naturally in Newfoundland, has more flavor and tastes better. The cooler climate in Newfoundland results in a longer growing season and a sweeter berry with more antioxidants. The blueberry industry has changed.

In 1985, Dr. Hilary Rodrigues, a dentist in Whitbourne, bought the vacant and vandalized Markland Hospital, with the goal of making wine from native berries. In 1993, he received a license to sell his wine. Today, Rodrigues Winery and Distillery is the largest primarily fruit winery in Canada, using blueberries, bakeapples, black currants, partridgeberries, raspberries, strawberries, cranberries, plums and pears which are handpicked and pesticide free. In 2005, his son, Lionel, introduced Sedna Nutraceuticals, derived from the words nutrition and pharmaceutical. The nutraceutical business produces wellness products such as antioxidant-rich powders and flakes made from berries which can be added to juices and smoothies. It supplies a global market.

SANGER

MERCER

DOWNTON

HIGDON

PINSENT

THORNE

THE EXTENDED FAMILY

Andrew Ralph Smith was the second of seven children born August 4, 1894, to William and Julia. He had a brother, Eldred, and five sisters, Beatrice, Nellie, Violet, Blanche and Sadie. Beatrice Irene, born in 1892, died of tuberculosis, at age 17.

THE SANGERS
VIOLET (Andrew's sister)

Violet was born November 15, 1898. When she was 12, she went to Bay Roberts as a domestic for Major Higdon, a Salvation Army officer, to look after his children and do light housework. After three years, she was hospitalized at the Fever Hospital in St. John's where she worked for two years upon recovery. In Grand Falls, she obtained a job at the new A.N.D. Company pulp and paper mill staff house for single men and met Timothy Sanger. They married November 15, 1916, on her eighteenth birthday. Tim was 22. They had 16 children in 23 years, Rea (Lester Powell), Lillian (Tom Martin), Andrew (1 Marjorie Belbin 2 Alma Hattie), Stella (Donald Bruce), Gladys (Douglas Osborne), Wilford, Maxwell, Bill (1 Marnie Spence

2 Donna Pearce), Annie (Raymond Thomas), Nettie (Richard Harkins), Fred (Jean Pinsent), Roy (Doris Beson), Carrie (Sonny Degeer), Harry, Norman (Yvonne Byrne), and Marjorie (1 Herb Wheeler 2 Terrance Ward). Wilford and Maxwell died in infancy.

Tim and Violet Sanger

Harry's was a breech birth which resulted in cerebral palsy. He was unable to walk or talk. His father made him a wooden seat with wheels so he was able to push himself around. Tim took him to the Notre Dame Bay Memorial Hospital in Twillingate under Dr. John Olds for treatment. Dr. Olds was a legend in Newfoundland for his success in treating what was thought to be impossible. Harry died in Twillingate on May 3, 1941. The cause of death was listed as Spastic Paraplegia, cerebral hemorrhage. He was four years old. Their mother grieved that Harry died of a broken heart because he was with strangers in a strange place. He is buried with his father.

Tim was a tall man who liked to read, with a strong work ethic, and high expectations of himself and his family. He was raised in a strict Methodist faith and was active in his church, the Orange Lodge and the Co-Operative Society. He was a unionist, one of the founders of, and the Secretary Treasurer of The Newfoundland Confederation of Labour for nine years until his death. He died suddenly on March 14, 1945, at the age of 51, of a burst appendix. Tim and Violet had been married 29 years.

After Tim's death, Violet worked at the Dry Cleaners across the street and ran back and forth to prepare meals. She took in boarders to make ends meet as she had nine children at home. There was no Government help. The boys walked the railway tracks to find discarded coal to supplement their heat. Violet made and sold cakes, Norm beat the batter and Carrie made the deliveries.Violet was a survivor. She was organized, a stickler for cleanliness. Daughter, Rea, wrote, "In the spring of the year, Jeyes Fluid scoured the corners, mattresses were put out to air and windows were polished to a fare-thee-well. No germ could survive."

Norm broke his elbow jumping off their back shed. Removing the cast, the doctor warned his mother he would never straighten the arm again. Undaunted, she taped a small bucket of rocks in his hand for a long time. His arm is perfectly normal and he has played hockey, like his brother Fred, for years.

For the First Avenue home, Tim had a table built so that all could be seated. Grace was said before every meal and thanks offered when it was finished. Meals were on time, at noon and at 5, and the children waited for their father to sit before they ate. Every day had its routine, a time and place for everything. Violet adopted Tim's strong Methodist beliefs in the value of religion, education, hard work and thriftiness. The Sanger children towed the line (followed the rules). There was no idleness amongst them. Fred thought they had a great life. He did not think they did without. His mother was amazing. "She made us what we are today."

Violet and Tim were Methodist friends with Hardy and Dorothy (Dicks) Rideout. The Rideouts had 13 children. After Dorothy died, Violet and Hardy married in 1950 and raised their younger children together. Violet's grandson, Ches, says, "It could be viewed as a natural evolution in a sense, an arrangement particularly favorable to Nan. The integration, according to Marjorie and Norm, was reasonably smooth and he was a good step father," although Norm admits he was unhappy when the relationship first began. Hardy died April 26, 1971 and Violet, on January 31, 1983. Sadly, daughter Stella was killed in a car accident enroute to her mother's funeral.

Violet Sanger named her first son after her brother, Andrew, my grandfather. Ches, Andrew's son, says, "It is fair to say that Dad (Andrew Sanger) idolized his Uncle Andrew (Smith) and remembered him with deep affection in Grand Falls and when he visited Dildo on several occasions as a boy and a young man. They went rabbit catching together. He remembered his Uncle Andrew as personable, a respected and natural leader." Ches and his son, Darryl, have written a book, "The Sanger Family in Newfoundland: Timothy and Violet - Roots and Offshoots."

THE MERCERS
BLANCHE (Andrew's sister)

Blanche

Blanche was born February 21, 1908. She came to Grand Falls at 15 to help her sister, Violet Sanger, with her babies. She worked at The Woods Candy Store on High Street across from the town hall for four years. Her Sanger nieces and nephews went to the movies on Saturday afternoons for 10 cents admission, and she gave them free candy for the event.

While sliding on Gilbert's Hill, she met Don Mercer from Bay Roberts. They married September 29, 1929 and had three children, Ruby (Harvey Feener), Bruce (Vera Stuckless) and Madeline (Earl Vokey). They lived at 25 Junction Road. Bruce and Vera added a piece to the house for their growing family.

Blanche had happy memories of growing up in Dildo. She was a tomboy, game for anything. She jigged squid with her father, fished for tomcods off the wharf and went on hayrides. She embraced life. Blanche would give the shirt off her back. She gave away more food and clothing than anyone will ever know to needy families. Don supported her, let her do as she pleased. She was outgoing, carefree and laughed a lot, like my grandfather, Andrew. She liked her smoke, a drink and a joke. She worked hard all day so she could enjoy her nights playing cards and Bingo. She was well known for her accuracy in telling fortunes by reading palms and tea leaves. She was young for her age. She had friends from all walks of life and they were welcome in her home and her trailer in Goodyear's Cove, near Springdale. Even when Blanche was hospitalized in old age, she was a character. She endeared herself to the nurses who slipped her a bit of brandy before she fell asleep. She said with a wink, "I pretends I spilled it so they gives me some more."

Daddy Don was a tall strapping (strong) man with a big laugh. He towered over Blanche. Daughter-in-law, Vera, says he was the sweetest man on earth, an angel. Never once did she hear him complain. Hilda reflects, "Uncle Don and Aunt Blanche were a great bit o' fun. Uncle Don was liable ta pick ya up and shove ya in the sink and turn the water on." In the evenings, he put his blind mother to bed at 10 o'clock, had two beers and picked up Blanche at Bingo. He worked as a millwright in the mill, as did his son, Bruce, who was an electrician. His mother was Granny Mercer, (Ann Mariah), a midwife and a healer. Don brought her myrrh bladders or balsam blisters from trees which she used to make salve for sores. When children came to have warts removed, she warned them, "Don't thank me fer this," for there was a belief you lost the ability if you accepted thanks, payment or compensation. Don died of cancer on November 15, 1970.

THE DOWNTONS
SADIE (Andrew's sister)

Sadie (middle), with sisters-in-law, Bessie and Mildred

Sadie Rebecca was born December 21, 1910. She also went to Grand Falls to help sister, Violet Sanger, for the birth of Violet's seventh child, Bill, in 1927. She married Harold William Downton from Lewisporte on August 27, 1934. They lived on Crescent Heights with Harold's mother, Jessica (Jewer) and their son, Reginald Grant.

Sadie's home was immaculate. Like many others, she covered her floors and countertops after cleaning with Grand Falls paper readily available from the mill. The beautiful shiny range in Sadie's kitchen looked like it had never been used but she loved to cook, bake and make preserves. She knit socks, mittens and sweaters. She was always at it. She was reserved, some say shy, the opposite of her sister, Blanche. She was content to be a homebody, taking joy in camping with her grandchildren and having them over for Christmas dinner, baking bread and playing bingo, the simple things in life.

Reg remembers his mother and Aunt Blanche laughing about the younger days when Blanche sneaked out her bedroom window. Blanche was a bit of a hard case. They sent boxes of new and used clothing to their Dildo relatives. Harold was the saver, Sadie the spender, generous to her family. She doted on Reg (Jean Collins) and her four grandchildren.

Harold worked at the mill as did his father, son, and grandson. He worked in wood handling, before the logs were stripped of their bark. He retired in 1977. In 1944, due to work shortage in Grand Falls, Harold, Sadie and Reg moved to Wellsville, New York, where he worked at a dairy farm for two and a half years.

Harold visited Blanche's husband, Don, most every day. They were great friends who enjoyed the outdoors. Reg says, "Father and Uncle Don were supposed to be back before dark but many times that did not happen, so Aunt Blanche and Mother were always there to guide them ashore on the Exploits with their flashlights. Many times Father got into trouble. One time his car got stuck in the snow while he checked rabbit snares. Long after dark when my son and I were looking for him, we spotted him dodging up the road. As far as he was concerned, it was just a normal day!" Harold loved berry picking, rabbit catching, moose hunting and fishing. As his eyesight diminished and he got lost fishing with his grandson, he said, "Don't tell Nan." He was undeterred.

Harold loved his family, his church and God's great outdoors. He was a religious man and spent many hours volunteering for the United Church. Sadie was not, she "didn't want ta hear tell o' it." He died in the woods. Those of strong faith would say God granted him this wish on November 1, 1992. He was 80 years old. Sadie died peacefully in her sleep, three years later, on September 27, 1995.

Harold Downton and Don Mercer

THE HIGDONS
NELLIE (Andrew's sister)

Heber and Nellie

Nellie was born September, 1897. She married Heber Higdon on August 23, 1916, and lived in New Harbour. Heber's parents were James and Willamina Higdon. Nellie and Heber had three children, Marjorie (Fred Williams), Grant (Margaret Higdon) and Bill (1. June Pollett 2. Betty).

Nellie and Heber were staunch supporters of the Salvation Army faith. In 1964, Nellie was recognized for 26 years as home secretary of the Dildo Corps. Heber served as Sergeant Major, reporting directly to the corps officer and taking command in his absence.

Heber was a gentle man who worked as a culler at Woodman's Store. When the merchant bought fish from the fishermen, the culler (inspector) separated the fish according to their size, quality and cure (salting). Undersize, broken or sun burnt fish were deemed cullage. The culler determined the prices paid the fishermen for their catch. After the downturn in the fishery, the store employed Heber as a clerk, a full time job he viewed as a privilege.

Grandson, Gerald Williams, remembers his grandfather crippled with arthritis using his crutch to carry a turn (a full load) of wood. Heber delighted his 25 grandchildren with gifts and candy. He gave Gerald a three wheel bike and a Champion sled, luxuries to a little boy at that time. A granddaughter, Gloria, was killed in a hit and run car accident when she was about 12, just before Christmas, getting a recipe for a cake. Heber died of a heart attack on January 18, 1957 at age 64.

Nellie was a tiny little thing and looked like she came out of a catalogue. Even her apron was spotless. She was strict, fastidious and obsessed about cleanliness. Despite having a stroke, being paralyzed on one side and not able to put two words together, Nellie sang like a trooper at Andrew's funeral. She died 15 months later, October 10, 1971. She was 75 years old.

ELDRED (Andrew's brother)

Eldred was Andrew's younger brother, born in 1906. He married Amelia (Smith) and they had 10 children, Blanche, Don, Erwin, Alfred, Bill, Stella, Nellie, Bruce, Phyllis and Elizabeth. Eldred worked as a blasting foreman for the Highways, in road construction. This was seasonal and he subsidized it cutting birch saplings and making barrel hoops to make extra money during the Depression and into the 1940s when salt fish was shipped in barrels. He was "more fer in the woods" than

Eldred with Lynx

Andrew. Aunt Mel was a good housekeeper, rising at the crack of dawn, the first to hang out her wash. This early rise meant dinner at 11, supper at 4:30 and bedtime at 9:30, when she locked her door, turned out the lights and went to bed. She did not like the dark.

Eldred was an exceptional singer, played the mouth organ and could tap dance like nobody else. He died of kidney cancer at the young age of 58. Like their father, the children were musically talented. Cousins, Bill and Bruce hung out with Hilda, singing on the wood horse, while Bruce played his guitar, impersonating Johnny Cash. Music was the most important thing in their lives.

JULIA ELIZABETH (REID) SMITH
(Andrew's mother)

Reuben (Read) Reid came to Dildo from Devon, England in 1830. Reuben and Julia (Chipman) had six children, Owen, Albert, Mary Ann, Levi, Elizabeth and Moses. Their son, Moses, married Catherine Thorne. They had four children, Samuel, Levi, Cleophus and Julia.

Moses was Andrew's grandfather. His gun burst while he was hunting in a boat. He bled to death from the wound in his side at age 28, April 24, 1870. He was not brought into his house because Catherine was pregnant and they wanted to spare her the pain of watching her husband die. Julia was the child born to Catherine two and a half months after his death. Catherine remarried James (Joseph) Hefford.

Julia (July 11, 1870) married William Smith, (November 10, 1866), one of eight children born to Martin and Sarah (George). She was a gentle grandmother, had a soft way about her. Her favorite treat was a cup of hot cocoa. She wouldn't go anywhere without her gloves to cover her chapped hands but she could do anything with those hands, sewing, knitting, crocheting. She made men's suits, something few women did at that time. On Saturday nights, she braided granddaughters Alma's and Rea's hair with a strip of cloth so they had ringlets when she took them to the Army church on Sunday. She was spotless clean. Late in life, Julia's sight was affected by cataracts. She died of Typhoid Fever October, 1940. Before she died, she unknowingly infected many of her grandchildren.

TOM SMITH
(Andrew's uncle)

Andrew's Uncle Tom lived with his invalid wife in a small two room structure, a kitchen and a bedroom. Violet said of Tom's wife, "I don't know nothin' 'bout her. When I come here, he lived by his self. We took him in fer a few years and I looked after him 'til he died. So I never had no easy task and don't tell me I did." Uncle Tom was in hard shape with an ulcerated leg and he did not have enough to eat. Violet remembers him fondly, "poor as e'er could be, lousy as a goat, and ridden with bed flies." Tom said to Andrew, "I can't go wit ya. I got the varmints." Andrew cleaned him up and turned their front room into a bedroom for the older man.

Uncle Tom was childless but he became a grandfather figure. Violet said, "He was sweet, good as gold. No one in the world better than he. He loved the youngsters, carried 'em 'round and played with 'em. No wonder we all loved him, poor old soul." He made small wooden boats and floated them in the washstand to occupy the children while Violet worked. Alma remembers their playing games with small stones in the dirt by the back door. When Eldred and Mel's children came, he would say, "The Germans are comin'."

He liked to smoke his pipe keeping warm in the corner by the stove. He never said much. He received a small quarterly pension, $6 every three months from the government with which he bought hard tobacco and a suit of long johns. Most men wore long johns year round. He developed dropsy, (hydropsy or edma), in most cases caused by heart or kidney problems. He died in his sleep. Andrew made his casket and put a Johnson's Baby Powder tin under his chin to keep his mouth closed and Newfoundland pennies on his eyes. Andrew did not stop his children from seeing the dead. His belief was, live and learn.

AUNT MILLIE AND UNCLE BILL PINSENT
(Andrew's aunt)

Millie and Bill Pinsent

Andrew's Aunt Millie (1875-1967) and her husband, Uncle Bill Pinsent (1877-1954) lived behind him, on the right side of Pinsent's Lane. Millie (Amelia) was his father's sister. They had five children, Mildred (Walter Mercer), Albert (Florence "Floss" Pollett), Marion (Jonathon Gosse), Walter (Lena Thorne) and Adolphus (Amanda Thorne). Uncle Bill's brother, Steve, was father to Canadian actor, Gordon Pinsent. The Pinsents are a creative bunch, successful actors, artists, writers, and musicians.

Millie's daughter, Mildred, and her husband, Walter, were transferred to New York by his employer, Western Union. They were a chatty couple and drew people like magnets. Daughter, Florence (Guy), recalls many visits by Newfoundlanders to their home. Her mother would exclaim, "My Lord, you must be a cousin!" Mildred was a wonderful baker and people flocked to buy her bread.

Marion married Jonathon Gosse, a war buddy of Andrew. She was witty, with a dry sense of humour and always a smile. Jonathon was tender hearted, a caring man. Marion and daughters, Daphne and Mildred, visited her sister, Mildred, in New York during World War II, quite an adventure at the time.

Uncle Bill and Aunt Millie were a good match, opposite to one another. As she told her stories, he sat with his pipe in his rocking chair laughing quietly. She was funny and made everybody happy. Granddaughter, Florence says, "Grandma was sweet and kind. She WAS the entertainment committee." Granddaughter, Audrey (George), recalls a family dinner when her grandmother, dressed in old clothes, knocked on the back door, begging, "Would any o' yas be willin' ta take an old woman in fer the night?" Millie wore her best dress and bonnet to get water from the well. She once put a dead mouse in Chester Reid's coat pocket in retaliation for his tricking her when they were playing cards. "She was one o' those people who ne'er cracked a smile," deadpan, so you did not suspect her wit and mischievous nature. She had her quirks. She was terrified of thunder and lightning storms, hiding under a bed or convenient cubby hole, and she didn't trust cows!

Millie, like many Newfoundland women, knit socks for the Newfoundland Regiment during World War I. They were a hot commodity in the trenches. Soldiers, even those from other countries, eagerly traded for a pair. Like cigarettes, they were better than money which was always in short supply. A soldier corresponded with her as she included her name and address in the toes of his socks. She was absolutely thrilled.

As was custom, Aunt Millie followed the rules for the Twelve Days of Christmas. The tree, which was brought into the home December 24, was removed January 6, Old Twelfth Night (Old Christmas Day). To not do so was unlucky. On January 6, Millie made the traditional Twelfth Buns, to bring to her best friend's, Polly Pretty, for the last night of mummering, a final chance to celebrate with friends. To her bowl, she added 12 ingredients, flour, sugar, shortening, eggs, molasses, raisins, currants, cherries, dates, mixed peel, cinnamon and allspice. Uncle Bill was tasked with finding 12 different kinds of wood for the fire used in the baking. Millie was superstitious and when she discovered one missing, son Dolph was the culprit, she was sure it meant bad luck. It was one of few times her friend, Florence Smith, saw her upset.

In the community, the young looked after the old. When Hilda went to Moore's store for groceries, Violet reminded her to check with Aunt Millie for her order. Hilda was rewarded with a soft ginger snap, a baking powder bun, dark fruitcake and cheese or an apple from Millie's apple tree. Lon Smith also shopped for Aunt Millie. She usually gave him two cents but one day she had only one. When next she asked Lonnie, he said, "No, Aunt Millie. Ya owe me a penny." Lon's brother, Mervin, and Albert sawed wood for Uncle Bill. Millie gave them pennies and advised them not to tell Uncle Bill in the hope he might give them more. As Bill got older and cutting wood was difficult, Lon's parents, Florence and Gordon, looked out for them and Gordon kept them warm with wood. Andrew and his cousin, Eli Rowe, visited most days.

THE HIGDONS
(Violet's family)

Violet's father and grandfather, both named Charles Higdon, were coopers who made wooden barrels for fish. A cooper was a highly skilled tradesman, an important person in the community. It was not uncommon for the art to be passed down from father and grandfather as it required a four to five year apprenticeship, the sons learning at their father's knee. For centuries, goods were stored and transported in sturdy wooden barrels which were watertight and withstood the rigors of sea travel around the world. With the arrival of plastic, cardboard and metal containers, it is fast becoming a lost art.

Violet had two sisters and four brothers. Her youngest brothers, Charles George and Llewellyn, (May 7, 1899 – 1917), died as young men, never married. There are conflicting stories as to the causes, pneumonia, tuberculosis and measles? Her oldest sister, Catherine, known as Kit, (1882 – 1929), married twice. Her first husband, William Cramm of Famish Gut (Fairhaven) may have drowned. During her second marriage to Richard Higdon, she had three children, Elsie Maude, Annie (Sullivan) and Thomas. Kit died two weeks shy of her 47th birthday.

EVELYN
(Violet's sister)

A sister, Evelyn, was born July 10, 1892. She was baptized Emilena but did not like it and changed it. She married William (Bill) Thorne. Their children were Annie (died of whooping cough at 18 months), Maisie (Fred Hefford), Harvey (Pearl Goonsey), Llewellyn (Lizzie Hefford) and Levi (Gertie Reid). Levi and Gertie lived with them and looked after them in their old age. Levi was a quiet man like his father. Lew, a successful entrepreneur in Argentia, "could talk ya blind."

Evelyn and Bill, Maisie,
Harvey and Llewellyn

Evelyn and Bill had a large property in New Harbour in on the tracks, with a two storey house, stables, sheep and cows. Evelyn kept up to 80 lambs and sold them for $10 each. Grand daughter, Gloria Thorne, rubbed their heads to keep them calm as her grandmother sheared them with household scissors, trussed on a table, their opposite legs tied together. Evelyn sold milk and made her own butter.

As a child, Alma helped her aunt in the barn in summertime. Evelyn ran a tight household and worked from morning 'til night. When Alma went home, Evelyn put fresh butter on cabbage leaves for her to take for there were no plastic containers! Alma was glad to go home because the Thornes did not have electricity. She was accustomed to lights and she found the evenings in New Harbour very dark.

Evelyn was not in want. Her small farm provided a good income and Uncle Bill had a railway job, but she was frugal, patched her flannelette nighties and stitched the runs in her stockings. Violet protested her behavior but Violet was just as nonchalant about her own appearance. Her apron often needed cleaning and her stockings were askew. Rea gave her mother earrings and Albert correctly noted, "It won't be long before they're out."

Evelyn did not go to church. Uncle Bill played drums with the Salvation Army. He was a gentle soul, with crossed eyes, older than Evelyn by 14 years. They had a strong marriage. Gloria "blames" her Pap for her love of animals. They had cows, sheep, horses, cats, dogs, pigs, rabbits, chickens and pet rats but the pigeons were his favorite. He often had one named Mickey perched on his shoulder.

Violet and Evelyn got along well. In the winter, Andrew took Violet by sled to New Harbour. When Evelyn came to visit them in Dildo, Andrew would say, "Evelyn's comin'. I'm leavin' 'cause no one will get a word in edgewise." Evelyn liked to talk! Evelyn died of cancer, age 77, in February, 1970. Uncle Bill predeceased her in 1963.

CHRIS and TOM
(Violet's brothers)

Violet had two other brothers, Tom (Sara Annie Thorne), and Chris (Dorianna Cranford). Chris worked as section foreman for the railway and Tom worked in Argentia. When Violet was a little girl, they gifted her with coats and laced up boots. Uncle Chris was so crippled with arthritis that he crawled to the wood pile, sat to chop the kindling and threw it to the house. He loved whittling wood. His many cats were everywhere, inside and outside his house. He was the joking kind.

THE NEIGHBORS
THE ROWES

Painting of Eli Rowe Jr. and
one of his wives

No record of Andrew and Violet's family would be complete without mention of Eli Rowe and his son, Albert Jim Rowe. Eli was raised by Andrew's grandparents, Martin and Sarah Smith. His mother was Rosanna Elizabeth (Rose), their daughter. Eli's biological father was Eli Rowe Sr., who came from Heart's Content to build the All Saints Church of England in Dildo. He was the master carpenter. He did not marry Rose. He married Mary Ann Cranford in 1881 and moved to the United States.

It is believed Eli Jr. was born December 20, 1879. He was christened a Smith but he was known as Eli Rowe Jr. He and Andrew were first cousins. Andrew's children did not know they were related to Eli, that he was their first cousin once removed. They thought of him only as a wonderful neighbor and friend, an important person in their lives. Eli Rowe Jr. was twice married. He and his first wife, Emily (Reid), had a son, Albert Jim, born November 13, 1908, when Eli was 29 years old. His second wife, Elizabeth (Smith), had a daughter Rosanna who lived only 12 hours. Eli named her after his mother. Elizabeth died four days later, complications of childbirth, on January 27, 1920. Eli raised Albert Jim by himself.

Eli Rowe and Hilda

Eli was, in Hilda's words, the most wonderful person who ever was. He was an intelligent man, often requested to write letters for the illiterate. He helped Rea with a poem for a contest on the Gerald S. Doyle News Bulletin. She did not win but was thrilled to hear her poem and name on the radio. He was a constant positive figure in the children's lives. Alma idolized him. He planted pennies along the lane and lit up with joy when they discovered them. Albert says Eli would take his foot off a penny when they passed and say, "What's the matter? Are ya blind today?" They stumbled upon ripe berries which he had previously scouted for them to eat. He treated them with peppermint knob candy. He liked to tease. He appointed himself the children's protector. His lip trembled when they were hurt or upset. They thought of him as a grandfather figure.

The Rowe House was begun by Andrew's grandfather, Martin Smith, in 1887. It was completed by Martin's son, Silas, and Eli, his grandson. Eli inherited the house when Silas moved to British Columbia and looked after Sarah when Martin died. The Rowe House is now The Inn by the Bay. The George House sits behind it. Impressive sister properties, they are operated as Bed and Breakfasts.

My Painting, " Albert Jim's Boat"

In winter, Eli left Whitbourne by train and travelled to Gander and Badger to snare rabbits. Gander was still a sawmill operation known as Hattie's Camp. The frozen rabbits were put in barrels to be sold upon return. Eli had a fishing stage, wharf, and a putt putt motor boat with an Acadia Make and Break engine to fish in summer. The boat was used by his son until it was left to rot in an adjacent field with the George house in the background. I painted it from an old photo. I call it "Albert Jim's Boat."

Eli and Albert Jim were slight men like Andrew but they were different. Eli was all for fun and Albert more serious. Albert had wild wavy hair. He married Amy Pinsent late in life and they had no children. Albert Jim and Amy lived with Eli in his house and got along well. Amy ran the Post Office from the home for 22 years. They added an addition for the post office as well as a sunroom with many windows to the front of the house. This is now the Sea Level Dining Room used by The Rowe House and the George House Bed and Breakfasts.

Amy was called "Emmy." She loved knitting and embroidery. She had a camera and left behind many old photos of people of Dildo but we do not know their identities. When she married Albert Jim, Eli's sparse house lacked a woman's touch. She was capable, neat and tidy, and filled the home with nice things.

In his last year, Eli had a stroke and walked with a cane. One late afternoon when Hilda was gathering splits for firewood and Albert was getting coal, Eli slipped and fell on ice. Albert saw him fall and shouted to Hilda who ran to her father and Albert Jim for help. Eli was never the same after he broke his hip. He became bedridden. Eli died October 18, 1954. He was 75.

Mom told me I met Eli when I was three years old. He was excited to meet me because I was Andrew and Violet's first grandchild. I was all dressed up, having arrived by train from Gander for a summer vacation. I was going up the lane to my grandparents' house. He bent down to me and Mom says I replied, "You have bad breath." She was embarrassed. I am embarrassed to be told the story, but she says he didn't hold it against me. He laughed to kill himself. I was five when he died.

After Eli died, Albert Jim and Amy continued to look out for our Albert, despite or because of his limitations, as Eli had requested. Everywhere Albert Jim went, he had our little Albert. Albert was named after Albert Jim, in gratitude for his devotion to the family during the Typhoid Fever crisis. Eli and Albert Jim repeatedly risked their lives by breaking the quarantine to check on them and see to their needs. Albert Jim died, age 70, in 1979. Amy continued to live in the Rowe House until 1993. She died in 2009.

THE GEORGES

Endymion Herbert (Dim or Dimmy) and his brother, Kenneth, were sons of Albert and Sarah Ann (Davis) George and lived next door to each other, up over the hill from Andrew and Violet. Albert was a successful businessman with schooners and a general store. An impressive house was built in 1885 under the supervision of Reuben Reid, before Albert's businesses failed in 1894. Albert landed on his feet with the establishment of a family farm. His son, Ken, married Ellen Duffitt from Clifton who was teaching in Dildo. They looked after Albert for his last 12 years, lived in his grand home and ran the farm. Ken and Ellen (Ellie) had six children, Lloyd, Vida, Munn, Roy, Edmund and Beryl.

Ellie and Ken George

Dimmy married Susannah Hunt from Harbour Grace. They had no children. He was the equivalent of a limousine or taxi driver in a time of no cars. He had a carriage house for his carriages and sleighs and a stable for his fine horse and cow. Dimmy and Susie ran a Bed and Breakfast and boarding rooms from their home. They supplemented their income with a small grocery store next to their house, selling staples like flour, molasses and salt pork and beef.

When Andrew and Violet's family were suffering from Typhoid Fever, nurses Kirby and Bretton boarded with Dimmy and Susie for four months. Rea's first summer job was working for Susie a few hours a day, dusting, wiping down the stairs and washing dishes. She was 13 and made $5 a month. Once, when she was putting away dishes in a cupboard under the stairs, she touched a wad of dollar bills. She quickly pulled her hand away, told no one and never went near the pantry again.

At 18, Vida married Magistrate George Trickett. George, who was nine years older, had been her teacher. Her Uncle Dim gave her away. Her sister, Beryl, was her flower girl, George's sister, Pearl, the maid of honor, and her brother, Lloyd, the best man. Rev. Cracknell performed the ceremony. Andrew and Violet attended the wedding.

The children were friends, Vida with Florence, Roy and Ed with Gerald, and Beryl with Alma. Alma remembers hiding under the front porch of the George house after Beryl sneaked a tin of plums. They kept it their secret. It did not occur to her mother to suspect Beryl. Days later, after she had searched high and low, Mrs. George went back to S.J. Pretty's store, convinced they had not included the plums in her order and got a new tin.

Friend, Florence Smith, called Ellie "Mrs. George" although they were good friends, because Ellie was the postmistress. Ellie ran the local Post Office for 36 years from their home. At a designated time, people waited outside her back porch to pick up their mail and their neighbor's mail when Ellie came to the door and called the names on the envelopes. Ellie played the organ at the All Saint's Anglican Church for 50 years and read the Bible every day. Florence asked if she understood everything she read and Ellie replied, "No, but I understand the Ten Commandments and they're plain enough."

In 2009, at Amy Rowe's funeral, Vida said to Hilda, "My dad, Ken George, would've been lost without your dad." There was a great deal of respect between Andrew, Ken and Dimmy. Alma remembers her father visiting Dimmy many times when Dimmy was dying. Andrew shaved him, cleaned him and kept him company. He said to Alma, "Today I must've hurt him 'cause he gave me one helluva look." Dimmy died, age 66, on

March 29, 1945. Ken died of a stroke, age 79, on September 18, 1964. When Vida and her brother, Lloyd, arrived from Clarenville, Andrew already had their father prepared for the funeral. Andrew said to them, "If that's dyin', that's how I wants ta go." Ken had slipped away peacefully.

In 1977, after Ellie died, the oldest son, Lloyd moved into the home from Clarenville. He and his wife, Virginia, married late in life. Lloyd became a father for the first time at 55. They had a son, Albert. Virginia died in 1981. Lloyd was well known and respected as the local historian with a wealth of information he was only too willing to share. Violet looked up to him, saying, "I wish I had his head," (knowledge). He died in 2002 at the age of 85.

Lloyd and Andrew were second cousins. They had the same great grandfather, Thomas George, and wife, Martha (Pretty). They are my great great great grandparents.

FLORENCE SMITH

Florence Smith and Marjorie and Lon

Florence (George) and Gordon Smith lived on the hill behind Andrew and Violet. Gordon was overseas with the Newfoundland Overseas Forestry Unit, in World War II, as was Pete Pretty, our Florence's boyfriend. The two girls met at the well to see who had received a letter from Scotland and exchange stories.

Gordon, #1595, Pete, #272, and Steve Higdon, #1570, were three of 3,680 Newfoundlanders who volunteered to work as loggers in wartime Scotland, over 50 from Dildo and New Harbour. They received the same pay as home, $2.00 a day, of which a compulsory $1.00 a day was sent to their families. Each agreed to work a minimum of six months. Gordon worked in Oban, a port in the West Highlands. Steve Higdon married a Scots lassie, Margaret Jamison. Florence remembers when he tied together all the clothing she had hung out to dry for devilment and the day he substituted her pillow with a full flour sack. That's the way it was. The fun was in the retaliation.

After nine months overseas, Gordon returned to Dildo, built a home and went to work for the railway. He and Florence had eight children, Marjorie (Day), Lon, nickname for Llewellyn (Lavinia Hooper), Mervin (Sheila Higdon), Sheila (Winsor), Verna (Elford), Beryl (Small), Terry and Linda (Delaney). Florence laughingly calls Hilda her sixth daughter!

The children of both families spent much time together. Lon says the community raised the kids. Every child could be chastised. They would get a bat (flick of the hand) beside the head from Florence or Violet if they did wrong. Neither mother discriminated between the children. If Violet's children got into a racket, Florence would say, "Go down the garden and stay in yer own yard." Violet would do the same. Hilda says, "If ya misbehaved, Florence could be yer mother as fast as ya could turn around. I was drove home more times than ya can shake a stick." Violet's reprimands to Lon were water off a duck's back. Andrew was always replacing insulators on the poles, usually broken by boys firing rocks. Florence said he was to deal sternly with her boys if they were the culprits.

When they were young, Lon, Merv and Albert were great friends. While playing cards at Albert's house, the phone rang. They knew, in all likelihood, that one of them would have to deliver a message. Albert told Mrs. Pollett, the switchboard operator, to stop phoning. She told Andrew and Albert never answered the phone again for a long time. Mervin and Albert got lost in the woods and were found at 3 AM by Clarence George. Albert played and got into scrapes like all little boys. Lon says they did youngster stuff. They chased the sheep but they knew better than to chase Albert Jim's sheep. They stole apples from Aunt Millie's apple tree the night Verd got married. Lon snared his first rabbit with Albert. Mervin walked to school each morning with Dulcie and Hilda says she never got into trouble with Sheila because Sheila was too good!

Florence credits Andrew's alertness to saving Lon, who climbed a ladder to the top of their two storey house when he was three. Andrew spotted him and pointed, not shouting for fear of scaring the boy. Florence forced herself to be calm as she retrieved her child who had no idea of the danger.

Florence is a natural story teller. She is funny and compelling. She tells me, "I'm the closest thing ya got ta a grandmother now." She says, "I knew Andrew all my life. He ne'er said an unkind word ta me. I thought I knew everythin' about him, but I didn't know what he done overseas. He could've bragged but that was not his way. I ne'er heard him talk 'bout the war." Florence recalls An and Vi as being the best of friends. She remembers my grandparents fondly. "I miss them," she says.

REFLECTION

My journey to fill in the blanks of the lives of my grandparents is comparable to working on a giant jigsaw puzzle without the final picture and with pieces missing. My first draft was 56 pages. It was shelved for over a year.

I saw them briefly once a year, my grandfather a distant memory. I believe he would have been surprised at the focus of our trip to France and Belgium. He often said, "As long as I lives, I hope ta God ne'er one o' my children or grandchildren has ta go ta war" and "Why the hell would anyone want ta know what we went through o'er there?" But Andrew was not bitter despite his time in the trenches. He had a positive outlook on life and most of all, he enjoyed a good story. He would smile and be pleased.

My grandmother, Violet, told Carla that I was a serious little girl who sat on her front step writing in my diary. It is a memory I had forgotten, the diary a fad at the time, but it must have struck a chord with her. She was a private person. But she was also open to new ideas. She believed, "It's a good day when ya learn somethin' new." Would she approve of my efforts to preserve the story of her family? I think she would say with a grin, "Ya talk about. Imagine that!"

Despite pages of detail, old and new, there are still many unanswered questions, puzzle pieces I may never find. What led to Andrew's decision to enlist? How was his life shaped by his war time experiences? He appears to have remained intact or he kept turmoil hidden. Hilda believes he may have come back a better man for he did not believe in fighting or arguing.

He thought it futile, saying it was a lot of foolishness. He was, by all accounts, a happy and affectionate man. He attracted people from all walks of life who enjoyed his company.

Andrew survived the trauma of war and witnessed the deaths of many soldiers. His sister died when he was 15. He was present at the deaths of his father and mother and other family and friends. Three of his children succumbed to Typhoid Fever. Death was not a mystery. He was all too familiar with it. He believed happiness is a choice. You are responsible for how you deal with the pitfalls of life. You work to make the best of it.

Would he have been different had he not been a soldier? Had he always been this way or did his time overseas strengthen his resolve to live for the moment? Andrew's childhood remains a mystery. The personalities of his sister Blanche and his Aunt Millie mirrored his own. His parents and other siblings did not exhibit the same uninhibited lust for life.

Rea, Alma and Hilda enjoyed a happy childhood. "Few were better off than everyone else. Most were in the same boat. Ya were lucky if ya had anythin' extra." Rea saw her life "as Heaven compared ta some, except for the time we had the Fever." The deaths of Larry, Florence and Gerald turned their lives upside down. The angst and sorrow marked them for the rest of their lives. Childhood ended abruptly for the surviving children.

For Violet, it was the beginning of a lengthy depression, a turning point in her life. Her faith in her ability to look after her family through hard work took a severe blow. She was unable to save them. Her confidence was shaken. To protect herself in future, she withdrew and felt guilty about being happy. She struggled to be optimistic about life. While Andrew also went through a time of grieving, he once again exhibited his amazing ability to overcome adversity. Violet's recovery was more painful. Was it that she lacked an outlet like Andrew created for himself, a laugh, a smoke, a beer, a game of cards and good times with friends? What were her options? Her relationship with her church was sorely tested if not ended by the Fever deaths. She dealt more than Andrew with the tedium of the multitude of tasks required to get through their everyday life.

Alma, Hilda and Rea at Peggy's Cove, Nova Scotia, 2002

Their son, Albert, survived a premature birth midst the Typhoid deaths of his three siblings. His survival was viewed as a miracle. Rea remembers seeing him after birth. He was so small. Bones showed through his blue skin. In his tiny face, all she could see was his mouth. When he tried to cry, he could not make a sound. For many weeks, Violet stayed in bed with him. Her world had spun out of control.

Albert's birth cast the family into uncharted waters. Today, most studies on premature infants confirm an increased risk for behavioural problems and ADHD, Attention Deficit Hyperactivity Disorder. Albert was easily distracted, unable to focus, impulsive and defiant. The blame for his inability to cope in school was often put on Andrew and Violet for spoiling him in their desperate efforts to see him through childhood. It was said their expectations were not high enough, that they had given into him too many times. Today, they would not have to bear the guilt of poor parenting for the medical profession and social services might have been able to offer support. Albert never had the opportunity for training in a special needs or adult education program. Who knows what a difference that might have made? He understands and remembers most things well. Who knows how different his life could have been had the pregnancy gone full term? When Albert was a boy and a young man, many in the community looked out for him for they knew the family and the circumstances of his birth. "Lil' Albert" was likeable and enjoyed being helpful. As the older people passed away, the next generation, as Violet said, "do not have the same understandin'."

In Albert's life he had control over little but his mother, who made allowances for him because of his shortcomings. All the grumbling in the world was not going to change that but there was no shortage of trying on both sides. Neither was capable of changing the dynamics of their complicated relationship. Violet was often at wits end. As his legal guardian, she could have arranged for him to go to a home but she feared he would not survive, uprooted from his surroundings. It was her wish that he remain in their house. Sadly, without a responsible person living there, the proud old house is in a state of utter disrepair. After Violet's death, Albert's relationship with his mother was transferred to Hilda, who lives nearby and has primary responsibility for him.

In January, 2012, Hilda was overwhelmed with the task. Her parents long dead, she prayed they help her resolve the dilemma with Albert. On February 11, Violet's birthday, Albert was admitted to hospital with a recurrent racing heart condition, 167 beats a minute, and was diagnosed with the family condition, hypertrophic cardiomyopathy. As a result of the hospital stay, Albert moved into a Rest Home. The family has some peace of mind and Hilda is convinced the timing, her mother's birthday, is not a coincidence.

Rea often wondered what happened to Nurses Kirby and Bretton. Her gratitude to them had not abated with time. When Justice Margaret Cameron was appointed in 2007 to head up an Inquiry into Hormone Receptor Testing, investigating reports of erroneous test results to breast cancer patients in Newfoundland, Rea believed it was more than a coincidence that she was a Cameron from Carbonear. In May, 2012, I received confirmation from Margaret Cameron that her mother was indeed Isabelle Kirby, a public health nurse, who married Duncan Cameron in the summer of 1941. She was 24 when assigned to my grandparents' case in November, 1940. She died in 2011 at the age of 95. She was of good mind. I missed a golden opportunity to query her on the Fever by one year.

The discovery of Bert Newhook in South Carolina while I was researching his father, Dr. William Newhook, was probably the most incredible stroke of luck, but there have been other coincidences. The research on Chester Reid took an unexpected twist when we found our only photo of Florence in Gertie Thorne's photos. Hilda met Owen Reid's daughter, Stella, as a result of a random comment at a funeral. Some things were simply meant to be.

What are the odds of my cousin, Rick, stumbling upon a treasure of black and white pictures while doing a carpentry job for Dave and Wendy Whitten? The photos, taken in the area in the 1930s and 40s, included unseen pictures of our family. What are the odds of our Vimy guide specializing in the role of the runner? What are the odds of finding the home of Andrew's Scottish girlfriend in Prestwick when all other homes on the block had been torn down for a supermarket? How can one explain that a single envelope in his military file in the Archives has Rea Scott's name and address, yet this particular page is missing in the same file online? What are the odds that when Andrew met his sister's second husband, Hardy Rideout, they would remember meeting in the trenches?

Why was I unable to find the death certificates of the three children in the Archives for the year 1941? Florence died in hospital. Her death should have been recorded. There were so many Smiths and they were not alphabetical but chronological. We scrolled pages of the 1940 and 1941 records several times to no avail but, in the process, I saw the name Harry Sanger. I found the details of the death of Andrew's nephew and nobody, not even his large family, had known the date of his early death. We did not know he died three months after Andrew and Violet's children.

When I began, I forgot Carla's tapes with Nan. I heard them 15 years ago, and was influenced by Carla's frustration in the sound quality and her effort to get answers from her great grandmother. How could I have not appreciated their value?

I tried to cross reference whenever possible. Mom's recollection of her Dad's memories of Captain Rendell's death was a gunshot to the throat. Imagine how I felt when this was confirmed, one time only, in Rendell's military file, a fact I might have missed had I not been looking for it.

I view this writing as an unexpected gift as it enabled me to relate to and bond with my mother in a new way. It made me appreciate not only her memory, but her memories, and it gave me some understanding of the circumstances that shaped her. As a child, most outdoor activities were off limits because of her asthma. What were her options inside the home? They were simply to excel at cooking and cleaning to help and please her mother, to emulate her sister, Florence.

I could not have predicted the interest of our grandson, Owen MacPherson. Naturally curious, his many questions alerted me to words which needed defining. Most 9 year olds do not have his awareness of their great, great grandparents.

I have amassed a wealth of detail. If it is lengthy, it is because I have been reluctant to cull it. How can I judge one memory to be more or less important than another? I missed out on the memories of Isabelle Kirby, my Uncle Lendo, and of Amy Rowe, Albert Jim's wife, who passed away after I began but before my research went in their direction.

I have tried to be as accurate as possible, difficult when the bulk of the material is based on hearsay or memories of events long past. I have been fortunate to have found people, besides my mother and her sisters, whose memories are impressive, their recall crisp. Together, their hundreds of stories made possible the story of my grandparents, Andrew and Violet Smith. Without this cooperation, the myriad of puzzle pieces could not have come together. My gratitude is great.

Enjoy!

AUTHOR BIO
Gloria (Hellier) Brown

A history buff since she learned to read the stories of Helen Keller and King Arthur, it was no surprise Gloria graduated with a history major from Memorial University of Newfoundland in 1970. She grew up in Gander and her maritime heritage is reflected in her paintings and recycled art, samplers and penny rugs. A keeper of memories and old photographs, it was predictable her first published book is a reflection of the past, her own.

You can find out more about Andrew and Violet at:
facebook.com/andrewandviolet